28

TRUTHS

TAUGHT BY THE BOOK OF MORMON

28
TRUTHS

TAUGHT BY THE BOOK OF MORMON

Monte S. Nyman

Sourced Media Books, LLC
20 Via Cristobal
San Clemente, CA 92673
www.sourcedmediabooks.com

ISBN-13: 978–1–937458–01–0
Printed in the United States of America.

This publication is designed to provide entertainment value and is sold with the understanding that the publisher is not engaged in rendering legal, accounting, or other professional advice of any kind. If legal advice or other expert assistance is required, the services of a competent professional person should be sought.

—From a Declaration of Principles jointly adopted by a Committee of the American Bar Association and a Committee of Publishers and Associations

For Mary Ann

Dear Tamara—   12·1·11

   This ~~book~~ isn't a fancy
Birthday gift but the words
inside are the best gift
I can give you — This is
the last ~~book~~ he wrote. —My
Dad once told me that I'd
look back on life and see
a few TRUE friends — you're
one of those true friends!
Love you Tamara

CONTENTS

CONTENTS

PREFACE

"By these things [The Book of Mormon] we know."
(D&C 20:17)

The importance of the Book of Mormon in interpreting the doctrines of The Church of Jesus Christ of Latter-day Saints was declared by the Lord at the time of the organization of the Church. In a series of revelations, published under the date of April 6, 1830, the Lord outlined the contents of the Book of Mormon, its purposes, and its effects upon both the Church collectively and upon the individual members (D&C 20:8–16). In these revelations (hereafter referred to as the April 6 revelation), the Lord gave twenty statements concerning doctrines that were definitely taught in the Book of Mormon (D&C 20:17–36). These verses that teach the doctrines referenced to in those twenty statements of the revelation are organized and analyzed in this book. Many of the statements require more than one chapter for full analysis.

It is not suggested that all doctrines taught in the Book of Mormon are included in this book, although the ones included are basic tenets of the faith of the Latter–day Saints. It is also noted that a few doctrines taught in the Book of Mormon are not mentioned in the April 6 revelation (i.e., the baptism of little children; see Moro. 8). Furthermore, because of the close relationship of many doctrines of the gospel, several of the Book of Mormon scriptures apply to more than one subject. Thus there are some duplications of several scriptures. The intent of the book is to help the readers come to a better understanding of the doctrines taught in the Book of Mormon and "liken all scriptures unto" themselves (see 1 Nephi 19:23). The Lord concluded the April 6 revelation with this anticipatory declaration:

> *35 And we know that these things are true and according to the revelations of John, neither adding to, nor diminishing from the prophecy of his book, the holy scriptures, or the revelations of God which shall come hereafter by the gift and power of the Holy Ghost, the voice of God, or the ministering of angels.*
>
> *36 And the Lord God has spoken it; and honor, power and glory be rendered to his holy name, both now and ever. Amen. (D&C 20:35–36)*

Many critics refer to Revelation 22:18–19 as a refutation of the Book of Mormon, claiming it adds to the Bible. This refutation and the April 6 revelation will be analyzed in the last chapter of this book.

The Book of Mormon clarifies and interprets the Bible. One of its purposes is "proving to the world that the holy scriptures are true" (D&C 20:11). Nephi, son of Lehi, was shown:

> *26 And after [the record of the Jews] go forth by the hand of the twelve apostles of the Lamb, from the Jews unto the Gentiles, thou seest the formation of that great and abominable church, which is most abominable above all other churches; for behold, they have taken away from the gospel of the Lamb many parts which are plain and most precious; and also many covenants of the Lord have they taken away.*
>
> *27 And all this have they done that they might pervert the right ways of the Lord, that they might blind the eyes and harden the hearts of the children of men. (1 Nephi 13:26–27)*

Nephi was then shown:

39 ... other books, which came forth by the power of the Lamb, from the Gentiles unto them, unto the convincing of the Gentiles and the remnant of the seed of my brethren, and also the Jews who were scattered upon all the face of the earth, that the records of the prophets and of the twelve apostles of the Lamb are true. (1 Nephi 13:39)

The Book of Mormon is one of those other books and restores many of the plain and precious parts that have been lost. These books give a second witness to the doctrines taught in the Bible and verify and enlarge upon these doctrines. In the words of President Harold B. Lee: "Many doctrines of the Bible that are only partially explained there are beautifully explained in the Book of Mormon, the Doctrine and Covenants, and Pearl of Great Price."[i]

The Bible itself foretold the doctrinal purpose of the purpose of the Book of Mormon. Isaiah, in prophesying of the coming forth of the Book of Mormon, testified: "They also that erred in spirit shall come to understanding, and they that murmured shall learn doctrine" (Isaiah 29:24, also quoted in 2 Nephi 27:35). The purpose of this book is to show the divinity and testimony of the great doctrines taught in the Book of Mormon and their application to the lives of those who will study and follow them. As President Boyd K. Packer has testified on several occasions:

True doctrine, understood, changes attitudes and behavior. The study of the doctrines of the gospel will improve behavior quicker than a study of behavior will improve behavior. Preoccupation with unworthy behavior can lead to unworthy behavior. That is why we stress so forcefully the study of the doctrines of the gospel.[ii]

i Williams, C. J., Ed. (1996). *The Teachings of Harold B. Lee.* Salt Lake City: Bookcraft, p. 155.
ii Packer, B. K. (1986). *Conference Report,* October, p. 20; (1997). *Conference Report,* April, p.8; (2004). *Conference Report,* April, p. 80.

1

THERE IS A GOD IN HEAVEN

"By these things we know that there is a God in heaven."

(D&C 20:17)

A knowledge of God's existence is a fundamental principle of religion and of individual faith. David Lawrence, former editor of *U.S. News and World Report,* states: "The acknowledgment of the existence of God is the beginning of human progress. Conversely it might be said also that the beginning of human retrogression is the rejection of the Supreme Being."[1] The Book of Mormon is a witness to the existence of God. The *Lectures on Faith* tell us the importance of knowing that God exists and how to come to that knowledge.

> ...For faith could not center in a being of whose existence we had no idea, because the idea of his existence, in the first instance, is essential to the exercise of faith in him. "How then shall they call on him in whom they have not believed? and how shall they believe in him of whom they have not heard? and how shall they hear without a preacher?" (or one sent to tell them?) (Romans 10:14). So, then, faith comes by hearing the word of God.

1 (1965). *Deseret News, Church News,* April 10, 1965, editorial page.

Let us here observe that three things are necessary for any rational and intelligent being to, exercise faith in God unto life and salvation.

First, the idea that he actually exists;

Secondly, a correct idea of his character, perfections, and attributes;

Thirdly, an actual knowledge that the course of life which one is pursuing is according to his will. (3:1–5)

The Book of Mormon testifies of the existence of God in its very first chapter (1 Nephi 1:8–10) and repeatedly bears testimony of him throughout the book.

The Book of Mormon further identifies the arguments people use against a belief in God and answers those arguments.[2] We will not attempt to enumerate all of the Nephite prophets' testimonies of God but will concentrate on two anti-Christ preachers who argue against God's existence and four prophets who refute the agnostic or atheistic arguments of the Nephite era.

These same arguments against the existence of God are used today, and the testimonies of these four prophets are therefore a warning to the modern–day readers against agnosticism and atheism. Since the existence of Jesus Christ is essentially evidence of his Father God, the existence of both will be considered together, although they lived approximately four hundred years part.[3]

Other chapters will differentiate between these two members of the Godhead.

---

2 The arguments against God's existence are an example of President Ezra Taft Benson's teachings that one of the major purposes of the Book of Mormon is to expose the enemies of God and the Church. Benson, E.T. (1988). *A Witness and a Warning.* Salt Lake City: Deseret Book, p. 3.

3 Sherem lived before "Jacob began to be old" and died (Jacob 7:26–27). Jacob was born in the wilderness after his father left Jerusalem in 600 B.C. (1 Nephi 18:7). His birth was therefore before about 590 B.C. Sherem's encounter with Jacob is at approximately 520–530 B.C. while Korihor, the second anti-Christ considered with Sherem, lived about 74 B.C. Therefore, the two men lived over four hundred years apart.

Furthermore, since the arguments of the two anti-Christs are basically the same, the two incidents will be considered together. Since the later account of Korihor goes into more detail, we will use it as the primary argument and Sherem's earlier account as the secondary one.

Sherem and Korihor—The Anti-Christs

There are four basic arguments used by both Sherem and/or Korihor to challenge or pervert the truth of the existence of a God or the coming of a Christ. These four arguments are all based on human reasoning and deny the revealed truths from God. All of these arguments are still in use today in one form or another and are still based on human reasoning. We will now consider each of these individual arguments against the existence of God.

The Foreknowledge of God

Korihor came into the land of Zarahemla preaching "against the prophecies which had been spoken by the prophets, concerning the coming of Christ" (Alma 30:6). He addressed the people as "ye that are bound down under a foolish and a vain hope," and asked, "why do ye yoke yourselves with such foolish things? Why do ye look for a Christ? For no man can know of anything which is to come" (Alma 30:13). Korihor went on to label the prophecies of the holy prophets as "foolish traditions of your fathers" (Alma 30:14). Earlier, Sherem had accused the prophet Jacob of perverting "the right way of God" and converting "the law of Moses into the worship of a being which ye say shall come many hundred years hence." He declared this "perversion" to be blasphemy; for no man knoweth of such things; for he cannot tell of things to come" (Jacob 7:7). Both Korihor and Sherem denied the foreknowledge of God and refuted the idea that God can reveal future events to the inhabitants of the earth through his holy prophets. The prophet Jacob had earlier warned the Nephites against the plan of the evil one that is based on the learning of men.

*O that cunning plan of the evil one! O the vainness, and
the frailties, and the foolishness of men! When they are
learned they think they are wise, and they hearken not
unto the counsel of God, for they set it aside, supposing they
know of themselves, wherefore, their wisdom is foolishness
and it profiteth them not; And they shall perish. But to be
learned is good if they hearken unto the counsels of God.
(2 Nephi 9:28–29)*

As already stated, these same arguments of Korihor and
Sherem are being taught in our world today. However, they are
taught more subtly and frequently are veiled in the world of
scholarship, more particularly in the field of biblical criticism.
Arguments against authorship and historicity of the biblical
prophets are prevalent in our society.[4]

Faith: Knowledge of Things Not Seen

Korihor's second argument against the existence of God was
that "Ye cannot know of things which ye do not see; therefore ye
cannot know that there shall be a Christ" (Alma 30:15). Since
Korihor himself had not seen the Christ, he assumed that no one
else had. In making that assumption, he rejected the testimonies
of the Nephite prophets and all the other prophets who had seen
Christ and recorded their witnesses on the plates of brass (see 1
Nephi 5:11–13; Jacob 4:4; Luke 24:27, 44).

When Sherem argued a similar point, Jacob testified that all
the scriptures testified of Christ, and that he had seen and heard
and had the knowledge that there was a Christ, manifested to him
by the power of the Holy Ghost (Jacob 7:11–13). When Sherem
asked for "a sign by the power of this Holy Ghost" (Jacob 7:11–
13), he unknowingly branded himself as a wicked and adulterous

---

4 Although the pendulum has swung back somewhat at the time of this
writing, an examination of biblical commentaries will reveal there still persists an
acceptance of man's reasoning against biblical authorship and historicity.

man,[5] and also denied faith, "a hope for things which are not seen, which are true" (Alma 32:21; D&C 42:23; 63:16).

We live in a world of doubting Thomases, among people who will not believe unless they see and feel; it is a world of empiricism that accepts only "scientific" proof. While many things can and should be proven, we must not neglect the Lord's law of establishing His word by the mouth of two or more witnesses (Deuteronomy 19:15; Matthew 18:16).

Man Is Accountable for His Sins

Korihor's third argument against the existence of God was that having sins remitted was "the effect of a frenzied mind; and this derangement of your minds comes because of the traditions of your fathers, which lead you away into a belief of things which are not so." He went on, "telling them that there could be no Atonement made for the sins of men" (Alma 30:16–17). This rejection of the Atonement, based upon the reasoning or learning of man, seems to be an attempt to blame others or even external forces for our actions rather than to take individual responsibility for failures, mistakes, and inadequacies.

Sherem accused Jacob of perverting the law of Moses and converting it into a worship of Jesus Christ (Jacob 7:7). The law of Moses was a "schoolmaster to bring us unto Christ, that we might be justified by faith" (Galatians 3:24). It was given to a people who had been in bondage to the Egyptians and had lost their freedom. It was expedient that the law was given to Israel, "even a very strict law; for they were a stiffnecked people, quick to do iniquity, and slow to remember the Lord their God." It was "a law of performances and of ordinances, a law which they were to observe strictly from day to

---

5 Jesus taught that "an evil and adulterous generation seeketh after a sign" (Matthew 12:39; 16:4). The Prophet Joseph declared: "The principle is as correct as the one that Jesus put forth in saying that he who seeketh a sign is an adulterous person; and that principle is eternal, undeviating, and firm as the pillars of heaven; for whenever you see a man seeking after a sign, you may set it down that he is an adulterous man. See Smith, J. (1972). *Teachings of the Prophet Joseph Smith*. Salt Lake City: Deseret Book, p. 157; see also p. 278.

day, to keep them in remembrance of God and their duty towards him" (Mosiah 13:29–30). The law taught them responsibility and was to prepare them to exercise their agency when the fullness of the gospel of Jesus Christ was restored among them.

In a world that refuses to take responsibility for its actions, many blame their environment, both human and physical, or hereditary factors, for the sins they commit against God.

Humans Prosper According to Genius and Strength

Korihor's fourth argument against the existence of God was that "every man fared in this life according to the management of the creature; therefore every man prospered according to his genius, and that every man conquered according to his strength; and whatsoever a man did was no crime" (Alma 30:17). This argument is a twin to his third argument against accountability for sin. It eliminates the laws of moral behavior given by God. It advocates that sin or unacceptable behavior is established by the neighborhood, community, or nation and that as people change, the morals or standards of the people are also subject to change. Man's accountability for his behavior at the bar of God is therefore eliminated. Korihor's argument further suggests that to overcome feelings of guilt, we merely need to change our attitude about the behavior we are following. The accepting of a new morality in place of the old immorality is a substitute for God's law of morality. Thus the decline of a society is hastened.

Although the record of Sherem does not include his teaching a philosophy pertaining to moral behavior, the rest of his arguments follow closely the teachings of Korihor. Such are the philosophies of men mingled with scripture. Remember that Sherem professed a belief in the scriptures, but as Jacob so aptly replied, "ye do not understand them; for they truly testify of Christ" (Jacob 7:10–11).

The teachings of these anti-Christs are apparent in our society today. The prosperity of man according to genius and strength is the forerunner of "the survival of the fittest" doctrine that surfaces periodically in the theories of men.

When a Man Is Dead, That Is the End

Korihor's final teaching was a denial of the resurrection. His preaching had led "away the hearts of many, causing them to lift up their heads in wickedness, yea, leading away many women, and also men, to commit whoredoms—telling them that when a man was dead, that was the end thereof" (Alma 30:18). The wording of this verse is important. Note that Korihor led away many women, and also men. Apparently he was a "womanizer," convincing the women that immoral acts were harmless because there was no afterlife. Furthermore, the wording suggests that men, in their carnal natures, saw the conquests of Korihor and followed his lascivious example. His teaching is an appeal to the animalistic nature of man, advocating that behavior that comes naturally cannot be harmful. Sherem, like Korihor, was a sign seeker (Jacob 7:13; Alma 30:43), which is connected with immorality (see footnote 5). Immorality is a by-product of disbelief in the hereafter. To deny the resurrection is to deny that man is fallen and in need of a savior to overcome death brought into the world by the Fall. Wherefore, they teach that "when a man [is] dead, that [is] the end thereof" (Alma 30:18).

The above teachings of Korihor and Sherem regarding death are everywhere noticeable, particularly on university campuses, in the entertainment world, and wherever God is forgotten or considered to be dead or nonexistent. Advocates of these philosophies hide behind the same arguments as Korihor, such as academic freedom; scriptures are traditions of men; and religious leaders are merely usurpers of authority who yoke down their followers. These advocates require empirical or scientific proof for any belief that they do not currently accept or advocate and ignore the Lord's law of witnesses that are amply provided by his scriptures, his prophets, or the Spirit of Christ and the Holy Ghost (see Alma 30:23–28). Many of these advocates fit the category of Paul, "ever learning, and never able to come to the knowledge of the truth" (2 Timothy 3:7). Korihor's teachings are found among all disciplines of learning and among most religious societies. Bear in mind that there are many truths that are advocated by these disciplines and societies, but all truths must be tested for validity by measuring them against the standard of truth (the scriptures and the revelations of God).

The teachings of Korihor and Sherem certainly expose the enemy, which is a purpose of the Book of Mormon, as stated by President Ezra Taft Benson in the beginning of this chapter. But more importantly, the Book of Mormon also answers and gives evidences against the enemies' arguments. In the case of Korihor and Sherem, prophets Alma and Jacob provide these answers and evidences.

Testimony of the Spirit

The most important evidence of God's existence is the personal witness of the Spirit. Alma bore testimony to Korihor: "I know there is a God, and also that Christ shall come" (Alma 30:39). This testimony had been given to Alma by the Holy Spirit after he had "fasted and prayed many days that [he] might know" (Alma 5:45–46). In contrast, Alma testified that Korihor had no evidence, "save it be your word only" (Alma 30:40).

Sherem had attempted to shake Jacob from his faith by the use of "much flattery, and much power of speech, according to the power of the devil." This, in spite of Jacob having received "many revelations and the many things which [he] had seen concerning these things; for [he] truly had seen angels, and they had ministered unto [him]. And also, [he] had heard the voice of the Lord speaking unto [him] in very word, from time to time; wherefore, [he] could not be shaken" (Jacob 7:4–5). Furthermore, "the Lord God poured in his Spirit into my soul, insomuch that I did confound [Sherem] in all his words" (v. 8). Jacob continued, testifying that "it [concerning Christ] has been manifest unto me, for I have heard and seen; and it also has been made manifest unto me by the power of the Holy Ghost (v. 12). Because of the strong personal testimonies of these two great prophets, the arguments of Korihor and Sherem were repudiated.

After all these witnesses (Alma 30:45), men still follow the devil. The devil will not support his followers at the last day but will speedily drag them down to hell (Alma 30:60).

All Things Testify of God

Alma bore testimony to Korihor: "I have all things as a testimony that these things [there is a God and Christ cometh] are true; and ye also have all things as a testimony unto you that they are true" (Alma 30:41). Then Alma identified four evidences that were available to Korihor: (1) the testimony of all these thy brethren; (2) the testimony of all the holy prophets; (3) the scriptures which are laid before thee; and (4) all things denote there is a God (Alma 30:44). A careful review of these four evidences reveals that three of them are of a spiritual nature and one physical. The Lord always seems to use both spiritual and physical witnesses in his law of witnesses.[6] Each of these four witnesses is unique in its own way and needs to be differentiated from the others.

The Testimony of Thy Brethren

While we often speak of "the brethren" as the general authorities of the Church, in the context of Alma's testimony, "all these thy brethren" (Alma 30:44) refers to the testimony of the lay membership of the Church. This constitutes the strength of the Church. Each and every member may, and most do, have a testimony of God, Christ, the restored Church, the Book of Mormon, and God's prophets. Through the gifts of the Spirit, "to some it is given by the Holy Ghost to know that Jesus Christ is the

---

6 The three witnesses of the Book of Mormon were given a spiritual witness by an angel and the voice of the Lord. The eight witnesses viewed, felt, and lifted the plates in broad daylight (see their testimonies in the front of the Book of Mormon). When the Savior appeared to the Nephites, they heard the voice of the Lord, they saw him descend out of heaven (spiritual), and then they were invited to physically touch him (3 Nephi 11:3–15).

Son of God, and that he was crucified for the sins of the world. To others it is given to believe on their words, that they also might have eternal life if they continue faithful" (D&C 46:13–14). In every ward and branch of the Church there are faithful members who know of God and his works. These members can and do testify to the other members of that ward or branch. The members who do not yet have this knowledge can lean on the testimony of the faithful until they obtain their own testimony.

The Testimony of the Holy Prophets

The holy prophets, in the context of Alma's evidences, compare to the present-day apostles and prophets. These men are sustained and function as "special witnesses of the name of Christ in all the world—thus differing from other officers in the Church in the duties of their calling" (D&C 107:23). Those who are in tune with the Spirit may know of God and Christ through the testimony borne by these special witnesses, for the Holy Ghost will carry that testimony into their hearts (2 Nephi 33:1).

The Testimony of the Scriptures

The scriptures are the writings of the apostles and prophets from past dispensations who bear testimony of their knowledge of God and Christ through personal appearances or the power of the Holy Ghost. God has provided apostles and prophets for all dispensations and has inspired them to leave their written testimonies for future generations. An example from the Book of Mormon is Nephi, son of Lehi. He proclaimed, "But there is a God, and he is Christ" (2 Nephi 11:7). The testimonies of prophets such as Nephi are readily available to us today through our reading of the Bible, the Book of Mormon, the Doctrine and Covenants, and the Pearl of Great Price.

The Earth and All Things upon It

Alma's statement that "all things *denote* there is a God" (Alma 30:44, italics added) has significance. The word "denote" means "to serve as an indication of; to serve as an arbitrary mark for; to make known, announce" (Webster's Seventh *New Collegiate Dictionary*). This definition suggests a less powerful evidence than the spiritual ones that precede it. However, when the question of God's existence arises, it is usually this argument to which men turn. It does not seem an accident that Alma lists it last. While there are many things to be considered, they are not as convincing as the other testimonies that are of a spiritual nature.

Alma enumerates "all things" such as "yea, even the earth, and all things that are upon the face of it, yea, and its motion, yea, and also all the planets which move in their regular form do witness that there is a Supreme Creator" (Alma 30:44). The arguments of the earth and its motion as evidence of God have been bantered around for centuries. This work will not attempt to review these evidences. Latter–day revelation confirms Alma's statement. The Book of Abraham in the Pearl of Great Price enlarges on God's systematic order of the planets and the universe (Abraham chapter 3 and Facsimile #2). The Lord revealed much about space and the kingdoms in a revelation to the Prophet Joseph Smith (D&C 88:36–45). This revelation declares that "any man who hath seen any or the least of these hath seen God moving in his majesty and power" (D&C 88:47). It is our responsibility to read the scriptures, study and accept what the Lord has revealed, and look for God's majesty and power in the physical evidences of the earth and its motion. On a lighter note, the following anonymous poem is offered.

Where God Ain't

He was just a little lad
and on the Sabbath day
was wandering home from Sunday School
and doddling on the way.
He scuffed his shoes on the grass,
he found a caterpillar,
he found a fluffy milkweed pod
And blew out all the filler.

A bird's nest in a tree
So wisely placed and high
was just another wonder
that caught his eager eye.
A neighbor watched his zig zag course
and hailed him from the lawn;
the neighbor asked with interest
what was going on.
Oh, I have been to Sunday School,
he carefully turned the sod
and found a snail beneath it,
that made him think of God.
"Hmmm, a very fine way," the neighbor said,
"for a boy to spend his time.
If you tell me where God is
I'll give you a brand new dime."
Quick as a flash his answer came
nor were his accents faint.
"I'll give you a dollar, mister,
If you tell me where God ain't!"

—Anonymous

Through the power of the Holy Ghost, both of the anti-Christs, Korihor and Sherem, were given a sign as they had requested. These signs turned to their condemnation rather than their salvation (Alma 30:48–50; Jacob 7:13–15; see also D&C 63:7). Both acknowledged that they had been deceived by the devil and had lied, knowing beforehand that there was a God (Alma 30:52–53; Jacob 7:18–19). Both Alma and Jacob had born testimony to these servants of the devil that they had indeed known there was a God and were possessed of the devil's spirit (Alma 30:42; Jacob 7:14). The Lord will sustain his prophets in disclosing the works of Satan, but it will be in his own due time and in his own way in order to bring justice and judgment upon the wicked (Alma 14:11; 60:13). In the meantime, we must follow the words: "Be still and know that I am God" (Psalm 46:10).

The Testimony of Aaron

Korihor would be categorized as an agnostic by today's definition. He did not believe that there was a God, but he did not deny his existence (Alma 30:48). Sherem denied that there was a Christ but did accept the existence of a God (Jacob 7:2, 7). The Book of Mormon records another category of unbeliever in the person of the father of King Lamoni, the king over all the land of the Lamanites (Alma 20:8; 22:1). The king first met Ammon, who was traveling with Lamoni's son to the land of Middoni (Alma 20:7–8). In defending Lamoni, Ammon was able to physically disable the Lamanite king but spared his life. The sparing of his life opened the way for Ammon's brothers, who had been imprisoned by the Lamanites, to come unto the Lamanite king in his place of reigning (Alma 20:9–27). After Ammon's brethren were released from prison, they were led by the Spirit to the house of the king (Alma 22:1). In their conversation, Aaron asked the king if he believed "that there is a God." The king's answer was "that the Amalekites [an apostate Nephite group] say that there is a God, and I have granted unto them that they should build sanctuaries, that they may assemble themselves together to worship him. And if thou now sayest there is a God, behold I will believe" (Alma 22:7). Of course, the king had been greatly influenced by his experience with Ammon, but he was not one who denied or argued about the existence of God. He was apparently one who had grown up in an environment where he had not been taught about God.

After Aaron had born testimony of the existence of God and had expounded the scriptures concerning the Creation, the Fall, and the Plan of Redemption through Christ, the king desired to know of the truth of these doctrines. In response, Aaron invited the king to "bow down before God, and call on his name in faith" (Alma 22:16). This is naturally difficult for an agnostic, because one of the arguments used by them or other nonbelievers in God, when they are invited to pray, is that they would be hypocrites to pray because they do not believe in a God. The prayer of Lamoni is an example of a prayer that anyone could ask and not be hypocritical.

As the king bowed down, he did cry mightily, saying: "O God, Aaron hath told me that there is a God; and if there is a God, and if thou art God, wilt thou make thyself known unto me, and I will give away all my sins to know thee, and that I may be raised from the dead, and be saved at the last day" (Alma 22:18).

In addition to the prayer not being hypocritical, there are some other important concepts to be noted. The king was willing to give away all of his sins to know God. When his physical life was at stake in his conflict with Ammon, he had been willing to give away half of his kingdom (Alma 20:23). With an understanding of eternal life, he was willing to do much, much more to obtain that life. This dedication comes only through the testimony of the Spirit that verifies the teaching of the gospel. When such an experience is had, those who are honest in heart [Korihor and Sherem weren't] and are "brought to believe and to know the truth, [are] firm and [will] suffer even unto death rather than commit sin" (Alma 24:19). The Book of Mormon teaches the existence of God to the agnostic [Korihor], to the perverter of the doctrines and principles of the gospel of Jesus Christ [Sherem], and to those who have grown up in a darkened society without a knowledge of God [King Lamoni and his father]. To those who reject the scriptures, the testimony of the Lord's living servants, and the Holy Spirit, there is still another witness of God and Christ.

Moroni's Testimony

As Moroni finished his father's record, he spoke concerning those who do not believe in Christ (Mormon 9:1). He was speaking to the reader in the latter days and posed several poignant questions.

2 Behold, will ye believe in the day of your visitation—behold, when the Lord shall come, yea, even that great day when the earth shall be rolled together as a scroll, and the elements shall melt with fervent heat, yea, in that great day when ye shall be brought to stand before the Lamb of God—then will ye say that there is no God?

3 Then will ye longer deny the Christ, or can ye behold the Lamb of God? Do ye suppose that ye shall dwell with him under a consciousness of your guilt? Do ye suppose that ye could be happy to dwell with that holy Being, when your souls are racked with a consciousness of guilt that ye have ever abused his laws? (Mormon 9:2–3)

By posing these questions, Moroni is also declaring what Isaiah and Paul also taught, that "every knee shall bow [to Christ], and every tongue shall confess to God" (Romans 14:11; Isaiah 45:23); and, as Paul adds, "So then every one of us shall give account of himself to God" (Romans 14:12).

It should be noted that there is a difference between a confession, or acknowledgment, and a testimony. Those who will study the Book of Mormon will receive a testimony of God and Christ, while those who reject the Book of Mormon and its teachings will eventually have to acknowledge Christ and God. This warning may sound like God is harsh or domineering, but Moroni points out that such is not the case. This life is the time to prepare to meet God (Alma 12:24). If we are not prepared to live with him, Moroni continues,

4 Behold, I say unto you that ye would be more miserable to dwell with a holy and just God, under a consciousness of your filthiness before him, than ye would to dwell with the damned souls in hell.

5 For behold, when ye shall be brought to see your nakedness before God, and also the glory of God, and the holiness of Jesus Christ, it will kindle a flame of unquenchable fire upon you. (Mormon 9:4–5)

It is for our own happiness that we should accept the testimony of the Book of Mormon concerning the existence of God. To the unbeliever, Mormon pleads: "O then ye unbelieving, turn ye unto the Lord; cry mightily unto the Father in the name of

Jesus, that perhaps ye may be found spotless, pure, fair, and white, having been cleansed by the blood of the Lamb, at that great and last day" (Mormon 9:6).

The New Testament apostle John warned of the anti-Christs in his own day (1 John 2:18). He identified the anti-Christs as those who deny the Father and the Son (v. 22; see also 2 John 1:7). Alma asked Korihor if he would "deny against all these witnesses" (Alma 30:45). As Mormon abridged the Korihor account, he inserted this editorial comment: "And thus we see the end of him who perverteth the ways of the Lord; and thus we see that the devil will not support his children at the last day, but doth speedily drag them down to hell" (Alma 30:60).

Both Sherem and Korihor were deceived by the power of the devil through his appealing to their carnal minds (Alma 30:53; Jacob 7:16–19). The power of the devil and the philosophies of man, often mingled with scripture, are again prevalent in our society today. May we accept the witness and warning of the Book of Mormon and gain a testimony or strengthen the one we already have of the existence of God and his Christ and of the Plan of Redemption he has given unto us.

2

GOD IS INFINITE AND ETERNAL

"God . . . is infinite and eternal, from everlasting to everlasting, the same unchanging God." (20:17)

We live in a changing world. In the twentieth century, we experienced an explosion of knowledge in almost every aspect of life. In our computer age, there seems no end to new discoveries and improvements. But there are some things that never change and never will. The Book of Mormon is a witness to the infinite and eternal nature of God. Infinite is to be immeasurable or beyond earthly determination. Eternal is to exist before and beyond the mortal existence of the earth and man. God and his attributes existed before mortality and will exist after mortality.

The Book of Mormon testifies of "the nature [character] of that righteousness which is in our great and Eternal Head" (Hel. 13:38). The Book of Mormon commands us to become perfect even as Christ and the Father who is in heaven is perfect (3 Nephi 12 48; see also *Lectures on Faith* 2:2, 4).[7]

---

7 For an exposition on the "Relative Perfection," the perfection of man compared to the perfection of God and Christ, see Talmage, J. E. (1951). *Jesus the Christ,* 19th ed., chapter 17, page 248. Salt Lake City: Deseret Bond Co. For an explanation of how men can attain perfection, see Kimball, S. W. (1974). Be ye therefore perfect. *Speeches of the Year,* pp. 231–242. Provo, Utah: BYU Press.

The Book of Mormon also teaches us of other attributes of God. For example, five attributes of God were specified by Ammon as he was "carried away, even unto boasting in [his] God; for he has all power, all wisdom, and all understanding; he comprehendeth all things, and he is a merciful Being" (Alma 26:35). The Book of Mormon gives other testimonies of God's attributes, but we will analyze Ammon's list and one other attribute in this chapter.

All Power

The first attribute of God listed above by Ammon is that he has all power. The Book of Mormon repeatedly testifies of God's power. In response to Laman and Lemuel's declaration that Laban was "a mighty man, and he can command fifty, yea, even he can slay fifty; then why not us?" (1 Nephi 3:31), Nephi bore witness that the Lord was "mightier than all the earth, then why not mightier than Laban and his fifty, yea, or even than his tens of thousands?" (1 Nephi 4:1). He then cited the example of Moses dividing the Red Sea by the power of God (see 1 Nephi 4:2). Later, Nephi warned Laman and Lemuel against touching him (because he was filled with the power of God) and withholding their labor from helping him to build the ship that God had commanded him to build (see 1 Nephi 17:48–49). He then declared:

> 50 If God had commanded me to do all things I could do them. If he should command me that I should say unto this water, be thou earth, it should be earth; and if I should say it, it would be done.
>
> 51 And now, if the Lord has such great power, and has wrought so many miracles among the children of men, how is it that he cannot instruct me, that I should build a ship? (1 Nephi 17:50–51)

The power of God was so great upon Nephi that Laman and Lemuel were confounded, could not contend against him, and durst not touch him for the space of many days. The Lord then commanded Nephi to stretch forth his hand and the Lord would shock them. After Nephi had done as the Lord commanded, Laman and Lemuel knew the power of the Lord was with Nephi (see 1 Nephi 17:52–55).

Jacob recorded, "we truly can command in the name of Jesus and the very trees obey us, or the mountains, or the waves of the sea" (Jacob 4:6). Jacob does not give specific examples of these powers, but Moroni gives one in his abridgment of the Jaredite records. Through faith in the power of God, the brother of Jared "said unto the mountain of Zerin, 'Remove'—and it was removed" (Ether 12:30). Jacob continued his testimony:

> *4 For behold, by the power of [God's] word man came upon the face of the earth, which earth was created by the power of his word. Wherefore if God being able to speak and the world was, and to speak and man was created, O then, why not able to command the earth, or the workmanship of his hands upon the face of it, according to his will and pleasure? (Jacob 4:9)*

Even the elements of the earth obey God's commands.

The prophet Abinadi warned King Noah that he and his men would not be able to destroy him until he had delivered his message. As he spake, the Spirit of the Lord came upon Abinadi, "and his face shone with exceeding luster, even as Moses' did while in the mount of Sinai, while speaking with the Lord. And he spake with power and authority from God" (Mosiah 13:5–6). Although man has his agency to obey or disobey, the power of God will protect his servants until their missions are completed.[8]

In a lengthy editorial comment, as he abridged the book of Helaman, Mormon compared the power of God with the power of men.

---

8 The Prophet Joseph Smith said, "I defy all the world to destroy the work of God; and I prophesy they never will have power to kill me till my work is accomplished, and I am ready to die" (*TPJS*, p. 328; see also pp. 258, 274, and 361).

7 O how great is the nothingness of the children of men; yea, even they are less than the dust of the earth.

8 For behold, the dust of the earth moveth hither and thither, to the dividing asunder, at the command of our great and everlasting God.

9 Yea, behold at his voice do the hills and the mountains tremble and quake.

10 And by the power of his voice they are broken up, and become smooth, yea, even like unto a valley.

11 Yea, by the power of his voice doth the whole earth shake;

12 Yea, by the power of his voice, do the foundations rock, even to the very center.

13 Yea, and if he say unto the earth—Move—it is moved.

14 Yea, if he say unto the earth—Thou shalt go back, that it lengthen out the day for many hours—it is done;

15 And thus, according to his word the earth goeth back, and it appeareth unto man that the sun standeth still; yea, and behold, this is so; for surely it is the earth that moveth and not the sun.

16 And behold, also, if he say unto the waters of the great deep—Be thou dried up—it is done.

17 Behold, if he say unto this mountain—Be thou raised up, and come over and fall upon that city, that it be buried up—behold it is done.

18 And behold, if a man hide up a treasure in the earth, and the Lord shall say—Let it be accursed, because of the iniquity of him who hath hid it up—behold, it shall be accursed.

19 And if the Lord shall say—Be thou accursed, that no man shall find thee from this time henceforth and forever—behold, no man getteth it henceforth and forever.

20 And behold, if the Lord shall say unto a man—Because of thine iniquities, thou shalt be accursed forever—it shall be done.

21 And if the Lord shall say—Because of thine iniquities thou shalt be cut off from my presence—he will cause that it shall be so. (Hel. 12:7–21)

As illustrated above, the Book of Mormon testifies of the power of God being able to control the earth, the elements of the earth, and the inhabitants of the earth. Faith in the power of God enables men to feel they have nothing to fear.

The Attribute of Wisdom (Truth)

The second attribute of God listed by Ammon was "all wisdom" (Alma 26:32). Alma admonished his son Shiblon, "I have told you [of Christ] that ye may learn wisdom, that ye may learn of me that there is no other way or means whereby man can be saved, only in and through Christ. Behold, he is the life and the light of the world. Behold, he is the word of *truth* and righteousness" (Alma 38:9, italics added). Alma's equating of wisdom and the truth with Christ is consistent with other scriptures. In a revelation to Joseph Smith, the Lord said, "I am the Spirit of truth, and John bore record of me, saying: He received a fulness of truth, yea, even of all truth" (D&C 93:26). In the New Testament, Jesus told Thomas, "I am the way, the truth, and the life" (John 14:6). Therefore, God's wisdom is here equated with truth.

Truth is defined by the Lord as a "knowledge of things as they are, and as they were, and as they are to come" (D&C 93:24). The Book of Mormon uses a similar definition. Jacob admonished his brethren [of the latter day] to:

> *... prophesy to the understanding of men; for the Spirit speaketh the truth and lieth not. Wherefore, it speaketh of things as they really are, and of things as they really will be; wherefore, these things are manifested unto us plainly, for the salvation of our souls. But behold, we are not witnesses alone in these things; for God also spake them unto prophets of old. (Jacob 4:13; see also 2 Nephi 6:4)*

God, having all truth, inspires his prophets to make known the truth that will bring salvation to the souls of men or turn to their condemnation. An example of the effects of the truth bringing people to salvation is the account of Ammon and his brethren teaching among the Lamanites:

> *6 And as sure as the Lord liveth, so sure as many as believed, or as many as were brought to the knowledge of the truth, through the preaching of Ammon and his brethren, according to the spirit of revelation and of prophecy, and the power of God working miracles in them—yea, I say unto you, as the Lord liveth, as many of the Lamanites as believed in their preaching, and were converted unto the Lord, never did fall away.*

> *7 For they became a righteous people; they did lay down the weapons of their rebellion, that they did not fight against God any more, neither against any of their brethren. (Alma 23:6–7)*

Of these same people it was said: "And thus we see that, when these Lamanites were brought to believe and to know the *truth*, they were firm, and would suffer even unto death rather than commit sin" (Alma 24:19, italics added; see also 3 Nephi 6:14). These converted Lamanites totally relied upon the teachings of the prophets. When Ammon inquired of the Lord, they accepted what the Lord said through him and obeyed (see Alma 27:4–15).

An example of the truth bringing condemnation upon a people is Amulek preaching to the wicked people and lawyers of

Ammonihah. After perceiving their thoughts [by the Spirit], he chastised them for their wickedness, making them more angry with him. Amulek

> *25 ...stretched forth his hand, and cried the mightier unto them, saying: O ye wicked and perverse generation, why hath Satan got such great hold upon your hearts? Why will ye yield yourselves unto him that he may have power over you, to blind your eyes, that ye will not understand the words which are spoken, according to their truth?*
>
> *26 For behold, have I testified against your law? Ye do not understand; ye say that I have spoken against your law; but I have not, but I have spoken in favor of your law, to your condemnation.*
>
> *27 And now behold, I say unto you, that the foundation of the destruction of this people is beginning to be laid by the unrighteousness of your lawyers and your judges. (Alma 10:25–27)*

Thus, from the Book of Mormon we learn the effects of truth upon a people. Faith in the wisdom and truth of God enables men to believe all things and to know of a certainty his word will be fulfilled (see *Lectures on Faith,* 4:16).

The Attribute of Knowledge (Understanding)

The third attribute of God, noted by Ammon, is that he has "all understanding" (Alma 26:35). To understand all things, God must know all things. Once more the Book of Mormon testifies of God's knowledge and understanding.

Nephi was commanded to make a second set of plates but did not know why (see 2 Nephi 5:28–30). In his early writing of the second set of plates he declared:

5 Wherefore, the Lord hath commanded me to make these plates for a wise purpose in him, which purpose I know not.

6 But the Lord knoweth all things from the beginning; wherefore, he prepareth a way to accomplish all his works among the children of men; for behold, he hath all power unto the fulfilling of all his words. And thus it is. Amen. (1 Nephi 9:5–6)

As he read the second set of plates while abridging the original plates, Mormon chose to include them in the abridged record with this comment: "And I do this for a wise purpose; for thus it whispereth me, according to the workings of the Spirit of the Lord which is in me. And now, I do not know all things; but the Lord knoweth all things which are to come; wherefore, he worketh in me to do according to his will" (W of M 1:7).

Today we see the understanding of the Lord in inspiring Mormon to include Nephi's second set of plates. He knew that the first 116 pages of translated manuscript would be lost, and Nephi's other record would cover the same time period with an even better account (see D&C 10:38–45). The prophet Isaiah had been given this same information over a thousand years before it happened (see 2 Nephi 27).

Jacob, the brother of Nephi, testified, in the context of the Atonement, that God "knoweth all things, and there is not anything save he knows it" (2 Nephi 9:20). The God spoken of by Jacob is Jesus Christ. Without a knowledge of the past, present, and future, he would not have been able to make the Atonement. A second witness of the Atonement requiring a knowledge of all things was borne by Alma: "Now the spirit knoweth all things; nevertheless the Son of God suffereth according to the flesh that he might take upon him the sins of his people, that he might blot out their transgressions according to the power of his deliverance; and now behold, this is the testimony which is in me" (Alma 7:13).

Another evidence that God knows all things is given in what is called the sealed portion of the Book of Mormon, a part of the plates given to Joseph Smith which he did not translate (2 Nephi 27:8–10). These plates contain "a revelation from God, from the beginning of the world to the ending thereof" (2 Nephi 27:7). This revelation is the one shown to the brother of Jared that included "all the inhabitants of the earth which had been, and also all that would be; and he withheld them not from his sight, even unto the ends of the earth" (Ether 3:25). The brother of Jared was shown these things that he "might know that he [Jesus] was God, because of the many great works which the Lord had showed unto him" (Ether 3:18; see also 3:19–4:3). The sealed portion of the plates will be translated and given to the world at some future day, and this will establish the foreknowledge of God once and for all. Moroni warned that "God knoweth all things; therefore, he that condemneth, let him be aware lest he shall be in danger of hell fire" (Morm. 8:17; see also Moro. 7:22).

The Book of Mormon bears witness that God has all understanding or all knowledge. In the words of Joseph Smith, "the past, the present, and the future were and are, with Him, one eternal 'now'" (*TPJS*, p. 220). Faith in the knowledge and understanding of God enables men to exercise faith unto salvation (see *Lectures on Faith*, 4:11).

The Attribute of Comprehension (Judgment)

The fourth attribute of God, given by Ammon, is that "he comprehendeth all things" (Alma 26:35). With complete comprehension, he is able to judge justly and show no partiality to any person; otherwise, he would be "a changeable God, and a respecter of persons" (Moro. 8:12). In order to render eternal judgment, God must bring all things into consideration. The past, the present, and the future effects upon others must be taken into account. He must comprehend all things to render impartial judgments on the inhabitants of the earth. Thus, comprehending all things is equated with the attribute of judgment.

All of the major engravers upon the Book of Mormon plates testified that they would see the reader at the judgment bar of God, and the reader would know of God's totally righteous judgment. Nephi spoke of many who would be spotless at his judgment bar and bid an everlasting farewell to those who would not partake of God's goodness and respect the words of the Jews [Bible] and his words [Book of Mormon] (see 2 Nephi 33:7, 13–15). Nephi testified that the Holy One of Israel "shall execute judgment in righteousness" (1 Nephi 22:21; see also 2 Nephi 9:46; Mosiah 3:18).

Jacob urged his readers to enter the strait gate and continue in the narrow way to eternal life. He bid a farewell to them until he met them "before the pleasing bar of God, which bar striketh the wicked with awful dread and fear" (Jacob 6:13). Earlier, Jacob had proclaimed concerning the judgment:

> *14 Wherefore, we shall have a perfect knowledge of all our guilt, and our uncleanness, and our nakedness; and the righteous shall have a perfect knowledge of their enjoyment, and their righteousness, being clothed with purity, yea, even with the robe of righteousness.*
>
> *15 And it shall come to pass that when all men shall have passed from this first death unto life, insomuch as they have become immortal, they must appear before the judgment-seat of the Holy One of Israel; and then cometh the judgment, and then must they be judged according to the holy judgment of God. (2 Nephi 9:14–15)*

Jacob testified further that "the keeper of the gate is the Holy One of Israel; and he employeth no servant there; and there is none other way save it be by the gate; for he cannot be deceived, for the Lord God is his name" (2 Nephi 9:41).

Mormon wrote to all the world, "And for this cause I write unto you, that ye may know that ye must all stand before the judgment-seat of Christ, yea, every soul who belongs to the whole human family of Adam; and ye must stand to be judged of our works, whether they be good or evil" (Morm. 3:20). Mormon's desire was to "persuade all ye ends of the earth to repent and prepare to stand before the judgment-seat of Christ" (Morm. 3:22).

Moroni also testified that the readers would "see [him] at the bar of God," where they would know that what he had written was true (Moro. 10:27). He likewise invited them to repent and "be perfected in [Christ]" (Moro. 10:32–33). Earlier, Moroni had quoted scripture where the Lord says, "judgment is mine, . . . and vengeance is mine also, and I will repay" (Morm. 8:20).

Thus, all four of the major writers testified of the coming judgment by Christ, which was committed to Him by the Father (John 5:22). These same writers speak of the righteous and just judgment that he exercises. Faith that God comprehends all things enables men to suffer tribulations and afflictions from their enemies, knowing that God will recompense them at the judgment bar. Jesus Christ comprehends all things. He revealed to the Prophet Joseph Smith that he "knoweth all things [comprehends] for all things are before [his] eyes" (D&C 38:2).

The Attribute of Mercy

Ammon's fifth attribute of God is that "he is a merciful Being" (Alma 26:35). The attribute of justice is almost always mentioned in conjunction with mercy, although Ammon does not mention it in the verse under consideration here. To be an impartial God, there must be a balance between justice and mercy. The Book of Mormon bears further witness of the attribute of mercy.

Jacob, the brother of Nephi, speaks of the greatness of God's mercy in his deliverance of his Saints from endless torment (see 2 Nephi 9:19). Alma testifies of Christ's bowels being "filled with mercy according to the flesh that he may know . . . how to succor his people according to their infirmities" (Alma 7:12). Mercy can satisfy the demands of justice, but those who do not repent are "exposed to the whole law of the demands of justice" (Alma 34:14–16). Alma says there must be a perfect balance between justice and mercy or "God would cease to be God" (Alma 42:24–25). But God is an eternal being, and mercy is an eternal principle that he has attained. It will only be exercised in total righteousness. God's mercy enables man to have faith that they will be fully rewarded with his love for their having endured suffering in this life (see *Lectures on Faith* 4:15).

The Character of God (Justice)

The sixth attribute of God taught in the Book of Mormon is justice. As Alma instructed his wayward son Corianton, he emphasized the work of justice and said three times that were justice destroyed, or robbed by mercy, "God would cease to be God" (Alma 42:13, 22, 25). Earlier, he had declared that "the works of justice could not be destroyed, according to the supreme goodness of God" (Alma 12:32). God's nature is "that righteousness which is in our great and Eternal head" (Hel. 13:38). He is "a God of truth and cannot lie" (Ether 3:12).

An expression well known to members of the Church was coined by Lorenzo Snow, given to him by revelation, "As man is now, God once was; as God is now, man may be."[9] The concept undoubtedly originated with the Prophet Joseph Smith who taught that:

> God himself was once as we are now, and is an exalted man, and sits enthroned in yonder heavens! That is the great secret. If the veil were rent today, and the great God who holds this world in its orbit, and who upholds all worlds and all things by his power, was to make himself visible,—I say, if you were to see him today, you would see him like a man in form— like yourselves in all the person, image, and very form as a man; for Adam was created in the very fashion,

---

9 Williams, C. J. (1984). *The Teachings of Lorenzo Snow*. Salt Lake City: Bookcraft, pp. 1–2.

image, and likeness of God, and received instruction from, and walked, talked and conversed with him, as one man talks and communes with another. (*TPJS,* p. 345)

The Prophet Joseph Smith went on to teach that in the council of the Gods, there was "concocted a plan to create the world and people it" (*TPJS,* p. 349). He taught that spirits are eternal and that "all the minds and spirits that God ever sent into the world are susceptible of enlargement" (*TPJS,* p. 354). He also taught that "it is the first principle of the Gospel to know for a certainty the Character of God, and to know that we may converse with him as one man converses with another, and that he was once a man like us; yea, that God himself, the Father of us all, dwelt on an earth, the same as Jesus Christ himself did; and I will show it from the Bible" (*TPJS,* pp. 345–46).

Alma and those baptized in the waters of Mormon were blessed for believing in and following the words of God spoken through his prophet (see Mosiah 26:15–16). Nephi, son of Helaman, was blessed for his steadiness in keeping God's commandments (see Hel. 10:4–5). Those who do not keep the commandments will be punished by the law of justice at the last day, if not before. Nephi warned of "the punishment of the law at the great and last day, according to the commandments which God hath given" (2 Nephi 2:26).

Alma beautifully explained to his wayward son Corianton the justice of God and the punishment of the law.

> *21 And if there was no law given, if men sinned what could justice do, or mercy either, for they would have no claim upon the creature?*

> *22 But there is a law given, and a punishment affixed, and a repentance granted; which repentance, mercy claimeth; otherwise, justice claimeth the creature and executeth the law, and the law inflicteth the punishment;*

if not so, the works of justice would be destroyed, and God would cease to be God.

23 But God ceaseth not to be God, and mercy claimeth the penitent, and mercy cometh because of the Atonement; and the Atonement bringeth to pass the resurrection of the dead; and the resurrection of the dead bringeth back men into the presence of God; and thus they are restored into his presence, to be judged according to their works, according to the law and justice (Alma 42:21–23).

The inflicting of punishment by the law illustrates the co-eternal nature of God and his law.[10] Both God and eternal law are unchangeable and represent the attribute of justice.

The law[11] is the standard by which God gives and reveals his will to man. The law is also eternal; it existed before this world and will exist after this earth's mortal probation. Just as the nature of God is perfect, so is the eternal law. Moroni said:

9 For do we not read that God is the same yesterday, today, and forever, and in him there is no variableness neither shadow of changing?

10 And now, if ye have imagined up unto yourselves a god who doth vary, and in whom there is shadow of changing, then have ye imagined up unto yourselves a god who is not a God of miracles. (Morm. 9:9–10; see also Heb. 13:8)

If God varied in his actions under the same situations, then he would cease to be God. But since God's nature has been perfected

---

10 Philosophers and other scholars have argued for years over which existed first: God or law. There is no revelation answering this question; therefore, this issue will not be considered here.

11 As used in both the Bible and the Book of Mormon, the "law" sometimes refers to the law of Moses. Only references to the law as the eternal law of God are considered in this chapter.

beyond changeability, he will not and cannot change. There is no possibility that he will cease to be God. As Jacob testified: "O the greatness and the justice of our God! For he executeth all his words, and they have gone forth out of his mouth, and his law must be fulfilled" (2 Nephi 9:17). The fulfillment of the law is thus referred to as the law of justice. The Book of Mormon consistently uses justice as the function of the law of God.

Therefore, God became God by conforming to eternal law. Thus God and law are co–eternal. He has given us laws that we may become like him. It is his "work and [his] glory—to bring to pass the immortality and eternal life of man" (Moses 1:39). The laws he has given us are eternal and are associated with either blessings or punishments. The Book of Mormon shows how the laws blessed or cursed the people.

The Functions of Justice

The Book of Mormon teaches that there are four functions of justice, or the law: (1) it blesses those who keep the law; (2) it awakens people to a sense of guilt; (3) it divides the righteous from the wicked; and (4) it punishes those who break the law. Each one of these functions is explained in the Book of Mormon and discussed below.

In one of his many editorial comments, Mormon explains the blessings of the law: "We can see that the Lord in his great infinite goodness doth bless and prosper those who put their trust in him" (Hel. 12:1). King Benjamin speaks of the Lord's creating us and preserving us from day to day, and further states that "all that he requires of you is to keep his commandments; and he has promised you that if ye would keep his commandments ye should prosper in the land; and he never doth vary from that which he hath said; therefore, if ye do keep his commandments he doth bless you and prosper you" (Mosiah 2:22; see also D&C 130:20–21). As this scripture shows, the blessings are conditional, based upon our keeping the commandments.

The Lord is desirous to give us every blessing possible; but, since blessings are conditional, he uses various means to get the people to remember him so he can bless them. "And thus we see that except the Lord doth chasten his people with many afflictions, yea, except he doth visit them with death and with terror, and with famine and with all manner of pestilence, they will not remember him" (Hel. 12:3).

King Benjamin teaches us the second function of justice. When people sin, the Spirit withdraws, but "the demands of divine justice do awaken his immortal soul to a lively sense of his own guilt" (Mosiah 2:38). Although this scripture describes those who come out in open rebellion against God, the Book of Mormon shows that the same things happen whenever people sin. Zeezrom, after being silenced by Alma and Amulek, "began to tremble under a consciousness of his guilt" (Alma 12:1, see also Alma 14:6).

The third function of justice is taught in the vision of the tree of life, which Nephi and his father had seen (see 1 Nephi 8). Nephi explained to his hardened brethren that the river of water in the vision "was an awful gulf, which separated the wicked from the tree of life, and also from the saints of God" (1 Nephi 15:28). He reported "that our father also saw that the justice of God did also divide the wicked from the righteous" (1 Nephi 15:30). Nephi told his inquiring brothers that justice was represented in both this life, their days of probation, as well as the "final state of the soul after the death of the temporal body" (1 Nephi 15:31–32). Earlier, Nephi had equated the people in the great and spacious building [in the vision of the tree of life] with those being divided by "the justice of God." Life experiences confirm these Book of Mormon principles: there is a natural separation of "the wicked from the righteous," and we see that this separation is caused by "the justice of God." The reason for the separation is probably to prevent the influence of the wicked upon the innocent.

The fourth function of justice is given in the great discourse of Alma to his son Corianton (referred to above). Alma states that humans in their fallen condition "were in the grasp of justice;

yea, the justice of God" (Alma 42:14). The law of justice inflicted punishment for the breaking of the law (see Alma 42:22). A punishment was affixed opposite to the plan of happiness which was also eternal "and a just law given, which brought remorse of conscience unto man" (Alma 42:18, #2 function of justice, awaken to a sense of guilt). Alma then summarized (as quoted above) that if there were no repentance, "justice claimeth the creature and executeth the law, and the law inflicteth the punishment; if not so, the works of justice would be destroyed, and God would cease to be God" (Alma 42:22). Again we see the eternal nature of the law: it inflicts punishment as justice requires. There is no alternative except the mercy of the Atonement.

Nephi spoke of "the punishment of the law at the great and last day" (2 Nephi 2:26). Punishment coming at the great and last day suggests that justice may not be fully met during mortality. The Book of Mormon further verifies this concept. Jacob admonished his hearers to "prepare [their] souls for that glorious day when justice shall be administered unto the righteous, even the day of judgment, that ye may not shrink with awful fear" (2 Nephi 9:46). Both the righteous and the wicked will reap full justice and mercy at that great day. The righteous "do enter into the rest of the Lord," and "justice and judgment" come upon the wicked (Alma 60:13; see also Alma 14:11 and 1 Cor. 15:19).

The rewards or punishments that come from justice are apparently relative, depending on our circumstances and opportunities. The people of Limhi were promised conditional blessings, and these were "according to his own will and pleasure" (Mosiah 7:33; see also D&C 82:10). King Benjamin taught that the Lord requires that we should do as he hath commanded, "which if ye do, he doth immediately bless you" (Mosiah 2:24). However, Joseph Smith made this qualification:

> A man can bear a heavy burden by practice and continuing to increase it. The inhabitants of this continent anciently were so constituted, and were so

determined and persevering, either in righteousness or wickedness, that God visited them immediately either with great judgments or blessings. But the present generation, if they were going to battle, if they got any assistance from God, they would have to obtain it by faith. (*TPJS*, p. 299)

The rewards and/or the punishments will come. The law of justice will be fulfilled. The Prophet Joseph Smith also taught:

But while one portion of the human race is judging and condemning the other without mercy, the Great Parent of the universe looks upon the whole of the human family with a fatherly care and paternal regard; He views them as His offspring, and without any of those contracted feelings that influence the children of men, causes "His sun to rise on the evil and on the good, and sendeth rain on the just and on the unjust." He holds the reins of judgment in His hands; He is a wise Lawgiver, and will judge all men, not according to the narrow, contracted notions of men, but, "according to the deeds done in the body whether they be good or evil," or whether these deeds were done in England, America, Spain, Turkey, or India. He will judge them, "not according to what they have not, but according to what they have," those who have lived without law, will be judged without law, and those who have a law, will be judged by that law. We need not doubt the wisdom and intelligence of the Great Jehovah; He will award judgment or mercy to all nations according to their several desserts, their means of obtaining intelligence, the laws by which they are governed, the facilities afforded them of obtaining correct information, and His inscrutable designs in relation to the human family; and when the designs of God shall be made manifest, and the curtain of futurity be withdrawn, we shall all of us eventually have to confess that the Judge of all the earth has done right. (*TPJS*, p. 218; see also *Lectures on Faith* 4:13)

Summary

The six attributes of God treated above show him to be an infinite and eternal being. Our acceptance of these attributes in him is vital to our exercising faith in him. King Benjamin admonished:

> *9 Believe in God; believe that he is, and that he created all things, both in heaven and in earth; believe that he has all wisdom, and all power, both in heaven and in earth; believe that man doth not comprehend all the things which the Lord can comprehend.*
>
> *10 And again, believe that ye must repent of your sins and forsake them, and humble yourselves before God; and ask in sincerity of heart that he would forgive you; and now, if you believe all these things see that ye do them. (Mosiah 4:9–10)*

It is one thing to believe in these attributes of God, but it is another thing to accept and live the plan of redemption he has given unto mankind. And it is the Book of Mormon which will help us to do this.

Faith in a God of justice enables men to place themselves under his guidance and direction. Nephi had an understanding of justice as exemplified in his response to father Lehi telling him the Lord required them to return to Jerusalem, to the house of Laban and seek the records (see 1 Nephi 3:4–6). Said he, "I will go and do the things which the Lord hath commanded, for I know that the Lord giveth no commandments unto the children of men, save he shall prepare a way for them that they may accomplish the thing which he commandeth them" (1 Nephi 3:7).

Men such as Corianton, son of Alma, questioned the justice of God, usually as a justification for their breaking the commandments of God. Alma's concluding remarks to Corianton on this point are a most appropriate answer to this kind of rationalization:

> *29 And now, my son, I desire that ye should let these things trouble you no more, and only let your sins trouble you, with that trouble which shall bring you down unto repentance.*
>
> *30 O my son, I desire that ye should deny the justice of God no more. Do not endeavor to excuse yourself in the least point because of your sins, by denying the justice of God; but do you let the justice of God, and his mercy, and his long-suffering have full sway in your heart; and let it bring you down to the dust in humility. (Alma 42:29–30)*

For those who are not treated fairly in this life, the Book of Mormon holds out hope. As partially quoted above, General Moroni wrote concerning those whose life was cut short because of the wickedness of others: "For the Lord suffereth the righteous to be slain that his justice and judgment may come upon the wicked; therefore ye need not suppose that the righteous are lost because they are slain; but behold, they do enter into the rest of the Lord their God" (Alma 60:13).

Ammon's final admonition to his brethren is a fitting conclusion to a discussion on the justice of God: "Now my brethren, we see that God is mindful of every people, whatsoever land they may be in; yea, he numbereth his people, and his bowels of mercy are over all the earth. Now this is my joy, and my great thanksgiving; yea, and I will give thanks unto my God forever. Amen" (Alma 26:37).

3

FRAMER OF HEAVEN AND EARTH

*"We know that there is a God in heaven . . .
the framer of heaven and earth, and all things
which are in them." (D&C 20:17)*

The Book of Mormon testifies that Jesus Christ was the Creator, but there are many things about the creation of the heaven and the earth that are yet to be revealed. In the early days of the restored Church, it was revealed to Joseph Smith,

32 Yea, verily I say unto you, in that day when the Lord shall come, he shall reveal all things—

33 Things which have passed, and hidden things which no man knew, things of the earth, by which it was made, and the purpose and the end thereof—

34 Things most precious, things that are above, and things that are beneath, things that are in the earth, and upon the earth, and in heaven. (D&C 101:32–34)

As noted by President Harold B. Lee:

Missionaries going out into the field often ask how we reconcile the teachings of the scriptures with the teachings of the scientists in accordance with the temple ordinances. In reply I occasionally refer to the revelation given to the Prophet Joseph Smith in Kirtland in 1833, concerning the great event that is to take place at the commencement of the millennial reign when the Lord shall come . . .

Then I say, "If you and I are there when the Lord reveals all this, then I'll answer your questions—how the earth was made, how man came to be placed upon the earth." Until that time all we have is the support and security that we have in the scriptures, and we must accept the rest by faith.[12]

Although there are many things about the creation that have not been revealed, the Book of Mormon bears witness of several important principles that have been revealed. As Moroni abridged the Book of Ether, he recorded the following:

> *3 And as I suppose that the first part of this record, which speaks concerning the creation of the world, and also of Adam, and an account from that time even to the great tower, and whatsoever things transpired among the children of men until that time, is had among the Jews—*

> *4 Therefore I do not write those things which transpired from the days of Adam until that time; but they are had upon the plates; and whoso findeth them, the same will have power that he may get the full account. (Ether 1:3–4)*

The Jaredites left the eastern continent long before the account of the creation was revealed to Moses. Therefore, it was an earlier account than the one "had among the Jews" (v. 3). Furthermore, the account of the creation revealed to Moses and recorded in the biblical record has suffered the loss of "many parts which are plain and most precious" (1 Nephi 13:26–29; see also Moses 1:41). The

---

12 (1972). First Presidency message. *Ensign,* December, p. 2.

Nephites had "an account of the creation of the world" revealed to Moses and recorded upon the plates of brass (1 Nephi 5:11) before parts were taken away. They also had the Jaredites' earlier record (Ether 1:3–4 quoted above). Our emphasis in this chapter will be on what the Book of Mormon teaches about the creation.

Father Lehi gave this warning:

> *10 But behold, when the time cometh that they shall dwindle in unbelief, after they have received so great blessings from the hand of the Lord—having a knowledge of the creation of the earth, and all men, knowing the great and marvelous works of the Lord from the creation of the world; having power given them to do all things by faith; having all the commandments from the beginning, and having been brought by his infinite goodness into this precious land of promise—behold, I say, if the day shall come that they will reject the Holy One of Israel, the true Messiah, their Redeemer and their God, behold, the judgments of him that is just shall rest upon them. (2 Nephi 1:10)*

This warning illustrates the importance of what the Book of Mormon teaches.

Jesus Was the Creator

Father Lehi testified to his sons that "there is a God, and he hath created all things, both the heavens and the earth, and all things that in them are" (2 Nephi 2:14). The father of king Lamoni asked about the Great Spirit, and Aaron said that the Great Spirit was God, "and he created all things both in heaven and in earth" (Alma 22:9–11). Although these testimonies do not identify which God, the Book of Mormon bears record repeatedly that Jesus was the God who created the heavens and the earth and all things that are in them.

Nephi bore testimony that without God "there could have been no creation. But there is a God, and he is Christ" (2 Nephi 11:7). King Benjamin spoke of "Jesus Christ, the Son of God, the Father of heaven and earth, the Creator of all things from the beginning" (Mosiah 3:8). Samuel the Lamanite foretold of "the coming of Jesus Christ, the Son of God, the Father of heaven and of earth, the Creator of all things from the beginning" (Hel. 14:12). The prophet Abinadi spoke of God himself, "the very Eternal Father of heaven and earth" (Mosiah 15:1, 4), coming down among the children of men to redeem his people. Zeezrom asked Amulek if the Son of God was the very Eternal Father. He replied that he was "the very Eternal Father of heaven and of earth, and all things which in them are" (Alma 11:38–39). A father is a creator, and thus the Son of God was the Father or creator of the earth. Moroni spoke of "that same God[13] who created the heavens and the earth, and all things that in them are" (Morm. 9:11). When Christ spoke to the Nephites, he identified himself as the creator: "Behold, I am Jesus Christ the Son of God. I created the heavens and the earth, and all things that in them are" (3 Nephi 9:15). Therefore, the Book of Mormon repeatedly establishes Christ as the "framer of heaven and earth."

Although the doctrine of Christ's being the creator of this world and even the creator of other worlds may be new doctrine to most of the Christian world, it is taught in the Bible. The gospel of St. John states concerning the Word [Jesus Christ]: "All things were made by him; and without him was not any thing made that was made. He was in the world, and the world was made by him, and the world knew him not" (John 1:3, 10). Paul, in writing to the Colossians, positively identified Jesus by calling him the Father's dear Son, the one through whom we have redemption and receive forgiveness of sins, who was in the image of the invisible God, and was the first born (see Col. 1:13–15). Paul then said: "For by him were all things created, that are in heaven, and that are in earth,

---

13 "That same God" to whom Moroni refers will be further identified as Christ in chapter five.

visible and invisible, whether they be thrones, or dominions, or principalities, or powers: all things were created by him, and for him" (Col. 1:16). In the book of Hebrews we read, God "hath in these last days spoken unto us by his Son, whom he hath appointed heir of all things, by whom also he made the worlds" (Heb. 1:2). The Hebrews passage extends Jesus' role from the creator of this world alone to being the creator of other worlds, as well. Thus there are three biblical witnesses of Christ being the creator of this world and other worlds.

Modern-day revelation confirms the creator of other worlds to be Christ. To Moses the Lord revealed: "And worlds without number have I created; and I also created them for mine own purpose; and by the Son I created them, which is mine Only Begotten" (Moses 1:33). Joseph Smith and Sidney Rigdon bore testimony of Christ and of his role in the creation:

> 23 For we saw him, even on the right hand of God; and we heard the voice bearing record that he is the Only Begotten of the Father—
>
> 24 That by him, and through him, and of him, the worlds are and were created, and the inhabitants thereof are begotten sons and daughters unto God. (D&C 76:23–24)

The phrase "by him" suggests that he was the administrator of the creation. The phrase "through him" suggests that others assisted in the creation. The idea that "others" assisted in the creation is confirmed in the Pearl of Great Price (see Abraham 4:1). The phrase "of him" suggests that it was created by his knowledge and power. Doctrine and Covenants 88:6–11 confirms this concept of the creation.

Thus, as the Lord revealed in the April 6 revelation, we know from the Book of Mormon that God was "the framer of heaven and earth, and all things which are in them." We also know that the God spoken of in this revelation is Jesus Christ. Therefore, the testimony of the Book of Mormon is supported by the Bible and modern-day revelation.

The Earth Was Created by the Power of God

The Book of Mormon states that the "earth was created by the power of [God's] word" (Jacob 4:9). The creation by the power of his word is a second witness to the biblical record of how the earth was created. In the Bible, the account of each day's creation is prefaced with, "and God said" and is usually concluded with "and it was so" (Gen. 1:3, 6–7, 9, 11, 14–15, 20, 24, 26–27). The Prophet Joseph clarifies the biblical meaning of creating by the power of God's word:

> . . . the word create came from the [Hebrew] word *baurau* which does not mean to create out of nothing; it means to organize; the same as a man would organize materials and build a ship. Hence, we infer that God had materials to organize the world out of chaos— chaotic matter, which is element, and in which dwells all the glory. Element had an existence from the time he had. The pure principles of element are principles which can never be destroyed; they may be organized and re-organized, but not destroyed. They had no beginning, and can have no end. (*TPJS*, p. 350–52)

From the Joseph Smith clarification, we conclude that God spoke, and the materials or elements obeyed his commands. Thus the earth was created—organized—by the power of God's word commanding the elements.

Although referring to a time after the creation, in an editorial comment (quoted in the previous chapter but repeated here for a different purpose), Mormon substantiated that the earth and its elements obey the voice of God.

> *8 For behold, the dust of the earth moveth hither and thither, to the dividing asunder, at the command of our great and everlasting God.*
>
> *9 Yea, behold at his voice do the hills and the mountains tremble and quake.*

10 And by the power of his voice they are broken up, and become smooth, yea, even like unto a valley.

11 Yea, by the power of his voice doth the whole earth shake;

12 Yea, by the power of his voice, do the foundations rock, even to the very center.

13 Yea, and if he say unto the earth—Move—it is moved.

14 Yea, if he say unto the earth—Thou shalt go back, that it lengthen out the day for many hours—it is done. (Hel. 12: 8–14)

The earth obeyed the voice of God before and after the creation.

Further insight into how the earth was created is given in the Pearl of Great Price. The KJV of the Bible states that "the earth was without form and void" (Gen. 1:2). The Book of Abraham translation is different from yet consistent with the concepts discussed above.

1 In the beginning God created the heaven and the earth.

2 And the earth was without form, and void; and darkness was upon the face of the deep. And the Spirit of God moved upon the face of the waters. (Gen. 1:1–2)

1 And then the Lord said: Let us go down. And they went down at the beginning, and they, that is the Gods, organized and formed the heavens and the earth.

2 And the earth, after it was formed, was empty and desolate, because they had not formed anything but the earth; and darkness reigned upon the face of the deep, and the Spirit of the Gods was brooding upon the face of the waters. (Abr. 4:1–2)

The Book of Abraham verifies that the earth was organized out of existing materials, but it was not yet ready to be inhabited. This was certainly the intended interpretation of the KJV "without form and void." The respective accounts detail for us what happened in the sequence of the days of creation.

When Was the Earth Created?

The biblical book of Genesis speaks of the earth being created in a period of six days. The traditional interpretation of these days is that each day is one thousand years according to the Lord's time (see Ps. 90:4; 2 Pet. 3:8). Consequently, some reason that the creation of the earth took six thousand years and the Lord rested on the seventh day, and that since Adam was placed on the earth about six thousand years ago, according to the biblical records, the earth should not be dated beyond thirteen thousand years. However, if the earth was organized out of existing materials, there should be no objection to the earth's being dated much older than this. In fact, the earth's material makeup is likely without beginning, since the elements are eternal.

Another consideration regarding the age of the earth is the difference in the wording of the Bible and the Pearl of Great Price with respect to the time periods of the creation. The book of Abraham speaks of the six "times" or time periods, "morning until evening that they called day; and this was the second time that they called night and day" (Abr. 4:8; see also Abr. 4:13, 19, 23, 31). As a result, some suggest the creation time periods may have been longer than 1000 years.

The Abraham account does not say directly how long the "time" period was, although it does say it was "after the Lord's time, which was after the time of Kolob" (Abr. 5:13). Earlier, the Lord's (and Kolob's) time is given as one thousand of "our days" for one of "God's days" (Abr. 3:4). Therefore, the argument for creation periods being longer than one thousand years is not verifiable.

The Book of Mormon does not say anything about the time of the creation of the earth, but it does offer some suggestions for the earth's present form or organization. It speaks of what would happen at the time of the crucifixion of the earth:

> *21 Yea, at the time that he shall yield up the ghost there shall be thunderings and lightnings for the space of many hours, and the earth shall shake and tremble; and the rocks which are upon the face of this earth, which are both above the earth and beneath, which ye know at this time are solid, or the more part of it is one solid mass, shall be broken up;*
>
> *22 Yea, they shall be rent in twain, and shall ever after be found in seams and in cracks, and in broken fragments upon the face of the whole earth, yea, both above the earth and beneath. (Hel. 14:21–22)*

This prophecy of Samuel the Lamanite was fulfilled when the earth was broken up at Christ's crucifixion (3 Nephi 10:9). Various dating theories such as sedimentation[14] could verify the evidence found in seams and in cracks. Such verification could indirectly verify the time of the crucifixion.

In a revelation to Joseph Smith, the Lord said that the seven seals in the book of Revelation each represented a thousand years of the earth's temporal existence (D&C 77:6). Therefore, the time of the completion of the creation of the earth would be about six thousand years ago. How long each of the six creative periods were would still remain unanswered, but Christ will reveal that when he comes a second time. Some of our LDS scientists should accept the challenge of verifying the time of the seams and cracks in the earth; but more importantly, we should learn of the purpose of the earth being created.

---

14 Sedimentation is a measurement of the rate of dirt or silt being deposited in an area of the earth or in a sea over a given period of time to determine how long it has been happening. It has been nearly two thousand years since the earth was broken up, and the determination that dirt or silt had been deposited for that length of time in areas of North or South America would be significant.

The Purpose of the Creation

The earth was created as a place for men to dwell: "And there stood one among them that was like unto God, and he said unto those who were with him: We will go down, for there is space there, and we will take of these materials, and we will make an earth whereon these may dwell" (Abr. 3:24). This information was given to Abraham about four thousand years ago [around 2000 B.C.]. It was revealed also to Nephi: "Behold, the Lord hath created the earth that it should be inhabited; and he hath created his children that they should possess it" (1 Nephi 17:36).

After the earth has served the purpose of man's mortal habitation, it will be inhabited by the celestial beings of this earth. The Lord revealed to the Prophet Joseph Smith:

> *17 And the redemption of the soul is through him that quickeneth all things, in whose bosom it is decreed that the poor and the meek of the earth shall inherit it.*
>
> *18 Therefore, it must needs be sanctified from all un-righteousness, that it may be prepared for the celestial glory;*
>
> *19 For after it hath filled the measure of its creation, it shall be crowned with glory, even with the presence of God the Father;*
>
> *20 That bodies who are of the celestial kingdom may possess it forever and ever; for, for this intent was it made and created, and for this intent are they sanctified. (D&C 88:17–20; see also D&C 88:25–26 and D&C 49:15–17)*

The inhabitants of the earth should be privileged to possess the earth in order that they may participate in the plan of salvation and return to God's presence (see Abr. 3:25–26). More of this plan is discussed in chapters that follow.

We may not know all the details of the creation, but we do know the overall purpose of the creation. We also know what the scriptures teach about the creation, and we should test all theories against what these scriptures say. As admonished by President Harold B. Lee, quoted above, "If you and I are there when the Lord reveals all this, then I'll answer your questions—how the earth was made, how man came to be placed upon the earth. Until that time all we have is the support and security that we have in the scriptures, and we must accept the rest by faith." When the Lord comes again, he will teach us much more about the creation. Until then, we must rely upon the truths he has already revealed.

4

GOD CREATED MALE AND FEMALE

*God "created man, male and female, after his own image
and in his own likeness, created he them." (D&C 20:18)*

We will not compare the Book of Mormon teachings
with scientific theories or with teachings of other religions but will merely let the Book of Mormon speak
for itself. We will supplement those teachings with other modern-
day revelation and with what the Prophet Joseph Smith and other
Church presidents have said.

We introduce our commentary concerning the creation of
man with an excerpt from President Harold B. Lee:

> I was somewhat sorrowed recently to hear
> someone, a sister who comes from a church family,
> ask, "What about the pre-Adamic people?" Here was
> someone who I thought was fully grounded in the
> faith.
>
> I asked, "What about the pre-Adamic people?"
> She replied, "Well, aren't there evidences that
> people preceded the Adamic period of the earth?"
> I said, "Have you forgotten the scripture that
> says, 'And I, the Lord God, formed man from the
> dust of the ground, and breathed into his nostrils the
> breath of life; and man became a living soul, the first

flesh upon the earth, the first man also . . . " (Moses 3:7).

I asked, "Do you believe that?"

I say that we need to teach our people to find their answers in the scriptures. If only each of us would be wise enough to say that we aren't able to answer any question unless we can find a doctrinal answer in the scriptures! And if we hear someone teaching something that is contrary to what is in the scriptures, each of us may know whether the things spoken are false—it is as simple as that. But the unfortunate thing is that so many of us are not reading the scriptures. We do not know what is in them, and therefore we speculate about the things that we ought to have found in the scriptures themselves. I think that therein is one of our biggest dangers of today.[15]

The teachings of the Book of Mormon are apparently based upon the Nephite people searching the plates of brass or other scripture. When Lehi's sons returned from Jerusalem to the valley of Lemuel with the plates of brass, Lehi searched them. "And he beheld that they did contain the five books of Moses, which gave an account of the creation of the world, and also of *Adam and Eve, who were our first parents*" (1 Nephi 5:11, italics added). Other teachings of the Nephite prophets were also from the plates of brass, Jaredite records, or earlier teachings that were given to them by revelation and later became scripture. Let us examine these teachings.

Who Created Adam?

There are many Book of Mormon references to God creating Adam, or humankind in general. According to what Lehi had read, he spoke of God giving commandments to man "after he had created *our first parents*, and the beasts of the field and the fowls of

15 (1972). First Presidency message. *Ensign,* December, p. 2.

the air, and in fine, all things which are created" (2 Nephi 2:15, italics added. See also 2 Nephi 9:9; 29:7; Jacob 2:21). In addition to these general statements, there is one very specific reference to the creation of Adam. Moroni, writing to those "who deny the revelations of God" (Morm. 9:7) in the latter days, declared:

> *11 But behold, I will show unto you a God of miracles, even the God of Abraham, and the God of Isaac, and the God of Jacob; and it is that same God who created the heavens and the earth, and all things that in them are.*
>
> *12 Behold, he created Adam, and by Adam came the fall of man. And because of the fall of man came Jesus Christ, even the Father and the Son; and because of Jesus Christ came the redemption of man. (Morm. 9:11–12)*

The Book of Mormon teaches that the God of Abraham, Isaac, and Jacob was Jesus Christ (see 1 Nephi 19:10). He is identified in the JST as Jehovah: "And I appeared unto Abraham, unto Isaac, and unto Jacob. I am the Lord God Almighty; the Lord JEHOVAH. And was not my name known unto them?" (JST Ex. 6:3). Jesus identified himself to the Jews during his earthly ministry as "I AM," or Jehovah (John 8:58; compare Ex. 3:15–16). Wherefore, Jesus Christ was the creator of Adam. This concept needs further explanation. The Book of Mormon speaks of the Son of God as "the very Eternal Father of heaven and of earth, and all things which in them are" (Alma 11:38–39; compare Mosiah 15:4). He was the father of "heaven and of earth" because he created them. As the father of the earth, Jehovah not only organized it, but was also responsible for what could happen on it after it was created. He was the administrator of the plan, presented by Eloheim in the premortal life, to populate an earth where men would dwell and be tested or prove themselves (Abr. 3:24–28). Thus Jehovah or Christ was responsible for Adam's coming to the earth with Eve and for their family that would follow. Therefore, as quoted above, the plates of brass "gave an account of the creation of the world, and also of Adam and Eve, who were our first parents" (1 Nephi 5:11). Lehi, according to the things he had read in the plates of brass, testified that Adam and Eve "brought forth children; yea, even the family of all the earth" (2 Nephi 2:20). The plan of redemption for these inhabitants of the earth was to be directed by Jesus Christ as the father of the earth (2 Nephi 2:26–27).

The Book of Mormon testifies that Adam and Eve were the first humans created by God through the administration of Christ on this earth. Alma, paraphrasing or quoting scripture, said that "God placed cherubim and a flaming sword on the east of the garden of Eden, lest our first parents should enter and partake of the fruit of the tree of life, and live forever" (Alma 12:21). He then speaks further of Adam "partaking of the forbidden fruit" and not partaking "of the fruit of the tree of life at that time" (vv. 22–23).

Ammon, son of king Mosiah, used the records and holy scriptures to teach the Lamanite king, beginning "at the creation of the world, and also the creation of Adam" (Alma 18:36). Aaron, son of king Mosiah, teaching another Lamanite king, "began from the creation of Adam, reading the scriptures unto the king—how God created man after his own image" (Alma 22:12; see also v. 13). Again Alma, explaining the scriptures to his son Corianton, speaks of "the Lord God [sending] our first parents forth from the garden of Eden" (Alma 42:2). The above quotes, undoubtedly taken from the plates of brass, the predecessor to the Old Testament before many plain and precious parts were lost (see 1 Nephi 13:24–29), show that they contained the knowledge of Adam and Eve being the first humans created on this earth. King Mosiah, who translated the Jaredite records, said they went "back until the creation of Adam" (Mosiah 28:17). Both of these ancient records originally taught much more about Adam's creation than is in the Bible today. Although Adam is not specifically called the first man in Genesis, the Pearl of Great Price restores much of the knowledge lost from the Genesis account in the Old Testament. Moses was shown that Adam was "the first man of all men" (Moses 1:34). The Lord God later told Moses that when Adam was created, he was "the first flesh upon the earth, the first man also" (Moses 3:7). In the Book of Abraham, Abraham says he received "the right of the firstborn, or the first man, who is Adam, or first father" (Abr. 1:3). Paul, in the New Testament, confirms what the Pearl of Great Price teaches. He refers to what was written: "The first man Adam was made a living soul" (1 Cor. 15:45). Finally, in a revelation to Joseph Smith, the Lord traces the Melchizedek priesthood back to Adam, "who was the first man" (D&C 84:16). Thus, all of the standard works bear testimony that Adam and Eve were the first humans created by God in this world.

The Book of Mormon also testifies of the creation of all men. Nephi quotes the Lord God as having "created all men" (2 Nephi 29:7). Jacob says that God created all flesh (Jacob 2:21). All of these creations were administered by Christ, through the plan of Eloheim, who thus speaks of Christ as the creator. However, it is recognized that it is sometimes difficult to determine which God is spoken of when the creation is mentioned, and must be further recognized that both the Father and Christ had been involved. Their plan was "to bring to pass the immortality and eternal life of man" (Moses 1:39).

Under the administration of Christ, all others born upon this earth were born into the family of Adam, the first man. Jacob testified that "by the power of his word man came upon the face of the earth" (Jacob 4:9). Lehi, according to the things he had read (from the plates of brass), had taught Jacob that "after Adam and Eve had partaken of the forbidden fruit they were driven out of the garden of Eden, to till the earth. And they have brought forth children; yea, even the family of all the earth" (2 Nephi 2:19–20). When Jacob later taught of the infinite Atonement, he declared that Christ suffered "the pains of every living creature, both men, women, and children, who belong to the family of Adam" (2 Nephi 9:21).

With the above review of scripture, Moroni's declaration that the God of Abraham, Isaac, and Jacob (Jesus Christ) "created Adam, and by Adam came the fall of man" (Morm. 9:12) should be more clearly understood.

How Man Was Created

Adam and Eve were created in the same way that the earth was created, by the power of God's word.[16] The Book of Mormon states, "by the power of his word man was created of the dust of the earth" (Morm. 9:17). King Benjamin taught that humans were not "even as much as the dust of the earth; yet ye were created of the dust of the earth; but behold, it belongeth to him who created you" (Mosiah 2:25). Our bodies were created from the dust of the earth as an earthly tabernacle for our eternal spirits.

The meaning of Adam being created of the dust of the earth was given an interesting explanation by President Brigham Young. President Young explained that bodies were first created spiritually: the Father begat spirits, and they lived with him. Then he created earthly tabernacles (just as he had been created in this flesh, himself) by partaking of the course material that was organized and composed this earth, until His system was charged with it. Consequently, the physical bodies of His children were organized from the materials of this earth (JD 4:218; see also JD 6:275 and 3:319).

Adam's spirit, begotten by the Father, was thus placed in the body created from the dust of the earth. This seems to be the context of the genealogy given by St. Luke, "of Seth and of Adam, who was formed of God, and the first man upon the earth" (JST Luke 3:45).

Mormon taught that our bodies return to the earth when we die. Speaking of the thousands who were slain in the last Nephite battle, he said, "their flesh, and bones, and blood lay upon the face of the earth . . . to crumble and to return to their mother earth" (Morm. 6:15). Upon the death of the body, the spirit returns to God (Eccl. 12:7; 2 Nephi 9:38; Alma 40:11).

---

16 See the discussion of the meaning of the power of God's word in chapter 3, "The Framer of Heaven and Earth."

Male and Female Created

Mankind being the literal offspring of God suggests that whether they were male or female was dependent upon the natural process of the creation. The Book of Mormon says nothing about the genetic process of creating males or females, but it does affirm that Adam and Eve "were [the] first parents" of our earthly tabernacles (see 1 Nephi 5:11; 2 Nephi 2:15).

Nephi also indirectly teaches us that we had a mother of our spirits: "And he said unto me: Behold, the virgin whom thou seest is the mother of the Son of God, after the manner of the flesh" (1 Nephi 11:18). If Christ had a mother after the manner of the flesh, the implication is that he had a mother after the manner of the spirit. Since Christ is the firstborn of every creature (Col.1:15; see also D&C 93:21), the other spirits would also be the offspring of those heavenly parents. Celestial beings of the highest degree who have entered into the new and everlasting covenant of marriage are able to "have an increase" or offspring (D&C 131:1–4). Thus God, an exalted celestial being, is the father of male and female spirits, and we also have a heavenly mother of our spirits. The words of Eliza R. Snow in the hymn, "O My Father," explain this doctrine:

> I had learned to call thee Father, Thru thy Spirit from on high,
> But, until the key of knowledge was restored, I knew not why.
> In the heav'ns are parents single? No the thought makes reason stare!
> Truth is reason; truth eternal, tells me I've a mother there.[17]

Since intelligences (spirits) are eternal (D&C 93:29, 33), it seems logical that spirits who enter into male or female bodies are also male and female spirits. This is further supported by the

---

17 (1985). *Hymns of The Church of Jesus Christ of Latter-day Saints*, p. 292.

doctrine taught by Alma that all males who hold the priesthood were foreordained to that holy calling in the first place or premortal state (see Alma 13:1–5). In "The Family: A Proclamation to the World," an official declaration from the First Presidency and the Council of the Twelve Apostles, the divine nature of all human beings was declared: "All human beings—male and female—are created in the image of God. Each is a divine son or daughter of heavenly parents, and as such, each has a divine nature and destiny. Gender is an essential characteristic of individual premortal, mortal, and eternal identity and purpose."[18]

An image is a reproduction or imitation. If we look in a mirror we see our image—it looks like us. A likeness is a copy in character, quantity, and appearance. In other words, the offspring of God look like he does and have his form and character. From this concept has come the phrase, "gods in embryo."

King Limhi taught his people that the prophet Abinadi had been slain because:

> . . . *Christ was the God, the Father of all things, and said that he should take upon him the image of man, and it should be the image after which man was created in the beginning; or in other words, he said that man was created after the image of God, and that God should come down among the children of men, and take upon him flesh and blood, and go forth upon the face of the earth.* (Mosiah 7:27)

From this scripture we can see that man was in the image of Christ who had not yet been born.

We learn further from the Book of Ether that our spirits are in the image and probably likeness of our bodies. When Christ appeared to the brother of Jared he told him: "Behold, this body, which ye now behold, is the body of my spirit; and man have I

18 Read by President Gordon B. Hinckley as a part of the message at the General Relief Society Meeting, Sept. 23, 1995, in Salt Lake City, Utah. (1995). *Conference Report,* October.

created after the body of my spirit; and even as I appear unto thee to be in the spirit will I appear unto my people in the flesh" (Ether 3:16). The brother of Jared had just previously been shown the finger of the Lord and had been told that Christ would take upon him "flesh and blood" (Ether 3:9). Christ's spirit body and the body he would have of flesh and blood apparently looked the same. They were both in the image of man and God the Father.

Nephite prophets learned that Christ was the God or creator of all things (on this earth) and was to come to earth to take upon him flesh and blood. Both Ammon and Aaron taught that "man in the beginning was created after the image of God" (Alma 18:34; 22:12). While neither of them say which God (the Father or Christ), it really doesn't matter because the Bible and undoubtedly the plates of brass teach that man was to be created "in our image, after our likeness" (Genesis 1:26). The plural pronoun *our* strongly suggests we were created in the image and likeness of both the Father and his son, Christ. Christ, the firstborn spirit, was created after the image of our Father in Heaven. He looked like him. Thus Christ's answer to Philip's request to show the disciples the Father was: "he that hath seen me has seen the Father" (John 14:8–9). Christ's response probably had two meanings: (1) if you have seen me, you see what the Father looks like; and (2) since I represent him on earth [divine investiture of authority], I am in his likeness, that is, my character and attributes are the same as his.

Lehi beheld "One descending out of the midst of heaven, and he beheld that his luster was above that of the sun at noonday" (1 Nephi 1:9). That personage is interpreted to be Christ as a premortal spirit. As a resurrected being, Christ indeed looked like a man. The Nephites "saw a Man descending out of heaven" (3 Nephi 11:8). He had a body of flesh and bones; they felt his hands, feet, and side. His body was in the likeness of man but in a perfected state (3 Nephi 11:15). He was also introduced by God the Father as his Beloved Son. He was in the likeness of his Father, and the Nephites were told to hear him (3 Nephi 11:7–8). He represented the Father on earth because he had the same attributes and character. Man is created in the image and likeness of Christ and God in both spirit and body. They are the offspring of God and are here to fulfill his purposes.

The Purpose of Man's Creation

Jacob, the younger brother of Nephi, teaches us the purpose of man's creation: "And all flesh is of the dust; and for the selfsame end hath he created them, that they should keep his commandments and glorify him forever" (Jacob 2:21). The way that man glorifies God is by "the continuation of the work of my Father" (D&C 132:31). As told to Moses, and quoted previously, "For behold, this is my work and my glory—to bring to pass the immortality and eternal life of man" (Moses 1:39). The Family Proclamation further explains this work: "In the premortal realm, spirit sons and daughters knew and worshipped God as their Eternal Father and accepted His plan by which His children could obtain a physical body and gain earthly experience to progress toward perfection and ultimately realize his or her divine destiny as an heir of eternal life."

As stated in the last chapter, the earth was created for man to possess it (1 Nephi 17:36). It must "be sanctified from all unrighteousness, that it may be prepared for the celestial glory" so that "the poor and the meek of the earth [can] inherit it" (D&C 88:17–18). Those who fully become in the image and likeness of God will be the possessors of the earth.

5

THE AGENCY OF MAN

God "gave unto them commandments that they should love and serve him, the only living and true God, and that he should be the only being whom they should worship." (D&C 20:19)

The first of the ten commandments given to Moses was, "Thou shalt have no other gods before me" (Exodus 20:3). Implied in these commandments is the concept that there are other beings or things that mankind might be tempted to worship. It further implies that humans have a choice or agency to choose whom or what they will worship. This agency or freedom of choice is a divine gift, as often taught by President David O. McKay: "Next to the bestowal of life itself, the right to direct our lives is God's greatest gift to man."[19]

Desire to Do: Free Will

When discussing the Book of Mormon's teachings about the subject of agency, or the freedom of choice, it is essential to establish some definitions of terms, since some of them are often used interchangeably. As used in this chapter, *free will* is the desire to act; *agency* is the ability to act; and *free agency* is the ability to act correctly. While we may be forced or coerced to do or not do something, our will or desire to do or not do may not change.

19 (1965). *Conference Report,* Oct. 1965, p. 8.

As eternal beings, we have our free will or individual desires. As rational beings, men weigh their alternatives in their thoughts, which often determine the choices they make. The proverb tells us, "For as he thinketh in his heart, so is he" (Proverbs 23:7). The Book of Mormon teaches us that we are accountable for our thoughts. Alma explained to the lawyer Zeezrom in the land of Ammonihah that God "knows all [our] thoughts" (Alma 12:3; see also 3 Nephi 28:6). To the people Alma warned, "our thoughts will also condemn us" (Alma 12:14). Therefore, we should follow the counsel given by Alma to his son Helaman: "Let all thy thoughts be directed unto the Lord" (Alma 37:36; see also Mosiah 4:30).

Agency is the gift of choice given to us by God. It was introduced on this earth when God warned Adam and Eve about eating of the tree of the knowledge of good and evil. Said he, "nevertheless, thou mayest choose for thyself" (Moses 3:17). As long as we make the right choices, our options for progress are unlimited. When we make wrong choices, we still have our agency to attempt to correct those choices, but our free agency may be limited. As Jesus taught, "ye shall know the truth, and the truth shall make you free" (John 8:32).[20] In order for a man to be an agent unto himself in keeping the commandments God has given him, three things are required: (1) a law must be given; (2) man must be an intelligent being capable of understanding the law; and (3) a knowledge of good and evil and the right to choose must exist.

Requirements for Agency

God commanded his children to worship him and keep his commandments (the law) so that he could bless them: "There is a law, irrevocably decreed in heaven before the foundations of this world, upon which all blessings are predicated—And when we obtain any blessing from God, it is by obedience to that law

---

20 While this teaching of truth is probably a statement about Jesus being the truth (D&C 93:26; John 14:6), the concept as used in this example is a true principle.

upon which it is predicated" (D&C 130:20–21). By keeping God's commandments, his children could eventually become perfect as he is perfect (3 Nephi 12:48). The commandments, or laws given to men, had blessings or punishments affixed to them (see Deut. 27:11–28:14). With independence comes accountability: "unto whom much is given much is required" (D&C 82:3; Luke 12:48; see also Romans 4:15). Lehi taught Jacob that "men are instructed sufficiently that they know good from evil. And the law [was] given unto man" (2 Nephi 2:5).

> And if ye shall say there is no law, ye shall also say there is no sin. If ye shall say there is no sin, ye shall also say there is no righteousness. And if there be no righteousness there be no happiness. And if there be no righteousness nor happiness there be no punishment nor misery. And if these things are not there is no God. And if there is no God we are not, neither the earth; for there could have been no creation of things, neither to act nor to be acted upon; wherefore, all things must have vanished away. (2 Nephi 2:13)

As Alma explained to Corianton, "How could [man] sin if there was no law? How could there be a law save there was a punishment? Now, there was a punishment affixed, and a just law given, which brought remorse of conscience unto man" (Alma 42:17–18).

Jacob taught: "Wherefore, he has given a law; and where there is no law given there is no punishment; and where there is no punishment there is no condemnation" (2 Nephi 9:25). Those who cannot understand the law such as little children and the mentally handicapped are not accountable (Moroni 8:22; D&C 29:47–50), "but wo unto him that has the law given, yea, that has all the commandments of God, like unto us, and that transgresseth them, and that wasteth the days of his probation, for awful is his state" (2 Nephi 9:27).

In addition to being able to understand the law, people must have a right to choose. This was also taught by Lehi to Jacob:

> *For it must needs be, that there is an opposition in all things. If not so, my first-born in the wilderness, righteousness could not be brought to pass, neither wickedness, neither holiness nor misery, neither good nor bad. Wherefore, all things must needs be a compound in one; wherefore, if it should be one body it must needs remain as dead, having no life neither death, nor corruption nor incorruption, happiness nor misery, neither sense nor insensibility. (2 Nephi 2:11)*

Without choices, Lehi explained, "there would have been no purpose in the end of [the earth's] creation" (2 Nephi 2:12). Lehi went on to explain God's plan to Jacob:

> *And to bring about his eternal purposes in the end of man, after he had created our first parents, and the beasts of the field and the fowls of the air, and in fine, all things which are created, it must needs be that there was an opposition; even the forbidden fruit in opposition to the tree of life; the one being sweet and the other bitter.*
>
> *Wherefore, the Lord God gave unto man that he should act for himself. Wherefore, man could not act for himself save it should be that he was enticed by the one or the other. (2 Nephi 2:15–16)*

While we are constantly enticed either positively or negatively, we must make choices and accept the consequences of those choices. As Alma said of the "tens of thousands of souls sent to the eternal world," they would "reap eternal happiness or eternal misery, according to the spirit which they listed to obey . . . and this according to the words of the spirit of prophecy; therefore let it be according to the truth" (Alma 3:26–27). The relationship of these principles to the Fall and the Atonement will be considered later.

Premortal Judgment

The blessings or condemnation resulting from the keeping or the breaking of God's laws or commandments began before we came to this earth. Alma taught that those who hold the priesthood in this life were foreordained because of their choices to do good in the premortal world:

> And this is the manner after which they were ordained— being called and prepared from the foundation of the world according to the foreknowledge of God, on account of their exceeding faith and good works; in the first place being left to choose good or evil; therefore they having chosen good, and exercising exceedingly great faith, are called with a holy calling, yea, with that holy calling which was prepared with, and according to, a preparatory redemption for such.
>
> And thus they have been called to this holy calling on account of their faith, while others would reject the Spirit of God on account of the hardness of their hearts and blindness of their minds, while, if it had not been for this they might have had as great privilege as their brethren.
>
> Or in fine, in the first place they were on the same standing with their brethren. (Alma 13:3–5)

This doctrine is consistent with biblical teachings. Paul stood on Mars hill and testified that God "hath made of one blood all nations of men for to dwell on all the face of the earth, and hath determined the times before appointed, and the bounds of their habitation" (Acts 17:26). Moses had earlier taught the children of Israel of their premortal assignments.

> Remember the days of old, consider the years of many generations: ask thy father, and he will shew thee; thy elders, and they will tell thee.

> *When the most High divided to the nations their*
> *inheritance, when he separated the sons of Adam, he set*
> *the bounds of the people according to the number of the*
> *children of Israel. (Deuteronomy 32:7–8)*

The Prophet Joseph Smith made this proclamation: "Every man who has a calling to minister to the inhabitants of the world was ordained to that very purpose in the Grand Council of heaven before this world was" (*TPJS*, p. 365). Thus, because of the principle of agency, many were given greater responsibilities in this life than others. Those who made right choices maintained their free agency to progress toward Godhood. Those who were limited in their opportunities on earth still maintained agency or the right to choose; and, through accepting the gospel here or in the spirit world, they could attain godhood, as well. Those who make wrong choices on earth, whether or not foreordained, may lose their free agency partially or permanently; but, through their agency to repent, they can gain it back (Alma 42:22).

There was a third part of the premortal spirits who permanently lost their free agency, or the right to progress to Godhood. These lost the opportunity to come to earth and obtain a body. As Joseph Smith explained:

> The first step in salvation of man is the laws of
> eternal and self–existent principles. Spirits are eternal.
> At the first organization in heaven we were all present,
> and saw the Savior chosen and appointed and the plan
> of salvation made, and we sanctioned it.
>
> We came to this earth that we might have a
> body and present it pure before God in the celestial
> kingdom. The great principle of happiness consists in
> having a body. The devil has no body, and herein is his
> punishment. (*TPJS*, p. 181)

Although the Book of Mormon does not talk about this group, the Bible and modern-day revelation do.

And there was war in heaven: Michael and his angels fought against the dragon; and the dragon fought and his angels,

And prevailed not; neither was their place found any more in heaven.

And the great dragon was cast out, that old serpent, called the Devil, and Satan, which deceiveth the whole world: he was cast out into the earth, and his angels were cast out with him. (Revelations 12:7–9)[21]

These were the spirits who followed Satan "because of their agency" (D&C 29:36). Satan's plan was "to destroy the agency of Man" (Moses 4:1–4).

The summation of the choices made in the premortal life is given in the book of Abraham: "And they who keep their first estate shall be added upon; and they who keep not their first estate shall not have glory in the same kingdom with those who keep their first estate; and they who keep their second estate shall have glory added upon their heads for ever and ever" (Abraham 3:26). Satan was cast out into the earth and is still seeking to destroy the agency of man. Because the devil "had fallen from heaven and had become miserable forever, he sought the misery of all mankind" (2 Nephi 2:17–18). Those who follow him are bound by the chains of hell:

And now Alma began to expound these things unto him, saying: It is given unto many to know the mysteries of God; nevertheless they are laid under a strict command that they shall not impart only according to the portion of his word which he doth grant unto the children of men, according to the heed and diligence which they give unto him.

And therefore, he that will harden his heart, the same receiveth the lesser portion of the word; and he that will

---

21 The JST makes several changes in these verses; but, since the changes do not alter the concept of Satan being cast out of heaven, the KJV is quoted.

*not harden his heart, to him is given the greater portion of
the word, until it is given unto him to know the mysteries
of God until he know them in full.*

*And they that will harden their hearts, to them is given
the lesser portion of the word until they know nothing
concerning his mysteries; and then they are taken captive
by the devil, and led by his will down to destruction.
Now this is what is meant by the chains of hell. (Alma
12:9–11)*

Nephi, quoting Isaiah, taught the same concept but gave
more emphasis to the positive side:

*For behold, thus saith the Lord God: I will give unto
the children of men line upon line, precept upon precept,
here a little and there a little; and blessed are those who
hearken unto my precepts, and lend an ear unto my
counsel, for they shall learn wisdom; for unto him that
receiveth I will give more; and from them that shall say,
We have enough, from them shall be taken away even
that which they have. (2 Nephi 28:30; see Isaiah 28:13)*

In the last days, Nephi described how Satan would work
upon the inhabitants of the earth:

*For behold, at that day shall he rage in the hearts of the
children of men, and stir them up to anger against that
which is good.*

*And others will he pacify, and lull them away into carnal
security, that they will say: All is well in Zion; yea, Zion
prospereth, all is well—and thus the devil cheateth their
souls, and leadeth them away carefully down to hell.*

*And behold, others he flattereth away, and telleth them
there is no hell; and he saith unto them: I am no devil, for
there is none—and thus he whispereth in their ears, until*

he grasps them with this awful chains, from whence there is no deliverance. (2 Nephi 28:20–22)

Therefore, we live in an environment where Satan entices us in various ways to not keep the commandments that God has given us.

Free Agency: The Ability to Attain Eternal Life

Lehi testified that God created all things, "both things to act and things to be acted upon" (2 Nephi 2:14). As eternal beings we are to act and not be acted upon. Man cannot act for himself unless he is enticed by choices (2 Nephi 2:16). We act as led by the spirit, the scriptures, the prophets, or other good examples in our associations. We are acted upon when we yield to Satan or the negative peer pressures of our culture and society. The Book of Mormon teaches us how to act and how not to be acted upon.

After the fall, Adam and his family were placed "in a state to act, or being placed in a state to act according to their wills and pleasures, whether to do evil or to do good—Therefore God gave unto them commandments, after having made known unto them the plan of redemption" (Alma 12:31–32). Three quotations from the Book of Mormon clearly show that the children of Adam were free to act because of the Atonement of Christ that would be made. As Lehi explained to his sons:

And the Messiah cometh in the fulness of time, that he may redeem the children of men from the fall. And because that they are redeemed from the fall they have become free forever, knowing good from evil; to act for themselves and not to be acted upon, save it be by the punishment of the law at the great and last day, according to the commandments which God hath given.

Wherefore, men are free according to the flesh; and all things are given them which are expedient unto man. And they are free to choose liberty and eternal life, through the great Mediator of all men, or to choose captivity and death, according to the captivity and power of the devil; for he seeketh that all men might be miserable like unto himself.

And now, my sons, I would that ye should look to the great Mediator, and hearken unto his great commandments; and be faithful unto his words, and choose eternal life, according to the will of his Holy Spirit;

And not choose eternal death, according to the will of the flesh and the evil which is therein, which giveth the spirit of the devil power to captivate, to bring you down to hell, that he may reign over you in his own kingdom.

I have spoken these few words unto you all, my sons, in the last days of my probation; and I have chosen the good part, according to the words of the prophet. And I have none other object save it be the everlasting welfare of your souls. (2 Nephi 2:26–30)

Jacob learned well the lesson of his father. He later taught the Nephite people:

Therefore, cheer up your hearts, and remember that ye are free to act for yourselves—to choose the way of everlasting death or the way of eternal life.

Wherefore, my beloved brethren, reconcile yourselves to the will of God, and not to the will of the devil and the flesh; and remember, after ye are reconciled unto God, that it is only in and through the grace of God that ye are saved. (2 Nephi 10:23–24)

Samuel the Lamanite reminded the people of Zarahemla of their freedom to act:

And now remember, remember, my brethren, that whosoever perisheth, perisheth unto himself; and whosoever doeth iniquity, doeth it unto himself; for behold, ye are free; ye are permitted to act for yourselves; for behold, God hath given unto you a knowledge and he hath made you free.

He hath given unto you that ye might know good from evil, and he hath given unto you that ye might choose life or death; and ye can do good and be restored unto that which is good, or have that which is good restored unto you; or ye can do evil, and have that which is evil restored unto you. (Helaman 14:30–31)

We are blessed with agency and the opportunity to maintain and expand our free agency by making right choices constantly. The following chapters will show us much more about how to do this. *Agency is the greatest of God's gifts, save the bestowal of life itself.* We must remember the choice is ours. The Prophet Joseph Smith gave a good summary of the above discussion:

. . . the kindness of our Heavenly Father called for our heartfelt gratitude. He then observed that Satan was generally blamed for the evils which we did, but if he was the cause of all our wickedness, men could not be condemned. The devil could not compel mankind to do evil; all was voluntary. Those who resisted the Spirit of God, would be liable to be led into temptation, and then the association of heaven would be withdrawn from those who refused to be made partakers of such great glory. God would not exert any compulsory means, and the devil could not; and such ideas as were entertained [on these subjects] by many were absurd. (*TPJS*, p. 187)

6

THE FALL OF ADAM AND EVE

"But by the transgression of these holy laws man became sensual and devilish, and became fallen man." (D&C 20:20)

The Church of Jesus Christ of Latter–day Saints has an entirely different point of view regarding Adam and Eve than does the Christian world. The Church's point of view comes from the teachings of the Book of Mormon and the Prophet Joseph Smith. We will not review the points of view of the Christian world; they range from there being no Fall, because man evolved from lower forms of life, to the Fall being the dastardly deed of Eve and Adam that brought evil and misery into the world. Our objective is to state what we learn from the Book of Mormon, other modern scriptures, Joseph Smith, and other latter-day prophets.

The Position of Adam

As discussed in chapter four, the Book of Mormon establishes Adam and Eve as the first humans of this earth and the parents of all inhabitants of the earth. The Prophet Joseph taught:

> Every man lives for himself [and is foreordained].
> Adam was made to open the way of the world, and for dressing the garden. . . .
>
> The Priesthood was first given to Adam; he obtained the First Presidency, and held the keys of it

from generation to generation. He obtained it in the Creation, before the world was formed, as in Genesis 1:26, 27, 28. He had dominion given him over every living creature. He is Michael the Archangel, spoken of in the Scriptures. . . .

The keys [of the priesthood] have to be brought from heaven whenever the Gospel is sent. When they are revealed from heaven, it is by Adam's authority . . .

He (Adam) is the father of the human family, and presides over the spirits of all men. (*TPJS*, pp. 12, 157; see also pp. 167–169)

The above statements are foreign, even startling, to the Christian world; but in summary, Adam was foreknown and foreordained to bring about the fall, which was part of the plan of salvation.

When Jesus Christ appeared to the brother of Jared, he said: "I am he who was prepared from the foundation of the world to redeem my people" (Ether 3:14). Why would Jesus have been prepared in the premortal life to redeem his people unless the fall of Adam was foreknown? The Bible teaches the same doctrine. The Apostle Peter wrote: "[Jesus Christ] verily was foreordained before the foundation of the world" (1 Pet. 1:20).

There is a difference between *foreknown* and *foreordained;* being foreknown does not necessarily mean it was foreordained. God knows things will happen but may not want them to happen; but because of the agency of man, he will allow it. However, Adam was foreknown and foreordained, as the above statements of the Prophet Joseph Smith strongly imply. He was given the keys before the creation. However, God placed a veil over Adam's mind that he might exercise his agency (see Moses 5:6–12). The Book of Mormon teaches the reason for the Fall: "Adam fell that man might be" (2 Nephi 2:25). It was an essential part of the plan of salvation.

The Book of Mormon also gives us many insights into the cause and the effect of the fall of Adam and Eve. We will first consider the cause.

The Cause of the Fall

The prophet Abinadi referred to "that old serpent that did beguile our first parents" (Mosiah 16:3). That old serpent was Satan, or the devil. Obtaining his knowledge from the plates of brass, Lehi testified to his son Jacob:

17 And I, Lehi, according to the things which I have read, must needs suppose that an angel of God, according to that which is written, had fallen from heaven; wherefore, he became a devil, having sought that which was evil before God.

18 And because he had fallen from heaven, and had become miserable forever, he sought also the misery of all mankind. Wherefore, he said unto Eve, yea, even that old serpent, who is the devil, who is the father of all lies, wherefore he said: Partake of the forbidden fruit, and ye shall not die, but ye shall be as God, knowing good and evil. (2 Nephi 2:17–18)

The Book of Mormon does not give the full account of Eve's yielding to Satan first; rather, it treats their fall as a joint venture (see Genesis 3; Moses 4). Lehi continues his explanation to Jacob: "And after Adam and Eve had partaken of the forbidden fruit they were driven out of the garden of Eden, to till the earth" (2 Nephi 2:19).

Alma explained to Antionah, a chief ruler in the land of Ammonihah, "Now we see that Adam did fall by the partaking of the forbidden fruit, according to the word of God" (Alma 12:22). President Joseph Fielding Smith taught that "the forbidden fruit had the power to create blood and change [Adam's] nature; and mortality took the place of immortality, and all things, partaking of the change, became mortal."[22] The change in Adam and Eve's bodies made them mortal and was in accordance with the

---

22 McConkie, B. R., ed. (1954). *Doctrines of Salvation* 1:77. Salt Lake City: Bookcraft.

foreknowledge and plan of God. As explained above, God knew there would be a fall and had prepared for it.

The Effects of the Fall

After Adam and Eve were driven out of the garden, the Lord had the tree of life guarded against Adam and Eve partaking of it. Partaking of the fruit of the tree of life would have caused them to be immortal again without having overcome their fallen condition. Alma explained this to his son Corianton:

2 Now behold, my son, I will explain this thing unto thee. For behold, after the Lord God sent our first parents forth from the garden of Eden, to till the ground, from whence they were taken—yea, he drew out the man, and he placed at the east end of the garden of Eden, cherubim, and a flaming sword which turned every way, to keep the tree of life—

3 Now, we see that the man had become as God, knowing good and evil; and lest he should put forth his hand, and take also of the tree of life, and eat and live forever, the Lord God placed cherubim and the flaming sword, that he should not partake of the fruit—

4 And thus we see, that there was a time granted unto man to repent, yea, a probationary time, a time to repent and serve God.

5 For behold, if Adam had put forth his hand immediately, and partaken of the tree of life, he would have lived forever, according to the word of God, having no space for repentance; yea, and also the word of God would have been void, and the great plan of salvation would have been frustrated.

6 But behold, it was appointed unto man to die— therefore, as they were cut off from the tree of life they should be cut off from the face of the earth—and man became lost forever, yea, they became fallen man. (Alma 42:2–6; see also Alma 12:21–22)

The great plan of salvation for all mankind will be discussed in a later chapter, but Adam's role in that plan is further explained in the Book of Mormon.

By becoming mortal, it was inevitable that Adam and Eve would die temporally. Alma explained to the ruler Antionah that without the Fall there would have been no death: "And now behold, I say unto you that if it had been possible for Adam to have partaken of the fruit of the tree of life at that time, there would have been no death, and the word would have been void, making God a liar, for he said: If thou eat thou shalt surely die" (Alma 12:23). Enoch also testified that "because that Adam fell, we are; and by his fall came death" (Moses 6:48). Enoch further testified that the Lord spake unto Adam commanding him to teach his children that the Fall brought death (see Moses 6:58–59).

Adam and Eve also died a spiritual death—they were cut off from the presence of the Lord.

7 And now, ye see by this that our first parents were cut off both temporally and spiritually from the presence of the Lord; and thus we see they became subjects to follow after their own will.

8 Now behold, it was not expedient that man should be reclaimed from this temporal death, for that would destroy the great plan of happiness.

9 Therefore, as the soul could never die, and the fall had brought upon all mankind a spiritual death as well as a temporal, that is, they were cut off from the presence of the Lord, it was expedient that mankind should be reclaimed from this spiritual death. (Alma 42:7–9)

Another testimony of Adam being "cut off from the presence of the Lord" was given by Jacob, who said that "the fall came by reason of transgression" (2 Nephi 9:6).[23] It is significant that Adam's fall is called a *transgression* rather than a *sin*. A transgression is a breaking of a law and the consequences following, but a sin is a wilful disobedience of one of God's laws (see Mosiah 2:33). A person may transgress a law without sinning, but he cannot sin without breaking a law (1 John 3:4). The partaking of the fruit being a transgression is another evidence that what Adam did was part of the plan of God. Paul told Timothy that "Adam was not deceived" (1 Tim. 2:14). Adam's partaking of the fruit is usually explained by saying that Adam broke a lesser commandment in order to fulfill the higher law to multiply and replenish the earth. While this explanation has merit, there are some further considerations. God commanded Adam and Eve not to partake "of the tree of the knowledge of good and evil" (Genesis 2:17). The Book of Moses gives a fuller account of the commandment given to them: "But of the tree of the knowledge of good and evil, thou shalt not eat of it, *nevertheless, thou mayest choose for thyself, for it is given unto thee; but, remember that I forbid it,* for in the day thou eatest thereof thou shalt surely die" (Moses 3:17, italics added). The tree was "given unto (them)" or made accessible. It was placed in "the midst of the garden" (Genesis 3:3; Moses 4:9), where it would be visible and tempting. But the Lord warned them against transgressing in their innocence, for the consequences of eating the fruit were spiritual and physical death.

President Joseph Fielding Smith gives this explanation:

> I never speak of the part Eve took in this fall as a sin, nor do I accuse Adam of a sin. One may say,

---

23 The Book of Mormon always refers to Adam's partaking of the fruit as a *transgression,* as subsequent quotes will show. The Doctrine and Covenants verse under consideration in this chapter also refers to "the *transgression* of these holy laws" (20:20, italics added). Paul, in writing to Timothy, says, "the woman being deceived was in the transgression" (1 Tim. 2:14).

"Well did they not break a commandment?" Yes. But let us examine the nature of that commandment and the results which came out of it.

In no other commandment the Lord ever gave to man, did he say: "But of the tree of the knowledge of good and evil, thou shalt not eat of it, *nevertheless, thou mayest choose for thyself.*"

It is true, the Lord warned Adam and Eve that to partake of the fruit they would transgress a law, and this happened. But it is not always a sin to transgress a law. I will try to illustrate this. The chemist in his laboratory takes different elements and combines them, and the result is that something very different results. He has *changed* the law. As an example in point: hydrogen, two parts, and oxygen, one part, passing through an electric spark will combine and form water. Hydrogen will burn, so will oxygen, but water will put out a fire. This may be subject to some disagreement by the critics who will say it is not transgressing a law. Well, *Adam's transgression was of a similar nature, that is, his transgression was in accordance with law.*[24]

The law that Adam and Eve transgressed had a temporal effect upon their bodies. It caused a chemical change—blood in their veins—making them mortal.[25] Alma apparently understood that the law given to Adam was temporal. In explaining the plan of redemption to the ruler Antionah, he said, "Wherefore, he gave commandments unto men, they [Adam and Eve] having first transgressed the first commandments as to things which were temporal, and becoming as Gods, knowing good from evil, placing themselves in a state to act, or being placed in a state to act

_____

24 *Doctrines of Salvation,* 1:114.

25 Although the Lord gives no temporal laws to man, he does speak in temporal terms to help us understand (D&C 29:31–35). Adam's fall had a temporal effect upon his body, but the effects were ultimately spiritual.

according to their wills and pleasures, whether to do evil or to do good" (Alma 12:31). Without the Fall, Adam and Eve would not have experienced mortality, a part of God's plan, nor would they have become the parents of the human race and provided their children an earthly experience.

Lehi explained that the transgression of Adam had a purpose in God's plan:

> *22 And now, behold, if Adam had not transgressed he would not have fallen, but he would have remained in the garden of Eden. And all things which were created must have remained in the same state in which they were after they were created; and they must have remained forever, and had no end.*
>
> *23 And they would have had no children; wherefore they would have remained in a state of innocence, having no joy, for they knew no misery; doing no good, for they knew no sin. (2 Nephi 2:22–23)*

Lehi does not explain the reason they would have had no children, but it strongly implies it was biologically impossible. Other teachings of the Book of Mormon—such as the Fall coming from the eating of the fruit—suggest that the change in the body caused by the fruit also enabled Adam and Eve to reproduce children. Being the first flesh and the first mortals, Adam and Eve "brought forth children; yea, even the family of all the earth" (2 Nephi 2:20). From Lehi's teachings to his son Jacob came the famous couplet already quoted above: "Adam fell that men might be; and men are, that they might have joy" (2 Nephi 2:25). Mother Eve learned, "Were it not for our transgression we never should have seed" (Moses 5:11). One of the key purposes for man's coming to the earth was to obtain a mortal body. This was made possible because Adam and Eve had become mortal. The Prophet Joseph Smith taught the same doctrine as Father Lehi: "We came to this earth that we might have a body and present it pure before God in the celestial kingdom. The great principle of happiness consists in having a body. The devil has no body, and herein is his punishment" (*TPJS*, 181). Although Adam and Eve had become mortal and had been driven out of the Garden of Eden, they were now in a state to further exercise their agency and bring about the plan of salvation for themselves and for the whole human family.

The fall of Adam and Eve was foreknown and foreordained. It was purposeful and essential to the plan of God. As stated by Elder Orson F. Whitney, it was a step downward but also a step forward.[26] The fall of Adam and Eve was universal. It affected all mankind—including the animals and the earth, itself.

Man Becomes Lost and Fallen

There are many different philosophies in the world pertaining to the nature of man. The two extremes of these philosophies are: (1) the depravity of man—he is born basically evil in nature, corrupt in thought and action; and (2) the goodness of man—he is born basically good, and any deviation from goodness is caused by his environment. The Doctrine and Covenants does not support either of these philosophies but declares: "Every spirit of man was innocent in the beginning; and God having redeemed man from the fall, men became again, in their infant state, innocent before God" (D&C 93:38). The Book of Mormon states that "by [Adam's] fall, all mankind became a lost and fallen people" (Alma 12:22; see also 2 Nephi 2:21; Alma 34:9; 42:6).

Father Lehi taught his people: "Wherefore, all mankind were in a lost and in a fallen state, and ever would be save they should rely on this Redeemer" (1 Nephi 10:6). To be lost suggests that they were out of the presence of their Father in Heaven. To be in a fallen state suggests that they were in a lower state than they had been before the Fall. They were now mortal and subject to death. Without the Fall, mankind would have lived forever as spirits. All spirits are innocent when they come into this mortal earth but are subject to Satan and experiences with other mortals:

---

26 See (1908). *Conference Report,* April, p. 90.

"And that wicked one cometh and taketh away light and truth, through disobedience, from the children of men, and because of the tradition of their fathers" (D&C 93:38–39).

How mankind responds to Satan and other mortals determines what they "become." The plan of God is to give mankind a probationary period. Alma taught Antionah that "there was a space granted unto man in which he might repent; therefore this life became a probationary state; a time to prepare to meet God; a time to prepare for that endless state which has been spoken of by us, which is after the resurrection of the dead" (Alma 12:24; see also Alma 42:4). Thus we are all born into an environment of good and evil and, through our choices, will be resurrected to the degree of glory that we have prepared ourselves. We will become what we have chosen to become.

Those who believe mankind is born evil often cite King David as evidence: "Behold, I was shapen in iniquity; and in sin did my mother conceive me" (Psalm 51:5). David, in grieving over his sin with Bathsheba, might have been paraphrasing the teaching of Enoch[27] when he spoke of Adam's transgression being forgiven through the Son of God, atoning for original guilt, and little children being "whole from the foundation of the world" (Moses 6:53–54). The Lord revealed to Enoch:

> *And the Lord spake unto Adam, saying: Inasmuch as thy children are conceived in sin, even so when they begin to grow up, sin conceiveth in their hearts, and they taste the bitter, that they may know to prize the good.*
>
> *And it is given unto them to know good from evil; wherefore they are agents unto themselves, and I have given unto you another law and commandment. (Moses 6:55–56)*

That King David was aware of Enoch's teaching is shown in a later Psalm: "The wicked are estranged from the womb: they

---

27 Exactly when the teachings of Enoch were lost from the Bible is not known. It is possible that David had access to his teachings.

go astray as soon as they be born, speaking lies" (Psalm 58:3). This psalm shows that David understood that children are born innocent, or without sin, but become wicked as they follow the influence of a world of evil and wickedness.

Fall by Nature

Living in an environment of evil and wickedness, it is natural for people to follow some of its ways. Thus the Book of Mormon teaches that we fall by nature. King Benjamin gave this insight with respect to the salvation of little children: "And even if it were possible that little children could sin they could not be saved; but I say unto you they are blessed; for behold, as in Adam, or by nature, they fall, even so the blood of Christ atoneth for their sins" (Mosiah 3:16). Alma gave further insight into this doctrine when he taught Corianton: "And now, my son, all men that are in a state of nature, or I would say, in a carnal state, are in the gall of bitterness and in the bonds of iniquity; they are without God in the world, and they have gone contrary to the nature of God; therefore, they are in a state contrary to the nature of happiness" (Alma 41:11). Living in mortality is living in a carnal state because of the temptations of the flesh. Man is less than the dust of the earth, because man does not obey the Lord's commands as does the earth (see Mosiah 4:2; Hel. 12:7–21). In another incident, the brother of Jared pleaded to the Lord for mercy, because their "natures have become evil continually" (Ether 3:2). Thus, in a mortal world, where we encounter sin and temptation, it is natural to follow the ways of that world.

Natural Man—An Enemy to God

One of the passages in the Book of Mormon that has caused serious reflection by many is King Benjamin's statement about the natural man:

For the natural man is an enemy to God, and has been from the fall of Adam, and will be, forever and ever, unless he yields to the enticings of the Holy Spirit, and putteth off the natural man and becometh a saint through the Atonement of Christ the Lord, and becometh as a child, submissive, meek, humble, patient, full of love, willing to submit to all things which the Lord seeth fit to inflict upon him, even as a child doth submit to his father. (Mosiah 3:19)

From the time of Adam's fall, following the natural tendencies of the flesh has meant going against God's will, not following God's plan for salvation. God refers to these people as "the inhabitants of the earth, or among the congregations of the wicked" (D&C 62:5; see also 60:13–14; 61:30–32; 68:1). They are called the congregations of the wicked because they are in large numbers and are unbaptized. The Lord said: "And the whole world lieth in sin, and groaneth under darkness and under the bondage of sin. And by this you may know they are under the bondage of sin, because they come not unto me. For whoso cometh not unto me is under the bondage of sin" (D&C 84:49–51). To come unto Christ is to be baptized for a remission of sins (see 3 Nephi 21:6; 27:20). Those baptized receive the Holy Ghost; and by yielding to the enticings of the Holy Ghost, they become Saints and obtain the attributes to become children of God. If the baptized do not do his will, they remain enemies to God.

54 And your minds in times past have been darkened because of unbelief, and because you have treated lightly the things you have received—

55 Which vanity and unbelief have brought the whole church under condemnation.

56 And this condemnation resteth upon the children of Zion, even all.

57 And they shall remain under this condemnation until they repent and remember the new covenant, even the Book of Mormon and the former commandments which I have given them, not only to say, but to do according to that which I have written. (D&C 84:54–57)

There is a third group of mortals that is an enemy of God. The first two groups may be unconsciously or naively failing to conform to the plan of God, but those who knowingly or wilfully rebel against God are his fiercest enemies. King Benjamin spoke of these:

36 And now, I say unto you, my brethren, that after ye have known and have been taught all these things, if ye should transgress and go contrary to that which has been spoken, that ye do withdraw yourselves from the Spirit of the Lord, That it may have no place in you to guide you in wisdom's paths that ye may be blessed, prospered, and preserved—

37 I say unto you, that the man that doeth this, the same cometh out in open rebellion against God; therefore he listeth to obey the evil spirit, and becometh an enemy to all righteousness; therefore, the Lord has no place in him, for he dwelleth not in unholy temples. (Mosiah 2:36–37)

The enemy who drives away the influence of the Holy Spirit will remain an enemy forever unless he repents and obtains that Spirit again.

Jacob, the brother of Nephi, also spoke of those who fight against God: "Wherefore, he that fighteth against Zion, both Jew and Gentile, both bond and free, both male and female, shall perish; for they are they who are the whore of all the earth; for they who are not for me are against me, saith our God" (2 Nephi 10:16). Jesus taught the same doctrine: "He that is not with me is against me; and he that gathereth not with me scattereth abroad" (Matt. 12:30). Those who fight God will not have the companionship of the Holy Spirit and cannot become children of God without repentance.

Carnal, Sensual, Devilish

Since it is by nature that mankind becomes carnal, sensual, and devilish, the Lord has given us a probationary state or preparatory state to overcome these desires and come back into our Heavenly Father's presence (see Alma 42:10). The devil will have power over the people who persist in their carnal or natural ways. The prophet Abinadi gave this stern warning concerning the wicked:

> *3 For they are carnal and devilish, and the devil has power over them; yea, even that old serpent that did beguile our first parents, which was the cause of their fall; which was the cause of all mankind becoming carnal, sensual, devilish, knowing evil from good, subjecting themselves to the devil.*
>
> *4 Thus all mankind were lost; and behold, they would have been endlessly lost were it not that God redeemed his people from their lost and fallen state.*
>
> *5 But remember that he that persists in his own carnal nature, and goes on in the ways of sin and rebellion against God, remaineth in his fallen state and the devil hath all power over him. Therefore he is as though there was no redemption made, being an enemy to God; and also is the devil an enemy to God. (Mosiah 16:3–5)*

The Fall was the cause of our becoming carnal, sensual, and devilish. However, the three distinct characteristics of fallen man may come upon us separately or collectively. We can be carnal or sensual without being devilish. To be carnal means to put undue emphasis upon the things of the flesh. Father Lehi warned his sons to follow the will of the Holy Spirit: "And not choose eternal death, according to the will of the flesh and the evil which is therein, which giveth the spirit of the devil power to captivate, to bring you down to hell, that he may reign over you in his own kingdom" (2 Nephi 2:29). The flesh itself is not evil, but yielding to the will of the flesh gives the spirit of the devil power to captivate. It is through the flesh that many of earth's temptations come. Nephi made a covenant and gave us a warning at the same time regarding the "arm of flesh": "Oh Lord, I have trusted in thee, and I will trust in thee forever. I will not put my trust in the arm of flesh; for I know that cursed is he that putteth his trust in the arm of flesh. Yea, cursed is he that putteth his trust in man or maketh flesh his arm" (2 Nephi 4:34). Christ was tempted by Satan to turn the stones into bread to satisfy his hunger (Matt. 4:2–3). This was a carnal temptation to satisfy the appetite or a temptation of the flesh. Christ gave us the formula for resisting carnal temptations of appetites and passions when he said, "It is written, Man shall not live by bread alone, but by every word that proceedeth out of the mouth of God" (Matt. 4:4).

To be sensual is to put undue emphasis on the senses. It is among other things the temptations of pride and fashions of the world. Jacob, brother of Nephi, warned:

> O that cunning plan of the evil one! O the vainness, and the frailties, and the foolishness of men! When they are learned they think they are wise, and they hearken not unto the counsel of God, for they set it aside, supposing they know of themselves, wherefore, their wisdom is foolishness and it profiteth them not. And they shall perish. (2 Nephi 9:28; see also 2 Nephi 7:10–11 [Isaiah 50:10–11]; 15:21 [Isaiah 5:21])

There are other senses besides learning, but reliance upon reason rather than revelation is a prime example of trusting in the senses of man. Again, the senses are not evil. In fact, they are essential but should be used within the framework of God. Jacob warned: "But to be learned is good if they hearken unto the counsels of God" (2 Nephi 9:29).

Learning is one of the purposes for coming to earth, and what we learn has eternal consequences. The Lord told us through the Prophet Joseph Smith: "Whatever principle of intelligence we attain unto in this life, it will rise with us in the resurrection. And if a person gains more knowledge and intelligence in this life through his diligence and obedience than another, he will have so much the advantage in the world to come" (D&C 130:18–19). But we must remember that the devil tempts us through the senses, as Jacob said: "O, that cunning plan of the evil one." Christ was tempted by Satan to jump from the pinnacle of the temple to appeal to the senses of the Jewish populace (Matt. 4:5–6). This temptation Christ also resisted. His response was, "Thou shalt not tempt the Lord thy God" (Matt. 4:7). We must follow the example of the Lord and not yield to peer pressure or the fear of men, or seek to be popular among men.

To be devilish is to give ourselves over to the power of the devil. We are within the grasp of his everlasting chains when we give in to the flesh and the senses. Nephi told of Satan's manner of operation:

20 For behold, at that day shall he rage in the hearts of the children of men, and stir them up to anger against that which is good.

21 And others will he pacify, and lull them away into carnal security, that they will say: All is well in Zion; yea, Zion prospereth, all is well—and thus the devil cheateth their souls, and leadeth them away carefully down to hell.

22 And behold, others he flattereth away, and telleth them there is no hell; and he saith unto them: I am no devil, for there is none—and thus he whispereth in their ears, until he grasps them with his awful chains, from whence there is no deliverance. (2 Nephi 28:20–22)

To be stirred up to anger is usually a temptation of the flesh. To pacify into carnal security is the use of reasoning or senses to feel secure in the flesh. Flattery is another appeal to the reasoning senses. All of these temptations must be resisted.

To follow the carnal or natural ways of man is often considered honorable or at least acceptable by the world, but it is not the way of God. Honorable men of the world are terrestrial men (see D&C 76:75). If they yield to the temptations of Satan they become telestial people. Christ was enticed by Satan to fall down and worship him (see Matt. 4:8–10). To yield to Satan is, in a sense, to worship him. It is placing the god of this world, the devil, ahead of Christ (2 Cor. 4:4). We can be carnal and sensual without being devilish, but we cannot be devilish unless we are also carnal and sensual.

Humans are in a fallen state, but they are not born evil. They are born innocent before God and are placed in an environment of both good and evil. They become either celestial beings through yielding to the enticing of the Spirit, the prophets, and the scriptures (see D&C 76:51–53); or they become honorable, terrestrial beings, because they give consideration to the rights and feelings of others but follow natural instincts. If they yield to the influence of Satan that comes through the desires and appetites of the flesh or the senses, they become telestial beings (see D&C 76:103), or even sons of perdition.

This earth is a probationary period in which we prepare for our endless or resurrected state (see Alma 12:24). The Lord desires to pour out his Spirit upon all flesh. Many are called but few are chosen, because "they are walking in darkness at noonday" (D&C 95:4–6). The Lord is pouring out his Spirit in abundance, as the sun at noonday, giving the opportunity to become the Saints of God. However, if they fail to put off the natural man, follow the temptations of Satan, and do not rely upon the Atonement of Christ, they will be endlessly lost (see Mosiah 16:4).

7

THE ALMIGHTY GAVE HIS SON

"Wherefore, the Almighty God gave his Only Begotten Son, as it is written in those scriptures which have been given of him."
(D&C 20:21)

In the above reference, "as it is written" must refer to the testimony of John in the New Testament: "For God so loved the world, that he gave his Only Begotten Son, that whosoever believeth in him should not perish, but have everlasting life" (John 3:16). Because of God's love for all of his spirit offspring (see Heb. 12:9), he was willing to offer his Only Begotten Son in the flesh as a payment for the sins of the world (see John 3:17). The Son himself was also willing to make this necessary sacrifice. As revealed to Orson Pratt in November of 1830, he "so loved the world that he gave his own life, that as many as would believe might become the sons of God" (D&C 34:3).

The word "wherefore" (D&C 20:21, under the title above) refers us back to D&C 20:20, which describes fallen man. Because men became sensual and devilish, God sent his Son to atone for their sins. The Atonement took place in the garden of Gethsemane, where Jesus sweat "as it were great drops of blood falling down to the ground" (Luke 22:44). While the New Testament tells us what happened, the Book of Mormon greatly enlarges our knowledge of the Atonement, telling us why and how his suffering brought about the opportunity for fallen man to gain everlasting life. We will here discuss why Jesus suffered and will reserve for the next chapter how he was able to atone for the sins of the world.

The Plan of Salvation

The Father's plan to bring his children back from their fallen state into his presence is called by various names in the Book of Mormon: "the plan of salvation" (Jarom 1:2); "the plan of redemption" (Alma 12:25); "the plan of happiness" (Alma 42:8); "the great plan" (Alma 34:9); and "the plan of mercy" (Alma 42:15). Whatever it is called, it refers to the plan for Jesus to atone for the sins of all mankind. There are many Book of Mormon prophets who spoke of the atoning plan in some detail: Lehi, Jacob, King Benjamin, Abinadi, Alma, Amulek, Samuel the Lamanite, the Savior himself, and others. Some of these prophets emphasized some parts of the Atonement and others emphasized other parts, but there are several essential elements that were understood by all who wrote. Collectively, they are multiple witnesses of the Atonement of Jesus Christ.

To Pay the Demands of Justice

As discussed earlier, the law of justice required that if a law were broken, a punishment would be affixed (see Alma 42:13, 17–22). Adam broke the law and thus a punishment was affixed. As the posterity of Adam broke laws, they were also subject to the punishment of the laws. The Atonement was the great plan of the Eternal God to pay the demands of justice. Alma bore witness of the Atonement: "And now, the plan of mercy could not be brought about except an Atonement should be made; therefore, God himself atoneth for the sins of the world, to bring about the plan of mercy, to appease the demands of justice, that God might be a perfect, just God, and a merciful God also" (Alma 42:15). In Amulek's words:

> 8 And now, behold, I will testify unto you of myself that
> these things are true. Behold, I say unto you, that I do

know that Christ shall come among the children of men, to take upon him the transgressions of his people, and that he shall atone for the sins of the world; for the Lord God hath spoken it.

9 For it is expedient that an Atonement should be made; for according to the great plan of the Eternal God there must be an Atonement made, or else all mankind must unavoidably perish; yea, all are hardened; yea, all are fallen and are lost, and must perish except it be through the Atonement which it is expedient should be made. (Alma 34:8–9)

Amulek bore further witness of the needed balance between mercy and justice: "And thus mercy can satisfy the demands of justice, and encircles them in the arms of safety, while he that exercises no faith unto repentance is exposed to the whole law of the demands of justice; therefore only unto him that has faith unto repentance is brought about the great and eternal plan of redemption" (Alma 34:16). The prophet Abinadi proclaimed that all of the Old Testament prophets had foretold of the Messiah (see Mosiah 13:33–35). He then quoted Isaiah 53 as an example of the prophets' teachings (see Mosiah 14). In that prophecy, Isaiah stated: "He [the Father] shall see the travail of his [Christ's] soul, and shall be satisfied" (Mosiah 14:11, Isa. 53:11). In Abinadi's commentary on Isaiah's prophecy, he declared:

8 And thus God breaketh the bands of death, having gained the victory over death; giving the Son power to make intercession for the children of men—

9 Having ascended into heaven, having the bowels of mercy; being filled with compassion towards the children of men; standing betwixt them and justice; having broken the bands of death, taken upon himself their iniquity and their transgressions, having redeemed them, and satisfied the demands of justice. (Mosiah 15:8–9)

Abinadi's commentary further shows that the relationship between mercy and justice is eternal. Lehi taught his son Jacob:

> 5 And men are instructed sufficiently that they know good from evil. And the law is given unto men. And by the law no flesh is justified; or, by the law men are cut off. Yea, by the temporal law they were cut off; and also, by the spiritual law they perish from that which is good, and become miserable forever.
>
> 6 Wherefore, redemption cometh in and through the Holy Messiah; for he is full of grace and truth.
>
> 7 Behold he offereth himself a sacrifice for sin, to answer the ends of the law, unto all those who have a broken heart and a contrite spirit; and unto none else can the ends of the law be answered. (2 Nephi 2:5–7)

"To answer the ends of the law" (v. 7) extends the Atonement to every aspect of the law. In other words, Christ atoned for the law broken by Adam and every other law of God broken by mankind. Thus, the first basic element of the Atonement, or law of mercy, was that it satisfied the demands of justice for the laws broken by Adam and his posterity.

An Infinite Atonement

The second basic element of the Atonement, as taught in the Book of Mormon, is that it was an infinite sacrifice. Although Lehi taught that the ends of the law were answered only for those who have a broken heart and a contrite spirit, the Atonement covers all of mankind. The condition given by Lehi will be considered after the infinite nature of the Atonement is established. It had to be an all-inclusive Atonement that paid for the sins of Adam and all his offspring. Jacob taught what the consequences would have been if it had not been infinite:

Wherefore, it must needs be an infinite Atonement—save it should be an infinite Atonement this corruption could not put on incorruption. Wherefore, the first judgment which came upon man must needs have remained to an endless duration. And if so, this flesh must have laid down to rot and to crumble to its mother earth, to rise no more. (2 Nephi 9:7)

The Atonement satisfied the demands of justice for the law broken by Adam that brought death into the world and is infinite in bringing about the resurrection of every inhabitant of the earth.

A second consequence that affected all mankind was also explained by Jacob:

8 O the wisdom of God, his mercy and grace! For behold, if the flesh should rise no more our spirits must become subject to that angel who fell from before the presence of the Eternal God, and became the devil, to rise no more.

9 And our spirits must have become like unto him, and we become devils, angels to a devil, to be shut out from the presence of our God, and to remain with the father of lies, in misery, like unto himself; yea, to that being who beguiled our first parents, who transformeth himself nigh unto an angel of light, and stirreth up the children of men unto secret combinations of murder and all manner of secret works of darkness. (2 Nephi 9:8–9)

Through the wisdom of God, the Atonement overpowers the influence of Satan upon men. Jacob further explains:

10 O how great the goodness of our God, who prepareth a way for our escape from the grasp of this awful monster; yea, that monster, death and hell, which I call the death of the body, and also the death of the spirit.

11 And because of the way of deliverance of our God, the Holy One of Israel, this death, of which I have spoken,

*which is the temporal, shall deliver up its dead; which
death is the grave.*

*12 And this death of which I have spoken, which is the
spiritual death shall deliver up its dead; which spiritual
death is hell; wherefore, death and hell must deliver up
their dead, and hell must deliver up its captive spirits,
and the grave must deliver up its captive bodies, and the
bodies and the spirits of men will be restored one to the
other; and it is by the power of the resurrection of the Holy
One of Israel.*

*13 O how great the plan of our God! For on the other
hand, the paradise of God must deliver up the spirits of
the righteous, and the grave deliver up the body of the
righteous; and the spirit and the body is restored to itself
again, and all men become incorruptible, and immortal,
and they are living souls, having a perfect knowledge like
unto us in the flesh, save it be that our knowledge shall be
perfect. (2 Nephi 9:10–13)*

Thus the Atonement, in satisfying the demands of justice,
overcomes the physical death and the spiritual death brought about
by the Fall.

An Unconditional Atonement

One of the elementary teachings of the Atonement is that
Christ made an unconditional sacrifice for all men to bring about
their resurrection. Some may interpret Father Lehi's statement
above, the Atonement answering the ends of the law "unto all those
who have a broken heart and a contrite spirit" (2 Nephi 2:7), to be
teaching a conditional concept. Yet this concept is not consistent
with the more complete Book of Mormon teachings of the third
basic element of the Atonement by Samuel the Lamanite:

15 For behold, he surely must die that salvation may come; yea, it behooveth him and becometh expedient that he dieth, to bring to pass the resurrection of the dead, that thereby men may be brought into the presence of the Lord.

16 Yea, behold, this death bringeth to pass the resurrection, and redeemeth all mankind from the first death—that spiritual death; for all mankind, by the fall of Adam being cut off from the presence of the Lord, are considered as dead, both as to things temporal and to things spiritual.

17 But behold, the resurrection of Christ redeemeth mankind, yea, even all mankind, and bringeth them back into the presence of the Lord.

18 Yea, and it bringeth to pass the condition of repentance, that whosoever repenteth the same is not hewn down and cast into the fire; but whosoever repenteth not is hewn down and cast into the fire; and there cometh upon them again a spiritual death, yea, a second death, for they are cut off again as to things pertaining to righteousness. (Hel. 14:15–18)

The Atonement was unconditional. All mankind will be resurrected and brought back into the presence of God. The conditional aspect upon man is whether he can remain in God's presence after the Atonement has brought him back there. Therefore, Father Lehi taught that those who had a broken heart and a contrite spirit would receive the full benefit of the Atonement, and those who did not meet that condition would not receive the benefit of remaining in the presence of God—as Samuel the Lamanite warned. Moroni taught the same doctrine:

And because of the redemption of man, which came by Jesus Christ, they are brought back into the presence of the Lord; yea, this is wherein all men are redeemed, because the death of Christ bringeth to pass the resurrection, which bringeth to pass a redemption from an endless sleep, from which sleep all men shall be awakened by the power of God when the trump shall sound; and they shall come forth, both small and great, and all shall stand before his bar, being redeemed and loosed from this eternal band of death, which death is a temporal death. (Morm. 9:13; see also Alma 42:23)

All will come into the presence of God and there be judged to see if they are able to remain.

An Eternal Sacrifice

A fourth element of the Atonement, as taught in the Book of Mormon, is that it was to be an eternal sacrifice, the sacrifice of a God. King Benjamin taught: "And lo, he shall suffer temptations, and pain of body, hunger, thirst, and fatigue, even *more than man can suffer,* except it be unto death; for behold, blood cometh from every pore, so great shall be his anguish for the wickedness and the abominations of his people" (Mosiah 3:7, italics added). He identifies the atoner as "Jesus Christ, the Son of God" (3:8). Amulek also identified him as the Son of God (see Alma 34:14) and stated that it was not a human sacrifice: "For it is expedient that there should be a great and last sacrifice; *yea, not a sacrifice of man, neither of beast, neither of any manner of fowl; for it shall not be a human sacrifice;* but it must be an infinite and *eternal* sacrifice" (Alma 34:10, italics added).

The Great and Last Sacrifice

The fifth element of the Atonement taught by the Book of Mormon prophets was that it was to be the great and last sacrifice to answer the ends of the law and to fulfill the law of Moses:

13 Therefore, it is expedient that there should be a great and last sacrifice, and then shall there be, or it is expedient there should be, a stop to the shedding of blood; then shall

*the law of Moses be fulfilled; yea, it shall be all fulfilled,
every jot and tittle, and none shall have passed away.*

*14 And behold, this is the whole meaning of the law,
every whit pointing to that great and last sacrifice; and
that great and last sacrifice will be the Son of God, yea,
infinite and eternal. (Alma 34:13–14)*

Sacrifices, whether under the law of Moses or before, were
a type and shadow of Christ (see Moses 5:57; Mosiah 3:15; Alma
33:19). Abraham's being commanded to offer Isaac was to teach
the Atonement, Abraham and Isaac being in the "similitude of God
and his Only Begotten Son" (Jacob 4:5). The meaning of the "great
and last sacrifice" is that it was the ultimate of all sacrifices, though
not that it would end all sacrifices. According to the Prophet Joseph
Smith there will be sacrifice again carried out in righteousness by
the sons of Levi, apparently when the ten tribes return from the
North:

> It will be necessary here to make a few
> observations on the doctrine set forth in the above
> quotation [Malachi 3:3], and it is generally supposed
> that sacrifice was entirely done away when the Great
> Sacrifice [i.e.,] the sacrifice of the Lord Jesus was
> offered up, and that there will be no necessity for the
> ordinance of sacrifice in future; but those who assert
> this are certainly not acquainted with the duties,
> privileges and authority of the Priesthood, or with the
> Prophets.
>
> The offering of sacrifice has ever been connected
> and forms a part of the duties of the Priesthood. It
> began with the Priesthood, and will be continued
> until after the coming of Christ, from generation to
> generation. We frequently have mention made of the
> offering of sacrifice by the servants of the Most High
> in ancient days, prior to the law of Moses; which

ordinances will be continued when the Priesthood is restored with all its authority, power and blessings. . . .

These sacrifices, as well as every ordinance belonging to the Priesthood, will, when the Temple of the Lord shall be built, and the sons of Levi be purified, be fully restored and attended to in all their powers, ramifications, and blessings. This ever did and ever will exist when the powers of the Melchizedek Priesthood are sufficiently manifest; else how can the restitution of all things spoken of by the Holy Prophets be brought to pass. It is not to be understood that the law of Moses will be established again with all its rites and variety of ceremonies; this has never been spoken of by the prophets; but those things which existed prior to Moses' day, namely, sacrifice, will be continued. (*TPJS,* pp. 172–73)

These sacrifices will undoubtedly be in memory of the sacrifice by God of his Only Begotten Son.

The great and last sacrifice did fulfill the law of Moses: it ended daily sacrifice and the shedding of blood under the law. When Jesus spoke to the Nephites after the period of total darkness, he declared:

17 And as many as have received me, to them have I given to become the sons of God; and even so will I to as many as shall believe on my name, for behold, by me redemption cometh, and in me is the law of Moses fulfilled.

18 I am the light and the life of the world. I am Alpha and Omega, the beginning and the end.

19 And ye shall offer up unto me no more the shedding of blood; yea, your sacrifices and your burnt offerings shall be done away, for I will accept none of your sacrifices and your burnt offerings. (3 Nephi 9:17–19)

Later, when Jesus visited and taught the Nephites, he said: "Behold, I say unto you that the law is fulfilled that was given unto Moses. Behold, I am he that gave the law, and I am he who covenanted with my people Israel; therefore, the law in me is fulfilled, for I have come to fulfill the law; therefore it hath an end" (3 Nephi 15:4–5). Since the Old Testament prophets had foretold of both Christ's first and second comings, the prophets were not all fulfilled at this time, "for as many as have not been fulfilled in me . . . shall all be fulfilled . . . but the law which was given unto Moses hath an end in me" (3 Nephi 15:6–8).

Every jot and tittle of the law was fulfilled through Christ (3 Nephi 12:18). The jot, or the yod, as it is called in the Hebrew language today, was the smallest of the twenty–two letters of the Hebrew alphabet. The tittle was a part of a letter that often differentiated two similar letters. Thus Christ fulfilled every letter of the law, and even every small part of the letter of the law. He completely fulfilled the law of Moses.

The Atonement satisfied the demands of justice through the plan of mercy. It was infinite, overcoming both physical and spiritual death for all mankind unconditionally. It was an eternal sacrifice and the ultimate or great and last sacrifice of the law of Moses.

The Law of Mercy

In an earlier chapter, justice was equated with eternal law. There are also laws which govern the exercise of mercy. Alma testified: "For behold, justice exerciseth all his demands, and also mercy claimeth all which is her own; and thus, none but the truly penitent are saved. What, do ye suppose that mercy can rob justice? I say unto you, Nay; not one whit. If so, God would cease to be God" (Alma 42:24–25).

There is no possibility that he will cease to be God but will always mete out justice and mercy to his children in perfect love (see 1 John 4:15–19). Since "all have sinned, and come short of the glory of God" (Rom. 3:23), we all need the law of mercy in our lives. The Book of Mormon tells us what must be done to get mercy to pay the demands of justice.

The first requirement for obtaining the full benefit of the Atonement, as taught in the Book of Mormon, is to be righteous or to keep the commandments of God. Nephi told his rebellious brothers Laman and Lemuel: "Behold, the Lord esteemeth all flesh in one; he that is righteous is favored of God" (1 Nephi 17:35). He said further, "And he loveth those who will have him to be their God" and then spoke of how he had loved their fathers (Abraham, Isaac, and Jacob) with whom he had covenanted (see 1 Nephi 17:40). The Lord loves the righteous, "those who love [him] and keep all [his] commandments, and him that seeketh so to do" (D&C 46:9). Those who are trying to live the gospel will be blessed accordingly.

The second requirement for the law of mercy to take effect, as taught in the Book of Mormon, is to have a broken heart and a contrite spirit. Christ told the Nephites that the sacrifice required after the law of Moses was fulfilled was "a broken heart and a contrite spirit" (3 Nephi 9:20). One who is broken hearted is saddened and subdued because of his or her contribution to the suffering of Jesus in the Garden of Gethsemane and the fact that his transgression frequently causes others to suffer, as well. One whose spirit is contrite grieves over and is penitent for his sins or transgressions; he is also humble and receptive to the Lord's Spirit that will show him what he must do to receive the mercy of the Atonement.

The third requirement for the Atonement to bring salvation was given by Jacob. Although there are two requirements mentioned, repentance and baptism, the two go together:

> 23 And he commandeth all men that they must repent, and be baptized in his name, having perfect faith in the Holy One of Israel, or they cannot be saved in the kingdom of God. (2 Nephi 9:23–24)

The ordinance of baptism was instituted to bring about a remission of sins. Therefore repentance is a prerequisite to baptism. As Helaman told his sons Nephi and Lehi: "And remember also the words which Amulek spake unto Zeezrom, in the city of Ammonihah; for he said unto him that the Lord surely should come to redeem his people, but that he should not come to redeem them in their sins, but to redeem them from their sins" (Hel. 5:10; see also Alma 11:34). Alma also declared:

> *33 But God did call on men, in the name of his Son, (this being the plan of redemption which was laid) saying: If ye will repent, and harden not your hearts, then will I have mercy upon you, through mine Only Begotten Son;*
>
> *34 Therefore, whosoever repenteth, and hardeneth not his heart, he shall have claim on mercy through mine Only Begotten Son, unto a remission of his sins; and these shall enter into my rest. (Alma 12:33–34)*

Those who comply with the law of repentance will receive the mercy of the Atonement.

A fourth requirement to obtain the blessings of the Atonement, as taught in the Book of Mormon, is to do good works. Mormon, in another one of his editorial comments, proclaimed:

> *23 Therefore, blessed are they who will repent and hearken unto the voice of the Lord their God; for these are they that shall be saved.*
>
> *24 And may God grant, in his great fulness, that men might be brought unto repentance and good works, that they might be restored unto grace for grace, according to their works. (Hel. 12:23–24)*

Receiving grace for grace is receiving the benefit of Christ's Atonement in return for our good deeds towards our fellow men. It is the concept of Jesus' teachings in his mortal ministry: "Inasmuch as ye have done it unto one of the least of these my brethren, ye have done it unto me" (Matt. 25:40). It is also an example of one of the beatitudes: "And blessed are the merciful, for they shall obtain mercy" (3 Nephi 12:7). Samuel the Lamanite taught the people of Zarahemla, "Ye can do good and be restored unto that which is good, or have that which is good restored unto you; or ye can do evil, and have that which is evil restored unto you" (Hel. 14:31; see also Alma 41:13–15). Those who are merciful to others will receive the mercy of the Atonement in their behalf.

A fifth requirement for receiving the law of mercy, or the benefits of the Atonement, as taught in the Book of Mormon, is to love God with all of our might, mind, and strength. Moroni concluded the Book of Mormon with this declaration:

> *Yea, come unto Christ, and be perfected in him, and deny yourselves of all ungodliness; and if ye shall deny yourselves of all ungodliness, and love God with all your might, mind and strength, then is his grace sufficient for you, that by his grace ye may be perfect in Christ; and if by the grace of God ye are perfect in Christ, ye can in nowise deny the power of God. (Moroni 10:32)*

Through Christ's grace, or through the law of mercy, comes salvation. Thus, the law of mercy requires five conditions to become perfect in Christ: (1) keep the commandments of God; (2) offer a sacrifice of a broken heart and a contrite spirit; (3) repent and be baptized; (4) do good deeds for our fellow man; and (5) love God with all of our might, mind, and strength.

Those Who Had No Law

There are some who will receive the benefits of the Atonement who do not meet any of the requirements outlined above. These include those who do not have the law given unto them; little children who are not accountable; and the mentally handicapped, who are also not accountable. The latter two groups will be discussed in a subsequent chapter, but those without law, as discussed by Jacob, will be treated here.

Wherefore, he has given a law; and where there is no law given there is no punishment; and where there is no punishment there is no condemnation; and where there is no condemnation the mercies of the Holy One of Israel have claim upon them, because of the Atonement; for they are delivered by the power of him. (2 Nephi 9:25)

However, the Prophet Joseph Smith and Sidney Rigdon were shown in "The Vision" (D&C 76) that the Atonement will only assure those without law a place in the terrestrial kingdom, not the celestial (see D&C 76:72). But those who did not have full opportunity for the law in their mortal probation will be given a full opportunity to hear and accept the gospel in the spirit world. Therefore, they may qualify themselves for the celestial kingdom (see D&C 137:7–8).

The Demands of Justice

Amulek, Alma's missionary companion, had earlier testified that "the wicked remain as though there had been no redemption made, except it be the loosing of the bands of death" (Alma 11:41). He went on to tell that all would be resurrected and then "arraigned before the bar of Christ the Son, and God the Father, and the Holy Spirit, which is one Eternal God, to be judged according to their works, whether they be good or whether they be evil" (Alma 11:44). Those who do evil are the wicked who will be cast out of God's presence and thus have no redemption except loosing the bands of death.

Earlier, Jacob, brother of Nephi, had warned: "And if they will not repent and believe in his name, and be baptized in his name, and endure to the end, they must be damned; for the Lord God, the Holy One of Israel, has spoken it" (2 Nephi 9:24). And, "But wo unto him that has the law given, yea, that has all the commandments of God, like unto us, and that transgresseth them,

and that wasteth the days of his probation, for awful is his state"
(2 Nephi 9:27). He clarified who these people were: the learned
who think they are wise and hearken not to the commandments of
God; the rich as to the things of the world who despise the poor;
the [spiritually] deaf who will not hear; the [spiritually] blind who
will not see; the uncircumcised of heart [those who do not have
their spirit cleansed]; the liar, the murderer, those who commit
whoredoms [the sexually immoral]; and those who worship idols
[follow after false gods] (see 2 Nephi 9:28–37). "And, in fine, wo
unto all those who die in their sins; for they shall return to God,
and behold his face, and remain in their sins" (2 Nephi 9:38).

Again the infinite Atonement is declared. Even the sinners
will return to God but will be cast out and remain in their sins.

Saved by Grace

An angel declared to King Benjamin that salvation is only
through Jesus Christ. "And moreover, I say unto you, that there
shall be no other name given nor any other way nor means whereby
salvation can come unto the children of men, only in and through
the name of Christ, the Lord Omnipotent" (Mosiah 3:17).

Father Lehi taught the same doctrine:

6 *Wherefore, redemption cometh in and through the Holy
Messiah; for he is full of grace and truth.* . . .

8 *Wherefore, how great the importance to make these
things known unto the inhabitants of the earth, that they
may know that there is no flesh that can dwell in the
presence of God, save it be through the merits, and mercy,
and grace of the Holy Messiah, who layeth down his life
according to the flesh, and taketh it again by the power of
the Spirit, that he may bring to pass the resurrection of the
dead, being the first that should rise.*

9 *Wherefore, he is the firstfruits unto God, inasmuch as
he shall make intercession for all the children of men; and
they that believe in him shall be saved.*

10 And because of the intercession for all, all men come unto God; wherefore, they stand in the presence of him, to be judged of him according to the truth and holiness which is in him. Wherefore, the ends of the law which the Holy One hath given, unto the inflicting of the punishment which is affixed, which punishment that is affixed is in opposition to that of the happiness which is affixed, to answer the ends of the Atonement. (2 Nephi 2:6, 8–10)

It is not faith alone that saves us, nor is it our works. Both of these principles are important and bring us to where the Atonement, through the grace of Christ, will take full effect.

One of the teachings of Paul is often misunderstood, but he was teaching the same message as the Book of Mormon teaches: "For by grace are ye saved through faith; and that not of yourselves: it is the gift of God: Not of works, lest any man should boast" (Eph. 2:8–9). Salvation by grace means that it comes as a gift from God. As quoted in the beginning of this chapter (John 3:16; D&C 34:3), the Atonement of Jesus Christ was a gift of both the Father and the Son. Because the Almighty God loved all his children, he commissioned his Son to make the Atonement. Because Jesus Christ loved all of his brothers and sisters, he was willing to carry out the great plan of the Almighty God to bring about their redemption.

One of the major reasons that Nephi kept his record was for the reader to understand this doctrine: "For we labor diligently to write, to persuade our children, and also our brethren, to believe in Christ, and to be reconciled to God; for we know that it is by grace that we are saved, *after all we can do*" (2 Nephi 25:23, italics added). This succinct statement clarifies what Paul taught to the Ephesians. Both Paul and Moroni taught that you must "work out your own salvation" (Philip. 2:12; Morm. 9:27), but our deeds will not save us without the Atonement of Jesus Christ. From the Book of Mormon we know why Jesus Christ suffered in Gethsemane and the effect of that eternal experience.

8

CHRIST SUFFERED TEMPTATION

"He suffered temptations but gave not heed unto them."

(D&C 20:22)

In the Christian world, the word *atonement* is primarily associated with the cross, which is Christianity's major symbol. The Church of Jesus Christ of Latter-day Saints extends the concept of the Atonement to the suffering that Christ experienced in the Garden of Gethsemane. If the Atonement is spoken of specifically, this is a correct concept; but if the word is used as a general overall description of the life and mission of Jesus Christ, it should include three aspects of his life: (1) his ministry; (2) suffering in Gethsemane; and (3) his suffering and dying on the cross. These three aspects are all taught in the Book of Mormon.

While various aspects of the Atonement are taught throughout the Book of Mormon, there are four prophets who spoke in detail about the Atonement. Jacob gave "one of the most enlightening discussions ever delivered in regard to the Atonement—it is found in the ninth chapter of 2 Nephi."[28] The part of King Benjamin's sermon made known to him by an angel of God is a second great source for understanding the Atonement (Mosiah 3). The third

---

28 Smith, J. F. (1963). *Answers to Gospel Questions*, 4:57–63. Salt Lake City: Deseret Book Company.

detailed analysis of the Atonement is by the prophet Abinadi as he quotes and comments on the Old Testament prophet Isaiah (Mosiah 14–15). The fourth great source in the Book of Mormon teaches the Atonement is more succinct but outlines the birth and three major areas of the Atonement made by Jesus Christ. This great source is Alma's sermon delivered to the people of Gideon (Alma 7). This last source will be the outline of this chapter, but it will include supplements from the other sermons.

The Foretold Birth of Christ

About eighty-three years before the birth of Christ, Alma spoke of one thing that was more important than all the many things to come: "that the Redeemer liveth and cometh among his people" (Alma 7:7). Alma went on to prophesy: "And behold, he shall be born of Mary, at Jerusalem which is the land of our forefathers, she being a virgin, a precious and chosen vessel, who shall be overshadowed and conceive by the power of the Holy Ghost, and bring forth a son, yea, even the Son of God" (Alma 7:10). The Redeemer's miraculous birth as the Son of God made him an eternal being qualified to make the Atonement. Little is recorded in the biblical account concerning Jesus' early life (see Luke 2:40–52), and nothing of it is mentioned in the Book of Mormon. The focus of both scriptural records is his ministry.

Jesus' Ministry

Alma summarized the mission of Jesus Christ's three-year ministry: "And he shall go forth, suffering pains and afflictions and temptations of every kind; and this that the word might be fulfilled which saith he will take upon him the pains and the sicknesses of his people" (Alma 7:11). Jesus' suffering of temptations and taking upon himself the pains and sicknesses of his people is the fulfillment of a prophecy of Isaiah quoted in the Book of Mormon by Abinadi:

3 He is despised and rejected of men; a man of sorrows, and acquainted with grief; and we hid as it were our faces from him; he was despised, and we esteemed him not.

4 Surely he has borne our griefs, and carried our sorrows; yet we did esteem him stricken, smitten of God, and afflicted.

5 But he was wounded for our transgressions, he was bruised for our iniquities; the chastisement of our peace was upon him; and with his stripes we are healed. (Mosiah 14:3–5; Isa. 53:3–5)

Although Alma does not acknowledge the source, the wording of the verse quoted above and the verse that follows (Alma 7:11–12) is very similar to the Isaiah prophecy. Alma does say it "would be" done "that the word might be fulfilled," indicating that he is quoting or paraphrasing the word of God, probably Isaiah.

The words of the angel quoted by King Benjamin are another prophecy of the ministry of Jesus:

5 For behold, the time cometh, and is not far distant, that with power, the Lord Omnipotent who reigneth, who was, and is from all eternity to all eternity, shall come down from heaven among the children of men, and shall dwell in a tabernacle of clay, and shall go forth amongst men, working mighty miracles, such as healing the sick, raising the dead, causing the lame to walk, the blind to receive their sight, and the deaf to hear, and curing all manner of diseases.

6 And he shall cast out devils, or the evil spirits which dwell in the hearts of the children of men. (Mosiah 3:5–6)

Jesus' being among the children of men, his going forth among them, and the miraculous events that are enumerated all describe his ministry conclusively.

Interpreting Isaiah, Abinadi also comments on Christ's suffering, afflictions, and miracles:

> [Jesus] … suffereth temptation, and yieldeth not to the temptation, but suffereth himself to be mocked, and scourged, and cast out, and disowned by his people.
>
> And after all this, after working many mighty miracles among the children of men, he shall be led, yea, even as Isaiah said, as a sheep before the shearer is dumb, so he opened not his mouth. (Mosiah 15:5–6)

Thus, during his ministry, Jesus experienced temptations of every kind. According to President David O. McKay, the three temptations presented by Satan following Jesus' forty-day fast represent nearly every temptation that comes to mankind. These are: "(1) a temptation of appetite or passion; (2) a yielding to the pride and fashion or vanity of those alienated from the things of God; or (3) a desire for the riches of men, or power among men."[29] These three, however, were not the end of the Savior's temptations. At the end of his ministry, Jesus praised those "which have continued with me in my temptations" (Luke 22:28). The Book of Mormon confirms the suffering, afflictions, and temptations of Jesus during his ministry.

The reason Jesus experienced suffering and afflictions was to set an example for us to follow. As Paul said, he "was in all points tempted like as we are, yet without sin" (Heb. 4:15). To the Nephite disciples, Christ posed and answered the question, "Therefore, what manner of men ought ye to be? Verily I say unto you, even as I am" (3 Nephi 27:27).

The Atonement in Gethsemane

Alma, in summarizing the mission of Jesus Christ, connects the Atonement to the knowledge of the Spirit: "Now the Spirit knoweth all things; nevertheless the Son of God suffereth according

---

29 McKay, D. O. (1953). Gospel ideals. The Improvement Era, pp. 154–55.

to the flesh that he might take upon him the sins of his people, that he might blot out their transgressions according to the power of his deliverance; and now behold, this is the testimony which is in me" (Alma 7:13). Through the Spirit, the Redeemer was able to know of the sins of all mankind and experience them or take them upon himself vicariously. Jacob bore similar testimony:

> *20 O how great the holiness of our God! For he knoweth all things, and there is not anything save he knows it.*
>
> *21 And he cometh into the world that he may save all men if they will hearken unto his voice; for behold, he suffereth the pains of all men, yea, the pains of every living creature, both men, women, and children, who belong to the family of Adam. (2 Nephi 9:20–21)*

Thus, Jesus was able to pay for the sins of all men, because he comprehended all of their sins. Without omniscience, he could not have made the Atonement; it was infinite, covering Adam and all of his offspring.

The suffering experienced by Jesus in the Garden of Gethsemane was the fulfillment of a shadow and type taught in the Old Testament. The bitter cup commemorated by the children of Israel's partaking of bitter herbs in the Passover meal (see Ex. 12:8) was to foreshadow the coming Atonement of Christ. It was in Gethsemane that "his sweat was as it were great drops of blood falling down to the ground" (Luke 22:44). The suffering in the garden was so great that an angel appeared "unto him from heaven, strengthening him" for the ordeal (Luke 22:43). Jesus had asked the Father, "if it be possible, let this cup pass from me: nevertheless not as I will, but as thou wilt" (Matt. 26:39). When Jesus appeared to the Nephites in America, he testified: "[I have] drunk out of that bitter cup which the Father hath given me, and have glorified the Father in taking upon me the sins of the world, in the which I have suffered the will of the Father in all things from the beginning"

(3 Nephi 11:11). In some vicarious way, not comprehended by mankind, Christ suffered for the sins, pains, and inadequacies of every inhabitant who had ever lived or would ever live on the earth. The Book of Mormon confirms and illuminates the great suffering he experienced in the garden.

The angel informed King Benjamin that "blood cometh from every pore, so great shall be his anguish for the wickedness and the abominations of his people" (Mosiah 3:7). Not only does this Book of Mormon passage confirm that Jesus sweat blood (see Luke 22:44), but it gives the reason—the (mental) anguish was so great that Jesus' pores shed blood. The Doctrine and Covenants gives a third witness of his sweating blood from every pore, suffering in both body and spirit, and drinking of the bitter cup (see D&C 19:18).

The prophet Isaiah foretold, "when thou shalt make his soul an offering for sin he shall see his seed" (Mosiah 14:10; Isa. 53:10). The "offering of his soul" apparently refers to his mental anguish or internal suffering as he experienced the sins of all mankind. Isaiah seems to be saying that when the Father [the Almighty God] "gave" his Only Begotten Son as an offering for the sins of the world, the Son had a vision of the beginning of the world to the end. He more than viewed the events; he somehow placed himself in them or "descended below them all" (D&C 122:8). Through his experience, he paid the demands of justice for the inhabitants of the earth. The prophet Abinadi, commenting on Isaiah's prophecy, tied a previous question by Isaiah, "who shall declare his generation?"(v. 8), with the Savior "see[ing] his seed." He then declared that those who hearken to the words of the prophets and believe that the Lord would redeem his people are Christ's seed and heirs of the kingdom of God (see Mosiah 15:10–11; see also vv. 12–13). Those who believe and accept Jesus' Atonement are spiritually adopted as the sons and daughters of Jesus Christ (see Mosiah 5:7). Those who would do so were seen by Christ as he suffered in Gethsemane.

But Christ saw more than just those who believed. Isaiah continued: "He shall see the travail of his soul, and shall be satisfied"

(Mosiah 14:11; or Isa. 53:11). The "he" in this reference is the Father, who will be satisfied with the suffering of the Savior. What it means to be satisfied is interpreted for us by Abinadi:

> *Having ascended into heaven, having the bowels of mercy; being filled with compassion towards the children of men; standing betwixt them and justice; having broken the bands of death, taken upon himself their iniquity and their transgressions, having redeemed them, and satisfied the demands of justice. (Mosiah 15:9)*

Isaiah continues: "By his knowledge shall my righteous servant justify many; for he shall bear their iniquities" (Mosiah 14:11; Isa. 53:11). A surface reading may suggest he suffered only for those who believed; but as discussed in the previous chapter, his Atonement was infinite (see 2 Nephi 25:21; Morm. 9:12–13; Hel. 14:17). In other words, it covered all people. Isaiah is apparently emphasizing the great number of people covered by Jesus' Atonement. When it is remembered that the Atonement covered other worlds, as well (see D&C 76:24), the "many" has to refer to great numbers, and not just a part of the whole. The enormity of his suffering is unfathomable.

As discussed earlier, Jesus' suffering was the suffering of a God—it was an eternal sacrifice. It was also a free will offering of both the Father and the Son (John 3:16; D&C 34:2–3). Gethsemane was the apex of the Atonement, the payment for the individual sins of the inhabitants of the world.

Suffering on the Cross

Alma said, "And he will take upon him death, that he may loose the bands of death which bind his people; and he will take upon him their infirmities, that his bowels may be filled with mercy, according to the flesh, that he may know according to the flesh how to succor his people according to their infirmities" (Alma 7:12). The suffering on the cross paid for the sin of Adam: "For as in Adam all die, even so in Christ shall all be made alive" (1 Cor. 15:22).

An angel appeared to King Benjamin and said: "And lo, he cometh unto his own, that salvation might come unto the children of men even through faith on his name; and even after all this they shall consider him a man, and say that he hath a devil, and shall scourge him, and shall crucify him" (Mosiah 3:9). While on the cross, Jesus gave up his life but took it up again to break the bands of death. Abinadi taught: "And thus God [Christ] breaketh the bands of death, having gained the victory over death; giving the Son power to make intercession for the children of men" (Mosiah 15:8). Through the agonizing pain of the crucifixion, Jesus again suffered; but this time, his suffering was in a physical sense. He did it on his own as the Father withdrew his Spirit. President Brigham Young gave this thought-provoking description:

> Then the greater the vision, the greater the display of the power of the enemy. And when such individuals are off their guard they are left to themselves, as Jesus was. For this express purpose the Father withdrew His spirit from His Son, at the time he was to be crucified. Jesus had been with his Father, talked with Him, dwelt in His bosom, and knew all about heaven, about making the earth, about the transgression of man, and what would redeem the people, and that he was the character who was to redeem the sons of earth, and the earth itself from all sin that had come upon it. The light, knowledge, power, and glory with which he was clothed were far above, or exceeded that of all others who had been upon the earth after the fall, consequently at the very moment, at the hour when the crisis came for him to offer up his life, the Father withdrew Himself, withdrew His Spirit, and cast a vail over him. That is what made him sweat blood. If he had had the power of God upon him, he would not

have sweat blood; but all was withdrawn from him, and a veil was cast over him, and he then plead with the Father not to forsake him. "No," says the Father, "you must have your trials, as well as others."[30]

Through the suffering in Gethsemane and on the cross, Jesus was and is able to say to any of us as he said to Joseph Smith: "The Son of Man hath descended below them all. Art thou greater than he?" (D&C 122:8).

In addition, Jesus set the example for us to follow. However, none of us are able to be justified by the law (2 Nephi 2:5), as we all sin "and come short of the glory of God" (Rom. 3:23). He atoned for us that we might not suffer:

> *16 For behold, I, God, have suffered these things for all, that they might not suffer if they would repent;*
>
> *17 But if they would not repent they must suffer even as I;*
>
> *18 Which suffering caused myself, even God, the greatest of all, to tremble because of pain, and to bleed at every pore, and to suffer both body and spirit—and would that I might not drink the bitter cup, and shrink. (D&C 19:16–18)*

The specific aspects of the Atonement were exemplified in Jacob's following invitation:

> *23 Therefore, cheer up your hearts, and remember that ye are free to act for yourselves—to choose the way of everlasting death or the way of eternal life.*
>
> *24 Wherefore, my beloved brethren, reconcile yourselves to the will of God, and not to the will of the devil and the flesh; and remember, after ye are reconciled unto God,*

---

30 *Journal of Discourses*, 3:206. London: Latter-day Saint Book Depot.

that it is only in and through the grace of God [Christ] that ye are saved.

25 Wherefore, may God raise you from death by the power of the resurrection, and also from everlasting death by the power of the Atonement, that ye may be received into the eternal kingdom of God, that ye may praise him through grace divine. Amen. (2 Nephi 10:23–25)

From the Book of Mormon we learn of the three phases of the Atonement made while Jesus lived upon the earth: his ministry, in Gethsemane, and on the cross. It gives insight into how the Atonement was made and clearly shows why it was made.

9

THE RESURRECTION

"He was crucified, died, and rose again the third day."

(D&C 20:23)

One of the many reasons that the Book of Mormon is "Another Testament of Jesus Christ" (subtitle) is that it testifies of his literal resurrection. The first testament is, of course, the Bible, but that testament has suffered the loss of plain and precious parts (see 1 Nephi 13:24–29). The Prophet Joseph Smith explained: "I believe the Bible as it came from the pen of the original writers. Ignorant translators, careless transcribers, or designing and corrupt priests have committed many errors" (*TPJS,* 327). The Book of Mormon resolves these losses by verifying and clarifying the biblical teachings.

Prophecies Foretold Christ's Resurrection

The Old Testament has a few prophecies of Christ's resurrection; but due to the losses mentioned above, these have become obscure. One of these obscure passages is from Hannah, the mother of the prophet Samuel. As she prayed to the Lord, she said: "The Lord killeth, and maketh alive: he bringeth down to the grave, and bringeth up" (1 Sam. 2:6). Another passage, although its interpretation is sometimes disputed, is from Isaiah: "Thy dead men shall live, together with my dead body shall they arise. Awake and sing, ye that dwell in dust: for thy dew is as the dew of herbs, and the earth shall cast out the dead" (Isa. 26:19). A third passage teaches that the power of the resurrection is centered in Christ: "I will ransom them from the power of the grave; I will redeem them from death: O death, I will be thy plagues; O grave, I will be thy destruction: repentance shall be hid from mine eyes" (Hosea 13:14). The arguments for and against the various interpretations of these scriptures will not be considered. We will focus, however, on the testimony of the resurrection of Christ given in the Book of Mormon.

Paul, in his letter to the Corinthians, quotes a passage of scripture "that is written" and fulfilled by Christ: "Death is swallowed up in victory. O death, where is thy sting? O grave, where is thy victory?" (1 Cor. 15:54–55). Because it is similar to Hosea's prophecy quoted above, the quote by Paul is usually considered a paraphrase of Hosea. However, the wording is quite different. That Paul is really quoting a passage now lost from the Old Testament is evidenced from the Book of Mormon. Abinadi testifies of the resurrection of Christ in words similar to Paul's terminology:

> *7 And if Christ had not risen from the dead, or have broken the bands of death that the grave should have no victory, and that death should have no sting, there could have been no resurrection.*
>
> *8 But there is a resurrection, therefore the grave hath no victory, and the sting of death is swallowed up in Christ. (Mosiah 16:7–8)*

Earlier, in the same declaration to the priests of Noah, Abinadi had questioned, "Yea, and have they [all the prophets] not said also that he should bring to pass the resurrection of the dead, and that he, himself, should be oppressed and afflicted?" (Mosiah 13:35). Abinadi's testimony of Christ's resurrection is only one of several found in the Book of Mormon.

King Benjamin rehearsed the words of an angel concerning Christ being crucified: "And he shall rise the third day from the dead" (Mosiah 3:9–10). Alma, after fleeing from the servants of king Noah, taught the words of Abinadi "concerning the resurrection of the dead, and the redemption of the people, which was to be brought to pass through the power, and sufferings, and death of Christ, and his resurrection and ascension into heaven" (Mosiah 18:2). As Mormon abridged the account of Alma and Amulek's teaching of the Nephites, he recorded: "And many of the people did inquire concerning the place where the Son of God should come; and they were taught that he would appear unto them after his resurrection; and this the people did hear with great joy and gladness" (Alma 16:20). As Aaron, one of the sons of Mosiah, expounded scriptures to the Lamanite king, he taught that Christ would break "the bands of death, that the grave shall have no victory, and that the sting of death should be swallowed up in the hopes of glory" (Alma 22:14). Again we note the similar wording of Paul and Abinadi in this passage, another evidence of an Old Testament prophecy, now lost, but well known to ancient Israel and the Nephites. Finally, Alma the younger testified to the Zoramites that Christ "shall rise again from the dead, which shall bring to pass the resurrection" (Alma 33:22). The Book of Mormon prophets knew and testified of Christ being resurrected and thus breaking the bands of death and gaining a victory over the grave.

Christ Was Literally Resurrected

The Book of Mormon bears further witness that the words of those prophets had been fulfilled through the literal resurrection of Jesus Christ. As Mormon was abridging the Nephite records, he inserted this editorial comment:

> *18 Behold, I will show unto you that the people of Nephi who were spared, and also those who had been called Lamanites, who had been spared, did have great favors shown unto them, and great blessings poured out upon*

their heads, insomuch that soon after the ascension of Christ into heaven he did truly manifest himself unto them—

19 Showing his body unto them, and ministering unto them. (3 Nephi 10:18–19)

As Mormon fulfilled his promise to show the reader of Christ's coming among the Nephites, there is a witness given that Christ was a resurrected being with a literal body of flesh and bones. First, the Nephites heard the Father bear witness of his Beloved Son:

1 And now it came to pass that there were a great multitude gathered together, of the people of Nephi, round about the temple which was in the land Bountiful; and they were marveling and wondering one with another, and were showing one to another the great and marvelous change which had taken place.

2 And they were also conversing about this Jesus Christ, of whom the sign had been given concerning his death.

3 And it came to pass that while they were thus conversing one with another, they heard a voice as if it came out of heaven; and they cast their eyes round about, for they understood not the voice which they heard; and it was not a harsh voice, neither was it a loud voice; nevertheless, and notwithstanding it being a small voice it did pierce them that did hear to the center, insomuch that there was no part of their frame that it did not cause to quake; yea, it did pierce them to the very soul, and did cause their hearts to burn.

4 And it came to pass that again they heard the voice, and they understood it not.

5 And again the third time they did hear the voice, and did open their ears to hear it; and their eyes were towards the sound thereof; and they did look steadfastly towards heaven, from whence the sound came.

6 And behold, the third time they did understand the voice which they heard; and it said unto them:

7 Behold my Beloved Son, in whom I am well pleased, in whom I have glorified my name—hear ye him. (3 Nephi 11:1–7)

Secondly, they saw him descend out of heaven and heard him testify that he was Jesus Christ:

8 And it came to pass, as they understood they cast their eyes up again towards heaven; and behold, they saw a Man descending out of heaven; and he was clothed in a white robe; and he came down and stood in the midst of them; and the eyes of the whole multitude were turned upon him, and they durst not open their mouths, even one to another, and wist not what it meant, for they thought it was an angel that had appeared unto them.

9 And it came to pass that he stretched forth his hand and spake unto the people, saying:

10 Behold, I am Jesus Christ, whom the prophets testified shall come into the world.

11 And behold, I am the light and the life of the world; and I have drunk out of that bitter cup which the Father hath given me, and have glorified the Father in taking upon me the sins of the world, in the which I have suffered the will of the Father in all things from the beginning.

12 And it came to pass that when Jesus had spoken these words the whole multitude fell to the earth; for they remembered that it had been prophesied among them that Christ should show himself unto them after his ascension into heaven. (3 Nephi 11:8–12)

Thirdly, they felt the wounds in his side and hands and his feet,[31] and did know of a surety that this was he of whom the prophets had prophesied:

> *13 And it came to pass that the Lord spake unto them saying:*
>
> *14 Arise and come forth unto me, that ye may thrust your hands into my side, and also that ye may feel the prints of the nails in my hands and in my feet, that ye may know that I am the God of Israel, and the God of the whole earth, and have been slain for the sins of the world.*
>
> *15 And it came to pass that the multitude went forth, and thrust their hands into his side, and did feel the prints of the nails in his hands and in his feet; and this they did do, going forth one by one until they had all gone forth, and did see with their eyes and did feel with their hands, and did know of a surety and did bear record, that it was he, of whom it was written by the prophets, that should come.*
>
> *16 And when they had all gone forth and had witnessed for themselves, they did cry out with one accord, saying:*
>
> *17 Hosanna! Blessed be the name of the Most High God! And they did fall down at the feet of Jesus, and did worship him. (3 Nephi 11:1–17)*

Thus through the perception of three of the physical senses—sound, sight, and touch—the Nephites had witness born to them that Christ was a resurrected being with a literal body. The Old Testament law of witnesses was followed in testifying to the Nephites, "at the mouth of two witnesses, or at the mouth of three witnesses, shall the matter be established" (Deut. 19:15; see also

---

31 For a treatise on why Christ still had the wounds after his resurrection, see Smith, J. F. (1955). *Doctrines of Salvation*, vol. 2, pp. 290–92. Salt Lake City: Bookcraft.

Matt. 18:16). But the stronger witness must certainly have been that born to their spirits when they "did know of a surety and did bear record" that they beheld and touched the living God.

There were twenty-five-hundred men, women, and children gathered at the temple in Bountiful for this glorious occasion (see 3 Nephi 17:25). It was also another testament of Christ given to a body of people. The first testament was to a body of five hundred brethren somewhere in Palestine (1 Cor. 15:6). If women and children were present at the Palestine gathering, the numbers may have been very similar to the Nephite gathering.

The law of witnesses is also illustrated in there being both a physical and spiritual verification. Today we have the law of witnesses for Christ's resurrection through two physical witnesses: the Bible and the Book of Mormon accounts of his resurrection. We may not have had the physical witnesses of hearing, seeing, and touching Christ, but the Bible and the Book of Mormon teach us that he was resurrected. We may also know of a surety ourselves, through the spiritual witness of the Holy Spirit, that Jesus Christ is a resurrected God (Mor. 10:5).

Christ Had Power over Death

The purpose of Christ being resurrected is taught in the Bible and the Book of Mormon. Paul taught the Corinthians: "For as in Adam all die, even so in Christ shall all be made alive. But every man in his own order: Christ the firstfruits; afterward they that are Christ's at his coming" (1 Cor. 15:22–23). Thus Paul testifies of Christ as the first to rise, breaking the bands of death for all mankind. Lehi also taught his son Jacob that the Holy Messiah brought about the resurrection and was the first to rise.

> *Wherefore, how great the importance to make these things known unto the inhabitants of the earth, that they may know that there is no flesh that can dwell in the presence of God, save it be through the merits, and mercy, and grace of the Holy Messiah, who layeth down his life according*

to the flesh, and taketh it again by the power of the Spirit, that he may bring to pass the resurrection of the dead, being the first that should rise (2 Nephi 2:8).

Jacob, in turn, taught of the power of the resurrection being in Christ.

Wherefore, beloved brethren, be reconciled unto him through the Atonement of Christ, his Only Begotten Son, and ye may obtain a resurrection, according to the power of the resurrection which is in Christ, and be presented as the first-fruits of Christ unto God, having faith, and obtained a good hope of glory in him before he manifesteth himself in the flesh. (Jacob 4:11)

Another aspect of the resurrection taught in the Bible, but enlarged upon in the Book of Mormon, is its connection with the judgment bar. In the book of Revelation John recorded:

12 And I saw the dead, small and great, stand before God; and the books were opened: and another book was opened, which is the book of life: and the dead were judged out of those things which were written in the books, according to their works.

13 And the sea gave up the dead which were in it; and death and hell delivered up the dead which were in them: and they were judged every man according to their works. (Rev. 20:12–13)

Jacob expounded greatly on the importance of Christ delivering up the body and the spirit from death and hell:

7 Wherefore, it must needs be an infinite Atonement—save it should be an infinite Atonement this corruption could not put on incorruption. Wherefore, the first judgment which came upon man must needs have remained to an endless duration. And if so, this flesh must have laid down to rot and to crumble to its mother earth, to rise no more.

8 O the wisdom of God, his mercy and grace! For behold, if the flesh should rise no more our spirits must become subject to that angel who fell from before the presence of the Eternal God, and became the devil, to rise no more.

9 And our spirits must have become like unto him, and we become devils, angels to a devil, to be shut out from the presence of our God, and to remain with the father of lies, in misery, like unto himself; yea, to that being who beguiled our first parents, who transformeth himself nigh unto an angel of light, and stirreth up the children of men unto secret combinations of murder and all manner of secret works of darkness.

10 O how great the goodness of our God, who prepareth a way for our escape from the grasp of this awful monster; yea, that monster, death and hell, which I call the death of the body, and also the death of the spirit.

11 And because of the way of deliverance of our God, the Holy One of Israel, this death, of which I have spoken, which is the temporal, shall deliver up its dead; which death is the grave.

12 And this death of which I have spoken, which is the spiritual death, shall deliver up its dead; which spiritual death is hell; wherefore, death and hell must deliver up their dead, and hell must deliver up its captive spirits, and the grave must deliver up its captive bodies, and the bodies and the spirits of men will be restored one to the other; and it is by the power of the resurrection of the Holy One of Israel.

13 O how great the plan of our God! For on the other hand, the paradise of God must deliver up the spirits of the righteous, and the grave deliver up the body of the righteous; and the spirit and the body is restored to itself again, and all men become incorruptible, and immortal, and they are living souls, having a perfect knowledge like unto us in the flesh, save it be that our knowledge shall be perfect. (2 Nephi 9:7–13)

On the day following, Jacob summarized his teachings: "Wherefore, may God raise you from death by the power of the resurrection, and also from everlasting death by the power of the Atonement, that ye may be received into the eternal kingdom of God, that ye may praise him through grace divine. Amen" (2 Nephi 10:25). Jesus himself testified of the power that he possessed to bring about the resurrection: "Therefore doth my Father love me, because I lay down my life, that I might take it again. No man taketh it from me, but I lay it down of myself. I have power to lay it down, and I have power to take it again. This commandment have I received of my Father" (John 10:17–18). Abinadi verifies what Jesus taught concerning his power to bring about the resurrection:

8 And thus God breaketh the bands of death, having gained the victory over death; giving the Son power to make intercession for the children of men—

9 Having ascended into heaven, having the bowels of mercy; being filled with compassion towards the children of men; standing betwixt them and justice; having broken the bands of death, taken upon himself their iniquity and their transgressions, having redeemed them, and satisfied the demands of justice. (Mosiah 15:8–9)

In addition to "Another Testament" of Christ and the resurrection as taught in the Bible, the Book of Mormon adds the doctrine of the resurrection of Christ enabling man to come back into the presence of God. Alma testified to his wayward son Corianton that "the Atonement bringeth to pass the resurrection of the dead; and the resurrection of the dead bringeth back men into the presence of God; and thus they are restored into his presence, to be judged according to their works, according to the law and justice" (Alma 42:23). Samuel the Lamanite gave a second witness to this doctrine:

> *15 For behold, he surely must die that salvation may come; yea, it behooveth him and becometh expedient that he dieth, to bring to pass the resurrection of the dead, that thereby men may be brought into the presence of the Lord.*

> *16 Yea, behold, this death bringeth to pass the resurrection, and redeemeth all mankind from the first death—that spiritual death; for all mankind, by the fall of Adam being cut off from the presence of the Lord, are considered as dead, both as to things temporal and to things spiritual.*

> *17 But behold, the resurrection of Christ redeemeth mankind, yea, even all mankind, and bringeth them back into the presence of the Lord. (Hel. 14:15–17)*

The importance of the resurrection is taught in the Book of Mormon. Joseph Smith adds another witness. Speaking about the resurrection at the funeral sermon of Lorenzo D. Barnes, the Prophet Joseph Smith made this interesting remark:

> Salvation is nothing more nor less than to triumph over all our enemies and put them under our feet. And when we have power to put all enemies under our feet in this world, and a knowledge to triumph over all evil spirits in the world to come, then we are saved, as in the case of Jesus, who was to reign until He had put all enemies under His feet, and the last enemy was death. (*TPJS,* 297)

Christ's conquering of death was his physical resurrection, which testifies to us that we also will overcome death through a physical resurrection.

Subsequent Appearances of Christ

After Christ's resurrection and forty-day ministry in Palestine, he appeared to Saul [Paul] on the road to Damascus (Acts 9:3–6; 1 Cor. 15:8). There were undoubtedly other appearances that weren't recorded or have been lost. The Book of Mormon bears witness "that he did show himself unto them oft" (3 Nephi 26:13). Mormon "was visited of the Lord" (Mormon 1:15), and Moroni saw him and "talked with [him] face to face" (Ether 12:39). It was Christ's Church, and he directed it through his apostles.

The Book of Mormon is "Another Testament of Jesus Christ"; it verifies and expounds upon his literal resurrection and clarifies the biblical teachings on the subject.

The Resurrection of Man

The resurrection of Christ broke the bands of death and brought about the resurrection of man. The resurrection of the dead was listed by the Prophet Joseph as one of the first principles of the gospel: "The Doctrines of the Resurrection of the Dead and the Eternal Judgment are necessary to preach among the first principles of the Gospel of Jesus Christ" (*TPJS,* 149; see also H.C. 3:396).

Who Will Be Resurrected

The Book of Mormon is once more a second witness to the Bible concerning the resurrection. Paul, writing to the Corinthians, declared: "For since by man came death, by man came also the resurrection of the dead. For as in Adam all die, even so in Christ shall all be made alive" (1 Cor. 15:21–22). Amulek bore a similar testimony: "Now, there is a death which is called a temporal death; and the death of Christ shall loose the bands of this temporal death, that all shall be raised from this temporal death" (Alma 11:42).

There are some who believe that only the righteous will be resurrected, but that is not the teaching of the Bible or the Book of Mormon. In the Gospel of John we read: "And shall come forth; they that have done good, unto the resurrection of life; and they that have done evil, unto the resurrection of damnation" (John 5:29, see also Acts 24:15).[32] Amulek, in speaking further on the resurrection, testified: "Now, this restoration shall come to all, both old and young, both bond and free, both male and female, both the wicked and the righteous" (Alma 11:44). Abinadi also taught the universal resurrection. "If they be good, to the resurrection of endless life and happiness; and if they be evil, to the resurrection of endless damnation, being delivered up to the devil, who hath subjected them, which is damnation" (Mosiah 16:11). Mormon, in summarizing the teachings of Jesus, recorded that all would be judged of their works: "If they be good, to the resurrection of everlasting life; and if they be evil, to the resurrection of damnation" (3 Nephi 26:5).[33] The scriptures definitely teach the unconditional resurrection of all mankind.

The Literalness and Completeness of the Resurrection

The Book of Mormon and the Bible also teach a literal resurrection. Our fallen nature includes a body of mortal, corruptible flesh. Paul taught that the resurrection will "change our vile body, that it may be fashioned like unto his glorious body" (Philip. 3:21, see also 1 Cor. 15:53). The Book of Mormon verifies and enlarges upon this doctrine. Enos, son of Jacob, rejoiced "in

---

32 The passage in John was the catalyst for Joseph Smith and Sidney Rigdon having a vision of the degrees of glory as recorded in the Doctrine and Covenants, as they were doing the work of translation. While the wording is slightly different (see D&C 76:16–17), the passage is another witness of all coming forth in the resurrection.

33 Some people have interpreted D&C 76:38, "the only ones who shall not be redeemed," as saying that the sons of perdition will not be resurrected. However, a careful reading of D&C 88:27–32 shows that all will be resurrected, including the sons of perdition. See also Smith, J. F. (1957). *Answers to Gospel Questions,* 1:38. Salt Lake City: Deseret Book.

the day when my mortal shall put on immortality" (Enos 1:27). Abinadi testified: "Even this mortal shall put on immortality, and this corruption shall put on incorruption" (Mosiah 16:10). But it is Amulek who really defined the resurrection:

> *Now, behold, I have spoken unto you concerning the death of the mortal body, and also concerning the resurrection of the mortal body. I say unto you that this mortal body is raised to an immortal body, that is from death, even from the first death unto life, that they can die no more; their spirits uniting with their bodies, never to be divided; thus the whole becoming spiritual and immortal, that they can no more see corruption. (Alma 11:45)*

The resurrection unites the previously mortal body with the eternal spirit into one eternal, immortal, spiritual whole. As the Lord revealed to Joseph Smith, "the elements are eternal, and spirit and element, inseparably connected, receive a fulness of joy" (D&C 93:33). This is the victory over death and the grave spoken of by Abinadi and the Apostle Paul (see Mosiah 15:7–8; 1 Cor. 15:54–55). The spirit and the body will be completely intertwined, becoming a spiritual entity that will no longer suffer death.

Alma, basing his statement upon what "has been spoken by the mouths of the prophets" (Alma 40:22), testified: "The soul [spirit] shall be restored to the body, and the body to the soul; yea, and every limb and joint shall be restored to its body; yea, even a hair of the head shall not be lost; but all things shall be restored to their proper and perfect frame" (Alma 40:23). Amulek also taught:

> *43 The spirit and the body shall be reunited again in its perfect form; both limb and joint shall be restored to its proper frame, even as we now are at this time . . .*

> *44 Now this restoration shall come to all, both old and young, both bond and free, both male and female, both the wicked and the righteous; and even there shall not so much as a hair of their heads be lost; but every thing shall*

be restored to its perfect frame, as it is now, or in the body.
(Alma 11:43–44)

Modern-day revelation confirms the teachings of Alma and Amulek: "They who are of a celestial spirit shall receive the same body which was a natural body; even ye shall receive your bodies, and your glory shall be that glory by which your bodies are quickened. Ye who are quickened by a portion of the celestial glory shall then receive of the same, even a fulness" (D&C 88:28–29). The word "quickened" is apparently used interchangeably with "resurrected" in this revelation. The fulness of the celestial glory would certainly bring about the perfect, proper, spiritually whole bodies spoken of by Alma and Amulek.

The word "restored" (Alma 11:44 above) means that we will have our same bodies returned to us. The Prophet Joseph Smith understood the resurrection to be a restoration of the literal, personal body we occupied in mortality. He taught:

> There is no fundamental principle belonging to a human system that ever goes into another in this world or in the world to come; I care not what the theories of men are. We have the testimony that God will raise us up, and he has the power to do it. If any one supposes that any part of our bodies, that is, the fundamental parts thereof, ever goes into another body, he is mistaken.[34]

How the very same bodies could be ours may be difficult to comprehend, but when we consider another teaching of the Prophet Joseph Smith, "There is no such thing as immaterial matter. All spirit is matter, but it is more fine or pure, and can only be discerned by purer eyes" (D&C 131:7), it is more easily understood. While our bodies will decompose into other materials,

---

34 *History of the Church,* 5:339.

those same materials, or the exact combinations of the original body materials, will be restored to a perfect and proper frame. A fuller understanding of this principle will come at the appropriate time.

The Time of the Resurrection

Paul declared that Christ was "the firstfruits; afterward they that are Christ's at his coming" (1 Cor. 15:23). Matthew recorded that after Christ was resurrected, "the graves were opened; and many bodies of the saints which slept arose" (Matt. 27:52–53). The Book of Mormon again confirms and adds to this concept. Alma said: "There is no resurrection—or, I would say, in other words, that this mortal does not put on immortality, this corruption does not put on incorruption—until after the coming of Christ" (Alma 40:2). Samuel the Lamanite prophesied that after the resurrection of Christ, "many graves shall be opened, and shall yield up many of their dead; and many saints shall appear unto many" (Hel. 14:25). The fulfillment of that prophecy was recorded in 3 Nephi 23:9–13.

The Bible speaks of the first resurrection (Rev. 20:6) and divides the resurrection of the just and the unjust as quoted above. The book of Revelation places a time period of one thousand years between these two resurrections (Rev. 20:5). The Book of Mormon once more adds to our knowledge on this subject. The prophet Abinadi outlined who would be in the first resurrection:

21 And there cometh a resurrection, even a first resurrection; yea, even a resurrection of those that have been, and who are, and who shall be, even until the resurrection of Christ—for so shall he be called.

22 And now, the resurrection of all the prophets, and all those that have believed in their words, or all those that have kept the commandments of God, shall come forth in the first resurrection; therefore, they are the first resurrection.

23 They are raised to dwell with God who has redeemed them; thus they have eternal life through Christ, who has broken the bands of death. . . .

25 And little children also have eternal life. (Mosiah 15:21–23, 25)³⁵

Those described by Abinadi are the celestial beings, as confirmed by revelation to the Prophet Joseph Smith (D&C 88:28–29). More specifically, as the Lord revealed in the Doctrine and Covenants, these are those who were with Christ in the beginning of the first resurrection:

54 Yea, and Enoch also, and they who were with him; the prophets who were before him; and Noah also, and they who were before him; and Moses also, and they who were before him;

55 And from Moses to Elijah, and from Elijah to John, who were with Christ in his resurrection, and the holy apostles, with Abraham, Isaac, and Jacob, shall be in the presence of the Lamb. (D&C 133:54–55)

Those resurrected beings mentioned in this revelation had certainly qualified themselves to become celestial beings.

The terrestrial beings will also be a part of the first resurrection, although their coming forth will not be until after the initial resurrection of the celestial beings (D&C 88:30, 99). Abinadi was undoubtedly including these in stating:

And these are those who have part in the first resurrection; and these are they that have died before Christ came, in their ignorance, not having salvation declared unto them. And thus the Lord bringeth about the restoration of these; and they have a part in the first resurrection, or have eternal life, being redeemed by the Lord. (Mosiah 15:24)

35 The resurrection of little children will be discussed in a later chapter.

The telestial beings and the sons of perdition will be resurrected after the thousand-year millennium as the Apostle John declared (Rev. 20:5–6). The Doctrine and Covenants confirms this (D&C 88:31–32; 100–102). Abinadi also spoke of this resurrection:

> But behold, and fear, and tremble before God, for ye ought to tremble; for the Lord redeemeth none such that rebel against him and die in their sins; yea, even all those that have perished in their sins ever since the world began, that have wilfully rebelled against God, that have known the commandments of God, and would not keep them; these are they that have no part in the first resurrection. (Mosiah 15:26)

While there may be various times of people coming forth from the graves within the two general resurrections, there are two major periods of the resurrection, the first and the last, or the just and the unjust. The variation within the two time periods will now be considered.

The Order of the Resurrection

Alma defined the first resurrection in a manner that is sometimes confusing to his readers:

> 16 And behold, again it hath been spoken, that there is a first resurrection, a resurrection of all those who have been, or who are, or who shall be, down to the resurrection of Christ from the dead.

> 17 Now, we do not suppose that this first resurrection, which is spoken of in this manner, can be the resurrection of the souls and their consignation to happiness or misery. Ye cannot suppose that this is what it meaneth.

> 18 Behold, I say unto you, Nay; but it meaneth the reuniting of the soul with the body, of those from the days of Adam down to the resurrection of Christ.

19 Now, whether the souls and the bodies of those of whom has been spoken shall all be reunited at once, the wicked as well as the righteous, I do not say; let it suffice, that I say that they all come forth; or in other words, their resurrection cometh to pass before the resurrection of those who die after the resurrection of Christ.

20 Now, my son, I do not say that their resurrection cometh at the resurrection of Christ; but behold, I give it as my opinion, that the souls and the bodies are reunited, of the righteous, at the resurrection of Christ, and his ascension into heaven. (Alma 40:16–20)

Alma's opinion given in the above statement is often misunderstood. The opinion or question that he does not answer is whether the righteous and the wicked will all be resurrected at once at the time of Christ's resurrection. The doctrine on which he does not equivocate is that all who lived before the time of Christ will be resurrected before all of those who live after the time of Christ. From other scriptures and latter-day prophets, we can discern more on this doctrine.

What Alma seems to be teaching above is a patriarchal order of the resurrection. We know there is a time period between the resurrection of the righteous and the wicked. From Alma's statement there is a sequential order of both the righteous and wicked. We know from the Prophet Joseph Smith that Moroni had been resurrected when he appeared to Joseph: "Moroni, who deposited the plates in a hill in Manchester, Ontario County, New York, being dead and raised again therefrom, appeared unto me, and told me where they were, and gave me directions how to obtain them" (*TPJS*, 119).

Moroni lived around A.D. 400. We know that many Saints were resurrected in Jerusalem and among the Nephites at the time of Christ's resurrection (see Matt. 27:52–53; 3 Nephi 23:9–13). Can we assume that all who lived before the time of Christ had been resurrected by the time of Moroni being resurrected? Probably not. Nor can we assume that all who lived before A.D. 400 had been resurrected. While Moroni and others may have been resurrected for a special purpose, it is also reasonable that there had been a righteous line of people resurrected up to the time of Moroni. This possibility is based on teachings of Joseph Smith and Brigham Young.

Joseph Smith connected the resurrection with the priesthood: "Salvation is for a man to be saved from all his enemies; for until a man can triumph over death, he is not saved. A knowledge of the priesthood alone will do this" (*TPJS*, 305). Joseph had witnessed the resurrection in a vision (see *TPJS*, 295–96). From Joseph's comments we can discern that the resurrection is a "family affair." Brigham Young gives further insight into this concept. Two quotes from President Young will establish his teachings on the subject.

> After the body and spirit are separated by death, what, pertaining to this earth, shall we receive first? The body; that is the first object of a divine affection beyond the grave. We first come in possession of the body. The spirit has overcome the body, and the body is made subject in every respect to that divine principle God has planted in the person. The spirit within is pure and holy, and goes back pure and holy to God, dwells in the spirit world pure and holy, and, by and by, will have the privilege of coming and taking the body again. Some person holding the keys of the resurrection, having previously passed through that ordeal, will be delegated to resurrect our bodies, and our spirits will be there and prepared to enter into their bodies. Then, when we are prepared to receive our bodies, they are the first earthly objects that bear divinity personified in the capacity of the man. Only the body dies; the spirit is looking forth.[36]

---

36 *Discourses of Brigham Young,* p. 373.

When the body comes forth again, it will be divine, God-like according to the capacity and ordinations of the Lord. Some are foreordained to one station, and some to another. We want a house, and when we get it and our spirits enter into it, then we can begin to look forth—for what? For our friends. We want them resurrected. Here is this friend and that friend, until by and by all are on the earth that has abided the law by which it was made. Then that which you and I respect, are fond of, and love with an earthly love, will become divine, and we can then love it with that affection which it is not now worthy of.

Our bodies are now mortal. In the resurrection there will be a reunion of the spirit and bodies, and they will walk, talk, eat, drink, and enjoy. Those who have passed these ordeals are society for angels—for the Gods, and are the ones who will come into the Temple of the Lord that is to be built in the latter days, when saviors shall come up upon Mount Zion, and will say, "Here, my children, I want this and this done. Here are the names of such and such ones, of our fathers, and mothers—our ancestors; we will bring them up. Go forth, you who have not passed the ordeals of death and the resurrection—you who live in the flesh, and attend to the ordinances for those who have died without the law." Those who are resurrected will thus dictate in the temple. When the Saints pass through death, they cannot officiate in this sinful world, but they will dictate those who are here. "Go, now, and be baptized for the honorable—for those who would have received the law of God and the true religion, if they had lived; be baptized for the heathen—for all who were honest; officiate for them, and save them, and bring them up. Be baptized for them, anointed

for them, washed and sealed for them, and fulfil all
the ordinances which cannot be dispensed with." They
will all be performed for the living and the dead upon
Mount Zion.[37]

Thus from the latter-day prophets we learn that the
resurrection is a priesthood ordinance and a patriarchal order of
sequence. President Spencer W. Kimball endorsed at least the
priesthood ordinance of the resurrection in a general conference by
using this quote by Brigham Young:

> It is supposed by this people that we have all
> the ordinances in our possession for life and salvation,
> and exaltation, and that we are administering in those
> ordinances. This is not the case. We are in possession of
> all the ordinances that can be administered in the flesh;
> but there are other ordinances and administrations
> that must be administered beyond this world. I know
> you would like to ask what they are. I will mention
> one. We have not, neither can we receive here, the
> ordinance and the keys of resurrection.
>
> Do we have the keys of resurrection? Could you
> return to the earth as ones who would never again die,
> your own parents, your grandparents, your ancestors?
> I buried my mother when I was eleven, my father
> when I was in my early twenties. I have missed my
> parents much. If I had the power of resurrection as did
> the Savior of the world, I would have been tempted to
> try to keep them longer. I have been called to speak in
> numerous funerals for people whom I have known,
> people whom I have served and helped in a limited
> way. We do not know of anyone who can resurrect

---

37 *Discourses of Brigham Young*, 375.

the dead as did Jesus the Christ when he came back to mortality.

[The keys] will be given to those who have passed off this stage of action and have received their bodies again. . . . They will be ordained, by those who hold the keys of the resurrection, to go forth and resurrect the Saints, just as we received the ordinance of baptism then receive the keys of authority to baptize others for the remission of their sins. This is one of the ordinances we can not receive here [on the earth], and there are many more.[38]

The patriarchal sequence ties in with the justice of God. To ensure an opportunity for all to be resurrected, the Lord has determined that the father will resurrect the family. To paraphrase Joseph Smith regarding salvation, "those Saints who neglect [the ordinances] in behalf of their deceased relatives do it at the peril of his own salvation [resurrection]" (see *TPJS,* 193). We must do the vicarious work for our deceased ancestors in order that they may be resurrected, and they in turn will resurrect us. As the Prophet Joseph Smith said on another occasion: "Hence the responsibility, the awful responsibility, that rests upon us in relation to our dead; for all the spirits who have not obeyed the Gospel in the flesh must either obey it in the spirit or be damned. . . . The greatest responsibility in this world that God has laid upon us is to seek after our dead" (*TPJS,* 355–356). Of course, when there is no worthy father to perform the priesthood ordinance for the resurrection, the mercy of God will delegate that responsibility to another worthy person, probably a relative in the same patriarchal order.

All will be resurrected. As Alma declared to Corianton: "There is a time appointed that all shall rise from the dead" (Alma 40:5).

---

38 *Journal of Discourses,* 15:137; quoted in (1977). *Conference Report,* April, p. 69.

The time of resurrection and the kingdom ultimately inherited is determined by each individual's own behavior. As stated earlier by Alma, "this life became a probationary state; a time to prepare to meet God; a time to prepare for that endless state which has been spoken of by us, which is after the resurrection of the dead" (Alma 12:24).

10

CHRIST REIGNS WITH ALMIGHTY POWER

Christ "ascended into heaven, to sit down on the right hand of the Father, to reign with Almighty power according to the will of the Father." (D&C 20:24)

There are those who believe that if we can learn enough about the earth, and the atmosphere, we will be able to govern this earth to our liking. While we ought to pursue knowledge of the earth incessantly, the only way to govern the earth is through coming to know about Christ and his power. The earth is Christ centered, he is the governor of it as well as its framer or creator. The father "hast given him power over all flesh" (John 17:2). The Book of Mormon testifies of the reign of Christ in heaven.

Ascended into Heaven

The prophet Abinadi spoke of Christ "having ascended into heaven" to exercise mercy and "compassion towards the children of men; standing betwixt them and justice" (Mosiah 15:9). Alma taught of the coming "redemption of the people, which was brought to pass through the power, and sufferings, and death of Christ, and his resurrection and ascension into heaven" (Mosiah 18:2; see also Alma 40:20).

The Book of Mormon testifies of his ascension into heaven after his resurrection in Jerusalem, and also of his ascension again after he ministered to the Nephites. As Mormon abridged the Nephite record, he recorded "that soon after the ascension of Christ into heaven he did truly manifest himself unto them" (3 Nephi 10:18). When Jesus did appear to the Nephites, "they remembered that it had been prophesied among them that Christ should show himself among them after his ascension into heaven" (3 Nephi 11:12). After Jesus had taught the Nephites the same things he had taught in Galilee, as recorded in the Sermon on the Mount (see Matthew 5–7; 3 Nephi 12–14), he declared: "Behold, ye have heard the things which I taught before I ascended to my Father" (3 Nephi 15:1).

Jesus taught the Nephites as a resurrected being. He taught them that he would ascend into heaven again (see 3 Nephi 11:21). At the end of his first day of teaching, "the disciples saw and did bear record that he ascended again into heaven" (3 Nephi 18:39). He also ascended into heaven after the second day of teaching (see 3 Nephi 26:15). Although Mormon does not mention Christ's ascension after the third day, he later testifies of his ascension and his reigning on the right hand of God (see Moro. 7:27). The Book of Mormon gives further insight into his reign on the Father's right hand.

The Administrator of the World

Being on the right hand of the Father designates Jesus Christ as he who carries out the will of the Father (see D&C 20:24 above). Carrying out the Father's will is to have the "power of attorney" or, as the First Presidency states, "Divine Investiture of Authority,"[39] to speak as if he were the Father (see D&C 29:1 and 42). Christ is thus the administrator God of this world upon which we dwell.

---

39 Clark, J. R. (1971). *Messages of the First Presidency, June 1916*, 5:31–34. Salt Lake City: Bookcraft.

When Christ spoke to the Nephites after the terrible destruction in A.D. 34, he identified himself: "I am the light and the life of the world. I am Alpha and Omega, the beginning and the end" (3 Nephi 9:18; see also 11:11). As the light of the world, every person born into the world is blessed with the light of Christ. Mormon enlightens us on the function of this light.

16 For behold, the Spirit of Christ is given to every man, that he may know good from evil; wherefore, I show unto you the way to judge; for every thing which inviteth to do good, and to persuade to believe in Christ, is sent forth by the power and gift of Christ; wherefore ye may know with a perfect knowledge it is of God.

17 But whatsoever thing persuadeth men to do evil, and believe not in Christ, and deny him, and serve not God, then ye may know with a perfect knowledge it is of the devil; for after this manner doth the devil work, for he persuadeth no man to do good, no, not one; neither do his angels; neither do they who subject themselves unto him. (Moro. 7:16–17; see also John 1:9; D&C 88:11)

As the life of the world, there is a glory or radiance that proceeds forth from him that governs all things. King Benjamin taught that he "is preserving you from day to day, by lending you breath, that ye may live and move and do according to your own will, and even supporting you from one moment to another" (Mosiah 2:21). This reminds us of Paul's proclamation on Mars Hill in Athens: "For in him we live, and move, and have our being" (Acts 17:28). In the Doctrine and Covenants, the Lord said:

12 Which light proceedeth forth from the presence of God to fill the immensity of space —

13 The light which is in all things, which giveth life to all things, which is the law by which all things are governed,

even the power of god who sitteth upon his throne, who is
in the bosom of eternity, who is in the midst of all things.
(D&C 88:12–13)

In identifying himself as "Alpha and Omega, the beginning and the end" (3 Nephi 9:18, cited previously), Christ is acknowledging that he is the creator and the finisher of this world and its destiny. Moroni later calls him "the author and the finisher of their faith" (Moro. 6:4; see also Heb. 12:2). He knew the end from the beginning and brought about his purposes through revelation to his servants on earth.

Lehi was carried away in a vision and "saw One descending out of the midst of heaven, and he beheld that his luster was above that of the sun at noon-day. And he also saw twelve others following him, and their brightness did exceed that of the stars in the firmament" (1 Nephi 1:9–10). Although the "One" is not named, it was obviously Christ. The "One" came to Lehi and gave him a book and "bade him that he should read." As he read, "he was filled with the Spirit of the Lord" and "read concerning Jerusalem—that it should be destroyed" (1 Nephi 1:11–13). Lehi was later commanded to take his family and depart into the wilderness" (1 Nephi 2:2). Therefore, Christ was the Administrator of the people leaving Jerusalem because of its apostate condition.

It was Christ who gave the law of Moses and led Israel through the wilderness (see 3 Nephi 15:5; 17:23–42; 1 Cor. 10:1–4). Christ organized, directed, and protected his Church among the Old Testament period Nephites (see Mosiah 18, 23, 27:13; Alma 36:9). Nephi was shown six hundred years before Christ's birth what would happen to the Americas in the latter days (1 Nephi 13–14). He saw also the destiny of Jerusalem and the Nephites (1 Nephi 11–12). The prophet Isaiah had been shown the future of the nations of the earth and also the restoration of the gospel through Joseph Smith. These chapters of Isaiah were quoted by Nephi in the Book of Mormon (see 2 Nephi 17–21).

Through Christ's appointment of people to come to the earth at designated times (see Abr. 3:22; Gen. 18:18–19), he was able to covenant with Abraham, Isaac, Jacob, and Joseph and fulfill those covenants. He designated the times and the sequence of events to Isaiah and explained them to the Nephites (see 3 Nephi 20:11–21). He outlined the proceedings of the remnant of Jacob among the Gentiles from the time of the coming forth of the Book of Mormon to the building of the New Jerusalem (3 Nephi 21). He inspired Mormon to issue a warning to the readers of the Book of Mormon concerning the fulfillment of that covenant and their reaction to the house of Israel (3 Nephi 29).[40] Christ does govern and "hold the destinies of all the armies of the nations of the earth" (D&C 117:6). In short, he is the administrator God of the nations of the earth.

Another role of Christ, as the administrator at the right hand of God, is to direct the affairs of his Church upon the earth. He established his Church among his people in both the eastern and western continent and called servants to preach his word unto them (see Alma 29:11–13). An angel of the Lord appeared to Alma as he went "about secretly with the sons of Mosiah seeking to destroy the church" (Mosiah 27:10). The angel spoke "saying: Alma, arise and stand forth, for why persecuteth thou the church of God? For the Lord hath said: This is my church, and I will establish it; and nothing shall overthrow it, save it is the transgression of my people" (Mosiah 27:13; see also Alma 36:9). Since it is his Church, he will establish it and protect it.

He Reigns with Almighty Power

Almighty power is the power of a God. His reign is confirmed in the Book of Mormon, and it illustrates several different ways that the power of Christ is manifest.

---

40 For a full explanation of the Book of Mormon teachings about the events mentioned above, see Nyman, M. S. (1987). *An ensign to all people.* Salt Lake City: Deseret Book.

Mormon warns that "the sword of justice is in his [the Lord's] right hand" (3 Nephi 29:4). When and how the Lord uses his sword is taught throughout the Book of Mormon. Nephi spoke of the children of Israel destroying the inhabitants of Canaan because they "had rejected every word of God, and they were ripe in iniquity" (1 Nephi 17:35; compare Gen. 15:16). Nephi continued:

> *37 And he raiseth up a righteous nation, and destroyeth the nations of the wicked.*
>
> *38 And he leadeth away the righteous into precious lands, and the wicked he destroyeth, and curseth the land unto them for their sakes.*
>
> *39 He ruleth high in the heavens, for it is his throne, and this earth is his footstool. (1 Nephi 17:37–39)*

Nephi then described the destruction that was soon to come upon the people of Judah. He spoke first of the Israelites being led by the matchless power of God in the wilderness:

> *42 And they did harden their hearts from time to time, and they did revile against Moses, and also against God; nevertheless, ye know that they were led forth by his matchless power into the land of promise.*
>
> *43 And now, after all these things, the time has come that they have become wicked, yea, nearly unto ripeness; and I know not but they are at this day about to be destroyed; for I know that the day must surely come that they must be destroyed, save a few only, who shall be led away into captivity. (1 Nephi 17:42–43)*

As we know from history, and the Book of Mormon, they were destroyed.

Another example of the Lord's almighty power is the destruction of many cities of the Nephites at the time of the crucifixion of Christ (3 Nephi 8). Following the destruction, he spoke to the surviving Nephites and explained that it was he who had destroyed them:

> *10 . . . because of their wickedness in casting out the prophets, and stoning those whom I did send to declare unto them concerning their wickedness and their abominations.*
>
> *11 And because they did cast them all out, that there were none righteous among them, I did send down fire and destroy them, that their wickedness and abominations might be hid from before my face, that the blood of the prophets and the saints whom I sent among them might not cry unto me from the ground against them.*
>
> *12 And many great destructions have I caused to come upon this land, and upon this people, because of their wickedness and their abominations. (3 Nephi 9:10–12)*

His almighty power brought a total destruction upon both the Nephites and the Jaredites who lived in the Americas. Mormon testified that the Nephites were destroyed (about A.D. 385) because "the day of grace was passed with them, both temporally and spiritually" (Morm. 2:15). The wickedness that caused the final downfall was described graphically by Mormon (see Moro. 9), and the destruction of the Jaredites (about 2200 B.C.) by Moroni (see Ether 13–15).

The Lord also uses his power to protect the righteous. Nephi quoted the prophet Isaiah[41] regarding the destruction of the wicked at the end of the world:

> *15 For behold, saith the prophet, the time cometh speedily that Satan shall have no more power over the hearts of*

---

41 Nephi merely quotes "the prophet," but all the previous verses of the chapter are his commentary or interpretation of Isaiah chapter 49. Therefore, he is apparently quoting from a text of Isaiah that was upon the plates of brass but is now a part of the plain and precious parts that were lost (1 Nephi 13:29).

the children of men; for the day soon cometh that all the proud and they who do wickedly shall be as stubble; and the day cometh that they must be burned.

16 For the time soon cometh that the fulness of the wrath of God shall be poured out upon all the children of men; for he will not suffer that the wicked shall destroy the righteous. (1 Nephi 22:15–16)

In this situation, the righteous will be protected by the Lord destroying the wicked. Nephi also saw the Saints of the Church protected in a different way in the last days. The glory of God upon the righteous would be so powerful that the wicked would be afraid to come upon them:

And it came to pass that I, Nephi, beheld the power of the Lamb of God, that it descended upon the saints of the church of the Lamb, and upon the covenant people of the Lord, who were scattered upon all the face of the earth; and they were armed with righteousness and with the power of God in great glory. (1 Nephi 14:14; see also vv. 15–16)

The Lord revealed to Joseph Smith how the latter-day New Jerusalem would be protected and be "a place of safety for the saints of the Most High God":

67 And the glory of the Lord shall be there, and the terror of the Lord also shall be there, insomuch that the wicked will not come unto it, and it shall be called Zion.

68 And it shall come to pass among the wicked, that every man that will not take his sword against his neighbor must needs flee unto Zion for safety.

69 And there shall be gathered unto it out of every nation under heaven; and it shall be the only people that shall not be at war one with another.

70 And it shall be said among the wicked: Let us not go up to battle against Zion, for the inhabitants of Zion are terrible; wherefore we cannot stand.

71 And it shall come to pass that the righteous shall be gathered out from among all nations, and shall come to Zion, singing with songs of everlasting joy. (D&C 45:66–71)

Isaiah saw the same time period and extended it to other gatherings of Saints in stakes of Zion.[42] Nephi recorded Isaiah's prophecy in the Book of Mormon:

5 And the Lord will create upon every dwelling-place of mount Zion, and upon her assemblies, a cloud and smoke by day and the shining of a flaming fire by night; for upon all the glory of Zion shall be a defense.

6 And there shall be a tabernacle for a shadow in the daytime from the heat, and for a place of refuge, and a covert from storm and from rain. (2 Nephi 14:5–6; Isa. 4:5–6)

The cloud by day and fire by night seem to symbolically represent the power of the Lord that is protecting his Saints. The children of Israel were similarly protected in the wilderness by the Lord in a cloud and pillar of fire (see Exodus 13:20–22).

Another interesting equation of the almighty power of God was given by Nephi. After mentioning many prophecies regarding Christ's ministry and death, he quoted the prophet Zenos: "And all these things must surely come, saith the prophet Zenos. And the rocks of the earth must rend; and because of the groanings of the earth, many of the kings of the isles of the sea shall be wrought upon by the Spirit of God, to exclaim: The God of nature suffers"

---

42 See D&C 115:5–6 and 124:36 for verification of the other dwelling places being stakes of Zion.

(1 Nephi 19:12). Note that it is the Spirit of God that moves the kings to call Christ the "God of nature." Being the God of nature explains how the destructive storms that followed the crucifixion of Christ led him to say "I caused" these cities to sink, or burn, or be buried (see 3 Nephi 9). His power is manifest through the elements. Mormon supports this concept: "And thus we see that except the Lord doth chasten his people with many afflictions, yea, except he doth visit them with death and with terror, and with famine and with all manner of pestilence, they will not remember him" (Hel. 12:3; see also Amos 4:6–13).

Today, Christ is still reigning with almighty power on the right hand of the Father. We will yet see more and more of his power manifest. We must acknowledge that this is a Christ-centered earth—He is governing the earth, its nations, and the destiny of his people.

11

BELIEVE AND BE BAPTIZED

*"That as many as would believe and be baptized
in his holy name, and endure in faith to the
end, should be saved." (D&C 20:25)*

Faith is the most talked about but probably the least understood principle of the gospel. At least one of the reasons for this is that there are three different principles of faith, as defined in the *Lectures on Faith* given at the school of the prophets in 1834–35. These three principles are 1) faith as a principle of action; 2) faith as a principle of power; and 3) faith as a principle of life and salvation (*Lectures on Faith* 1:9–12). The Book of Mormon teaches and exemplifies all three of these principles. To "believe and be baptized" (D&C 20:25) is to exercise faith as a principle of action. This will be the topic of this chapter. Further chapters will discuss the other two principles of faith.

Definitions of Faith

Concerning faith as a principle of action, Alma defined it: "And now as I said concerning faith—faith is not to have a perfect knowledge of things; therefore if ye have faith ye hope for things which are not seen, which are true" (Alma 32:21). As Alma goes on to explain, faith is not to have a perfect knowledge (vv. 26–27), it is to proceed with hope based on the truths that have been taught.

The Bible gives a similar definition. In the Book of Hebrews we read: "Now faith is the substance [assurance] of things hoped for, the evidence of things not seen" (Heb. 11:1). The word "assurance," inserted in the biblical definition, is a JST change.

To believe and be baptized, as stated above, illustrates the action that follows faith. If one believes but is not baptized, he is not exercising faith. As Elder Howard W. Hunter stated, "We cannot have faith without belief but we may believe and still lack faith."[43] Thus faith is necessary for salvation.

When Jesus ministered among the Nephites, he declared: "And whoso believeth in me, and is baptized, the same shall be saved; and they are they who shall inherit the kingdom of God. And whoso believeth not in me, and is not baptized, shall be damned" (3 Nephi 11:33–34). He taught the same doctrine in his Jerusalem ministry (see Mark 16:15–16). Biblical criticism has questioned the authenticity of these verses in the Testimony of Mark,[44] but the Book of Mormon verifies that Jesus did indeed teach what is recorded in Mark:

> *22 For behold, thus said Jesus Christ, the Son of God, unto his disciples who should tarry, yea, and also to all his disciples, in the hearing of the multitude:*
>
> *23 Go ye into all the world, and preach the gospel to every creature; And he that believeth and is baptized shall be saved, but he that believeth not shall be damned. (Morm. 9:22–23)*

The first principle of the gospel is to believe [have faith] and be baptized (Article of Faith 4).

---

43 *Instructor,* Feb. 1960, p. 42.

44 See Grant, F. C. (1951). The Gospel According to St. Mark, Exegesis. *The Interpreter's Bible,* ed. G. A. Buttrick. 7:915–16.

Steps in Acquiring Faith

The Book of Mormon teaches us how to attain the motivating faith for being baptized. Alma's well-known speech to the outcast Zoramites is an excellent example. Alma told these people who were cast out of their synagogues because of the "coarseness of their apparel" (Alma 32:2–3) that it was "well that ye are cast out of your synagogues, that ye may be humble" and be brought to "a lowliness [poor] of heart" (Alma 32:12). Alma went on to teach that it is more blessed to be humble "without being compelled to be humble; or rather, in other words, blessed is he that believeth in the word of God, and is baptized without stubbornness of heart" (Alma 32:16).

On his visit to the Nephites, the Savior declared unto them his doctrine:

> 37 And again I say unto you, ye must repent, and become as a little child, and be baptized in my name, or ye can in nowise receive these things.

> 38 And again I say unto you, ye must repent, and be baptized in my name, and become as a little child, or ye can in nowise inherit the kingdom of God. (3 Nephi 11:37–38)

To become as a little child requires that we swallow our pride and recognize the need of a savior. Thus we become broken hearted, or poor in heart.

The second step taught by Alma is to "remember, that God is merciful unto all who believe on his name; therefore he desireth, in the first place, that ye should believe, yea, even on his word" (Alma 32:22). To believe on the word of God, one must be able to recognize the various sources of his word. These sources Alma gave as follows: "And now, he imparteth his word by angels unto men, yea, not only men but women also. Now this is not all; little children do have words given unto them many times, which confound the wise and the learned" (Alma 32:23).

Alma went on to caution the Zoramites:

37 Ye cannot know of their [the words of God] surety at first, unto perfection, any more than faith is a perfect knowledge.

38 But behold, if ye will awake and arouse your faculties, even to an experiment upon my words, and exercise a particle of faith, yea, even if ye can no more than desire to believe, let this desire work in you, even until ye believe in a manner that ye can give place for a portion of my words. (Alma 32:26–27)

Aaron, one of the sons of Mosiah, taught the words of God to the Lamanite king. The king was humbled and believed and asked what he should do to obtain eternal life (see Alma 22:5–15). "Aaron said unto him: If thou desirest this thing [eternal life], if thou wilt bow down before God, yea, if thou wilt repent of all thy sins, and will bow down before God, and call on his name in faith, believing that ye shall receive, then shalt thou receive the hope which thou desirest" (Alma 22:16). Thus, after one is humble, the second step is to have a desire in the heart to believe the words of God and come to a knowledge of the truth. This was compared by Alma to planting a seed in your heart:

Now, we will compare the word unto a seed. Now, if ye give place, that a seed may be planted in your heart, behold, if it be a true seed, or a good seed, if ye do not cast it out by your unbelief, that ye will resist the Spirit of the Lord, behold, it will begin to swell within your breasts; and when you feel these swelling motions, ye will begin to say within yourselves—It must needs be that this is a good seed, or that the word is good, for it beginneth to enlarge my soul; yea, it beginneth to enlighten my understanding, yea, it beginneth to be delicious to me. (Alma 32:28)

Through the planting of the word of God in one's heart, it may be known that the word is a good seed. As one continues to believe and to exercise faith, the seed or the word of God begins to take root and grow. This process produces the faith necessary to desire to be baptized. Thus faith is a principle of action. As Paul said to the Romans, "Faith cometh by hearing, and hearing by the word of God" (Rom. 10:17). Joseph Smith clarified the principle: "Faith comes by hearing the word of God, through the testimony of the servants of God; that testimony is always attended by the Spirit of prophecy and revelation" (*TPJS,* 148).

The Book of Mormon has many examples of faith as a motivating principle of action. Nephi, desiring to know of the mysteries of God, cried "unto the Lord; and behold he did visit me, and did soften my heart that I did believe all the words which had been spoken by my father" (1 Nephi 2:16). Sam believed on Nephi's words as Nephi spoke to him (see 1 Nephi 2:17). Nephi responded to Lehi's request to return to Jerusalem and obtain the plates of brass (see 1 Nephi 3:7). Nephi persuaded his brethren not to give up on obtaining the plates after Laban threatened to slay Laman (see 1 Nephi 3:11–21). Zoram agreed to accompany Nephi and his brethren based upon the oath given him by Nephi (see 1 Nephi 4:32–35). They were all humble, believed on the words of God, and were motivated to take action.

Faith as a principle of action is identified when people are persuaded to take action without having knowledge. One chapter in the Book of Mormon, which is similar to Hebrews 11 in the New Testament, lists many examples of faith. As Moroni abridged the record of the Jaredites, he paused to declare: "And now, I, Moroni, would speak somewhat concerning these things; I would show unto the world that faith is things which are hoped for and not seen; wherefore, dispute not because ye see not, for ye receive no witness until after the trial of your faith" (Ether 12:6). The examples of faith that are cited by Moroni (Ether 12) include examples of faith as a principle of power and life and salvation, but we will only note those here that exemplify the principle of action.

Christ appeared to the Nephites because of their faith (see Ether 12:7–8). They had not seen Christ but had gathered [action] because they believed the prophets that testified of him. Moroni believed callings unto the holy order of God (the priesthood) were a result of faith (see Ether 12:10). These men were foreordained to hold the priesthood because of their faith and good works in the first place [premortal life] (see Alma 13:1–5). Through continued faith and good works [action], they received the priesthood. Moroni also equated the giving of the law of Moses and its fulfillment with faith (see Ether 12:11).

Mormon's great sermon on hope, faith, and charity was addressed to the peaceable followers of Christ who had "obtained a sufficient hope by which ye can enter into the rest of the Lord" (Moro. 7:3). In other words, they were baptized members of the Church. This teaches us that we need faith as a motivating principle of action even after we are baptized. Faith is an ongoing principle. Mormon reminded the faithful followers, "For I remember the word of God which saith by their works ye shall know them; for if their works be good, then they are good also" (Moro. 7:5).

The Jaredite prophet Ether taught his people "that by faith all things are fulfilled" (Ether 12:3) and then testified: "Wherefore, whoso believeth in God might with surety hope for a better world, yea, even a place at the right hand of God, which hope cometh of faith, maketh an anchor to the souls of men, which would make them sure and steadfast, always abounding in good works, being led to glorify God" (Ether 12:4). Those who produce good works are good people and are motivated by their faith in Christ.

People who do good works for self-serving reasons are not doing acts of faith and may be inspired of Satan. Mormon warned: "All things which are good cometh of God; and that which is evil cometh of the devil" (Moro. 7:12; see also James 1:17). Through the inspiration of God and the light of Christ given to every man born into the world, we can exercise our faith unto the doing of good works (see Moro. 7:13–19).

The first step in obtaining faith as a principle of action is to be humble. A second step is to have a desire to believe on the word of God. After we have received the word of God in our hearts and nourished it, we are ready to believe and be baptized. After baptism, our faith must increase, and we must continue to do those things which are good and seek to come to know for a surety of Christ's gift of eternal life. In Moroni's words: "Wherefore, ye may also have hope, and be partakers of the gift, if ye will but have faith" (Ether 12:9).

The devil has a counter plan for each of the above steps. He would have us be lifted up in pride instead of being humble. He would pacify us into a state of apathy instead of having a desire to believe. He would have us rationalize the word of God in our minds instead of receiving it in our hearts. He would stir us up to anger against that which is good (see 2 Nephi 28:19–24). When we have been governed by Satan in these ways, rather than obtaining a hope in Christ, we end up in a state of despair.

Through a study of the Book of Mormon we can gain a hope in Christ; and through that hope, or the motivating principle of action, we may come to know of those things that are not seen but are true. As we believe and are baptized, we are on the path to eternal life. As we continue to exercise faith, we progress along the path to eternal life. Nephi summarized the process of traveling along the path in these succinct words:

19 And now, my beloved brethren, after ye have gotten into this strait and narrow path, I would ask if all is done? Behold, I say unto you, Nay; for ye have not come thus far save it were by the word of Christ with unshaken faith in him, relying wholly upon the merits of him who is mighty to save.

20 Wherefore, ye must press forward with a steadfastness in Christ, having a perfect brightness of hope, and a love of God and of all men. Wherefore, if ye shall press forward, feasting upon the word of Christ, and endure to the end, behold, thus saith the Father: Ye shall have eternal life. (2 Nephi 31:19–20)

As Nephi further testified: "This is the way; and there is none other way nor name given under heaven whereby man can be saved in the kingdom of God" (2 Nephi 31:21).

Be Baptized

Baptism is a commandment. And whoso believeth in me, and is baptized, the same shall be saved" (3 Nephi 11:33). Baptism has always been and will always be a part of the doctrine of Christ. As taught by Joseph Smith, God "set the ordinances to be the same forever and ever, and set Adam to watch over them, to reveal them from heaven to man, or to send angels to reveal them" (*TPJS*, 168). Adam himself was baptized (see Moses 6:64–65). Some have supposed that baptism was only a New Testament ordinance, a substitute for the law of circumcision, but the Prophet Joseph taught: "Circumcision is not baptism, neither was baptism instituted in the place of circumcision" (*TPJS*, 314). The purposes, the mode, and the significance of baptism are clearly taught in the Book of Mormon.

Necessity and Purposes of Baptism

From 2 Nephi 31 we learn that there are four purposes for baptism: 1) baptism brings us a remission of our past sins; 2) baptism gives us admittance into the Church and Kingdom of God on earth; 3) baptism opens the gate to the straight and narrow path that leads to eternal life; 4) baptism gives us the opportunity to receive the gift of the Holy Ghost

Baptism for Remission of Sins

Nephi emphasized our need of baptism by showing that even the Savior, who was holy, was baptized: "And now, if the Lamb of God, he being holy, should have need to be baptized by water, to fulfill all righteousness, O then, how much more need have we, being unholy, to be baptized, yea, even by water" (2 Nephi 31:5).

Jacob, in emphasizing the Atonement of Christ, noted: "And he commandeth all men that they must repent, and be baptized in his name, having perfect faith in the Holy One of Israel, or they cannot be saved in the kingdom of God. And if they will not repent and believe in his name, and be baptized in his name, and endure to the end, they must be damned; for the Lord God, the Holy One of Israel, has spoken it" (2 Nephi 9:23–24). To have perfect faith is to rely totally upon Jesus Christ and his atoning sacrifice. The usual theological interpretation of the word "damned" is to condemn to a punishment. However, in LDS theology, it is interpreted to have one's progression stopped, similar to the damming of a ditch of water.

The Prophet Joseph Smith, speaking of being born again and of baptism being an initial step in that experience, declared: "A man may be saved, after the judgment, in the terrestrial kingdom, or in the telestial kingdom, but he can never see the celestial kingdom of God, without being born of water and the Spirit" (*TPJS,* 12). Alma taught the people of Gideon that they could not inherit the kingdom of heaven without baptism:

> *Now I say unto you that ye must repent, and be born again; for the Spirit saith if ye are not born again ye cannot inherit the kingdom of heaven; therefore come and be baptized unto repentance, that ye may be washed from your sins, that ye may have faith on the Lamb of God, who taketh away the sins of the world, who is mighty to save and to cleanse from all unrighteousness. (Alma 7:14)*

The ordinance of baptism is a requirement to be cleansed from all unrighteousness, and the Lord "hath said that no unclean thing can inherit the kingdom of Heaven" (Alma 11:37; see also 7:21; 40:26).

By fulfilling the commandments, the Holy Ghost will be given and cleanse us of our sins (as will be discussed later). In the New Testament, Peter gave a similar emphasis: "even baptism doth also now save us (not the putting away of the filth of the flesh, but the answer of a good conscience toward God)" (1 Pet. 3:21). Therefore, through the ordinance of baptism, men receive a remission of their sins and a fresh start towards their goal of eternal life.

Baptism into the Church and Kingdom of God

When we are baptized, we witness "unto the Father that [we] are willing to take upon [us] the name of Christ, by baptism" (2 Nephi 31:13). Taking his name by baptism is to enter his Church (3 Nephi 27:5–8). Those who accepted Alma's challenge at the waters of Mormon were baptized into the Church:

> *16 And after this manner he did baptize every one that went forth to the place of Mormon; and they were in number about two hundred and four souls; yea, and they were baptized in the waters of Mormon, and were filled with the grace of God.*
>
> *17 And they were called the Church of God, or the Church of Christ, from that time forward. And it came to pass that whosoever was baptized by the power and authority of God was added to his Church. (Mosiah 18:16–17)*

Some people, becoming confused over the number and variety of claims made by the many different churches, have decided that they will endeavor to live the teachings of Christ in their own lives and not affiliate with any church. But the Book of Mormon teaches that the proper way to follow Christ begins with baptism as a witness to the Father:

> *6 And now, I would ask of you, my beloved brethren, wherein the Lamb of God did fulfill all righteousness in being baptized by water?*
>
> *7 Know ye not that he was holy? But notwithstanding he being holy, he showeth unto the children of men that,*

according to the flesh he humbleth himself before the Father, and witnesseth unto the Father that he would be obedient unto him in keeping his commandments. (2 Nephi 31:6–7)

Alma asked the people who were gathered at the place of Mormon: "Now I say unto you, if this be the desire of your hearts [to follow Christ], what have you against being baptized in the name of the Lord, as a witness before him that ye have entered into a covenant with him?" (Mosiah 18:10). The essential details of this most important covenant, as outlined by Alma, give ample reason for any person to be willing to enter into it.

Alma taught the same principle to the people of Gideon:

15 Yea, I say unto you come and fear not, and lay aside every sin, which easily doth beset you, which doth bind you down to destruction, yea, come and go forth, and show unto your God that ye are willing to repent of your sins and enter into a covenant with him to keep his commandments, and witness it unto him this day by going into the waters of baptism.

16 And whosoever doeth this, and keepeth the commandments of God from thenceforth, the same will remember that I say unto him, yea, he will remember that I have said unto him, he shall have eternal life, according to the testimony of the Holy Spirit, which testifieth in me. (Alma 7:15–16)

The way to eternal life begins with the covenant of baptism.

The Covenant of Baptism

The covenant of baptism is an agreement between God [Christ] and man that each party will perform certain actions. This covenant was undoubtedly originally agreed upon in the pre-earth council of heaven as part of the condition for keeping the second estate (see Abr. 3:25–26). God [Christ] has already fulfilled his part of that agreement by making possible the resurrection and the Atonement. Man makes his covenant at the waters of baptism and must endeavor to fulfill his part of the agreement throughout his lifetime.

God's Part of the Covenant

God promises three specific blessings to those who will take the name of Christ upon them in the waters of baptism. Alma preached "unto them repentance, and redemption, and faith on the Lord" (Mosiah 18:7). We may paraphrase this scripture to say that those who have faith on the Lord can overcome their fallen state and receive a remission of their past sins through the ordinance of baptism. This ordinance has always been the first step preached by God's servants (see Mark 1:4; 16:15–16).

The second part of Christ's agreement, as taught by Alma, was "that ye may be redeemed of God, and be numbered with those of the first resurrection, that ye may have eternal life" (Mosiah 18:9). All men will unconditionally be resurrected (see 1 Cor. 15:21–23; John 5:29; Acts 24:15), but the covenant of baptism carries the promise of coming forth in the first resurrection unto eternal life, or the resurrection of celestial beings (see D&C 76:64–65).

The third promise given by Alma in the baptismal covenant was "that [Christ] may pour out his Spirit more abundantly upon you" (Mosiah 18:10). This outpouring of the Spirit is executed through the gift of the Holy Ghost given to the baptized person. Thus we see that the three specific blessings promised by Christ to those who will enter into the baptismal covenant are (1) a remission of past sins; (2) a resurrection with the celestial Saints; and (3) the outpouring of his Spirit upon the individual. One of these blessings, the remission of sins, is for the past; one is for the future, the resurrection unto eternal life; and the third, the outpouring of the Spirit, is for the present. Therefore, Christ literally agrees to care for all of our spiritual needs, through this covenant, as a father cares for his children.

Man's Part of the Covenant

The specific things that man agrees to do in the covenant of baptism, in order to receive the above blessings, may be categorized into five parts. The first part constitutes membership in the Church of Jesus Christ: those who are baptized should be "desirous to come into the fold of God, and be called his people" (Mosiah 18:8). Being a member of Christ's Church means we are willing to take upon us his name. This becomes a family name, with Christ as the Father and we as his children. In the covenant, we agree to honor and uphold that name and to do nothing that would desecrate the name of Christ.

The second part of the covenant is an extension of the first. When we take Christ's name upon us, we accept certain responsibilities towards others who have also taken upon themselves Christ's name. We are "willing to bear one another's burdens, that they may be light; Yea, and [being] willing to mourn with those that mourn; yea, and comfort those that stand in need of comfort" (Mosiah 18:8–9). It is common within the Church to refer to other members of the Church as "brother" or "sister." They are our brothers and sisters in the family of Christ. Just as we share in the trials and tribulations of our immediate families, we extend that sharing into the family of Christ through baptism.

The third part of the covenant is that as a member of Christ's family, we have a mission to extend the opportunity for others to also become a member of the family. Through precept and proclamation we bear witness of Christ. As Alma states, we agree "to stand as witnesses of God at all times and in all things, and in all places that ye may be in, *even until death*" (Mosiah 18:9, emphasis added). Being an example "at all times" means just that: it includes our conduct in our occupations, social engagements, recreational activities, and all other secular functions, as well as all Church activities and programs. "In all places" includes activities among all people and cultures, in every locality and traveling between those localities, and in every environment as well as at Church functions.

As God's part of the covenant covers all areas of our lives, the past, the present, and the future, we must give total commitment to follow him in every phase of our lives.

That we will serve Christ is the fourth part of our baptismal agreement (see Mosiah 18:10). Though there are many ways to serve, King Benjamin summarized the epitome of service: "And behold, I tell you these things that ye may learn wisdom; that ye may learn that when ye are in the service of your fellow beings ye are only in the service of your God" (Mosiah 2:17; see also v. 21). This service to man has been misconstrued by some to be accomplished through service and fraternal organizations outside the Church. While these acts of service are commendable, and we ought to do them, the Lord has always taught that service to our fellow Saints was to be the heart of the Church, and in the particular way and time that was to be determined by the Lord through his chosen servants, not by the individual person.

A father, as the head of a household, designates to his children various tasks he expects them to perform. Christ is the head of the Church as a father is the head of a household (see Eph. 5:23–25), and he directs our stewardships through revelation to the Church leaders. We serve to perfect ourselves and to perfect the Saints. As Jesus taught in his mortal ministry, "he that is greatest among you shall be your servant" (Matt. 23:11).

The final part of man's agreement is that he will keep Christ's commandments (Mosiah 18:10). As the head of the Church, Christ has given us the rules by which we should live, even as an earthly father administers rules for his household. Christ's rules are given to us in the scriptures and through his chosen servants. The fulfillment of these rules, or commandments, brings blessings to us for our own good (see Mosiah 2:22–24). The keeping of the commandments is also for the perfecting of ourselves through obedience. It is submitting to the will of Christ as a child submits to the will of his father (see Mosiah 3:19).

In short, man's covenant includes five elements of agreement: (1) to enter the Church and take Christ's name; (2) to fellowship compassionately the members of the Church; (3) to stand as a witness of Christ at all times, in all things, in all places; (4) to serve our fellow men through the church; and (5) to keep Christ's commandments.

As in a temporal contract or covenant, the baptismal covenant requires witnesses and an official validation. The witnesses are other temporal beings who view the baptism, to assure it is performed properly, and the validation comes by the ordinance being sealed or approved by the Holy Spirit of promise, the Holy Ghost (see D&C 132:7). In order for the ordinance to be sealed, the person being baptized must have faith, have repented of his sins, and have come forth with a broken heart and a contrite spirit (see Moro. 6:1–3; D&C 20:37).

Through the Church, Christ receives the individual as a member of his family, his son or his daughter:

> 21 And he that will hear my voice shall be my sheep; and him shall ye receive into the church, and him will I also receive.
>
> 22 For behold, this is my church; whosoever is baptized shall be baptized unto repentance. And whomsoever ye receive shall believe in my name; and him will I freely forgive. (Mosiah 26:21–22)

As a member of Christ's family, man receives the counsel, guidance, and blessings of his spiritual father, Christ.

Baptism As the Gate to the Straight and Narrow Path

Nephi taught the purposes of the Savior's baptism: "And again, it showeth unto the children of men the straitness of the path, and the narrowness of the gate, by which they should enter, he having set the example before them" (2 Nephi 31:9). Nephi emphasized the importance of getting on the path to eternal life:

17 Wherefore, do the things which I have told you I have seen that your Lord and your Redeemer should do; for, for this cause have they been shown unto me, that ye might know the gate by which ye should enter. For the gate by which ye should enter is repentance and baptism by water; and then cometh a remission of your sins by fire and by the Holy Ghost.

18 And then are ye in this strait and narrow path which leads to eternal life; yea, ye have entered in by the gate; ye have done according to the commandments of the Father and the Son. (2 Nephi 31:17–18)

The gate is narrow. In the biblical Sermon on the Mount, and in the same sermon given to the Nephites, Christ defined the way to eternal life: "Because strait is the gate, and narrow is the way, which leadeth unto life, and few there be that find it" (3 Nephi 14:14; Matt. 7:14). The spelling of the word "strait" signifies a restricted way or passage.

This narrow, strait, or restricted gate of baptism shows the importance of baptism being performed by the proper methods and authority. Alma had received the authority to baptize into the newly organized Church at the waters of Mormon (Mosiah 18:13, 17). He baptized those who came forth by immersing them in water (v. 14). When the Savior visited the Nephites, he gave the authority to baptize to Nephi and others and instructed them in the method and prayer to be followed. His instructions were consistent with those given to Alma:

21 And the Lord said unto him: I give unto you power that ye shall baptize this people when I am again ascended into heaven.

22 And again the Lord called others, and said unto them likewise; and he gave unto them power to baptize. And he said unto them: On this wise shall ye baptize; and there shall be no disputations among you.

23 Verily I say unto you, that whoso repenteth of his sins through your words, and desireth to be baptized in my name, on this wise shall ye baptize them—Behold, ye shall go down and stand in the water, and in my name shall ye baptize them.

24 And now behold, these are the words which ye shall say, calling them by name, saying:

25 Having authority given me of Jesus Christ, I baptize you in the name of the Father, and of the Son, and of the Holy Ghost. Amen.

26 And then shall ye immerse them in the water, and come forth again out of the water. (3 Nephi 11:21–26)

Again, the Book of Mormon emphasizes that there is only one correct way to really follow Christ. They must enter into the path to eternal life through baptism by immersion under the hands of one holding the authority from God.

Baptism to Receive the Gift of the Holy Ghost

Nephi foresaw that when Jesus was baptized, the Holy Ghost came upon him: "Wherefore, after he was baptized with water the Holy Ghost descended upon him in the form of a dove" (2 Nephi 31:8; see also Luke 3:22).[45]

Nephi was taught by revelation that those who were baptized in the name of Christ would be given the gift of the Holy Ghost.

45 The Prophet Joseph Smith explained the meaning of the form of the dove: "The sign of the dove was instituted before the creation of the world, a witness for the Holy Ghost, and the devil cannot come in the sign of a dove. The Holy Ghost is a personage, and is in the form of a personage. It does not confine itself to the *form* of the dove, but in *sign* of the dove. The Holy Ghost cannot be transformed into a dove; but the sign of a dove was given to John to signify the truth of the deed, as the dove is an emblem or token of truth and innocence" (*TPJS*, 276).

And also, the voice of the Son came unto me, saying: He that is baptized in my name, to him will the Father give the Holy Ghost, like unto me; wherefore, follow me, and do the things which ye have seen me do. (2 Nephi 31:12)

The receiving of this gift is dependent upon one's worthiness and sincerity. Nephi taught:

Wherefore, my beloved brethren, I know that if ye shall follow the Son, with full purpose of heart, acting no hypocrisy and no deception before God, but with real intent, repenting of your sins, witnessing unto the Father that ye are willing to take upon you the name of Christ, by baptism—yea, by following your Lord and your Savior down into the water, according to his word, behold, then shall ye receive the Holy Ghost; yea, then cometh the baptism of fire and of the Holy Ghost; and then can ye speak with the tongue of angels, and shout praises unto the Holy One of Israel. (2 Nephi 31:13)

The baptism of fire and the Holy Ghost is the crowning point of being baptized by water. As taught by the Prophet Joseph, "Baptism by water is but half a baptism, and is good for nothing without the other half—that is, the baptism of the Holy Ghost" (*TPJS*, 314). The baptism of fire is the cleansing power that brings a remission of sins. In continuing to explain the doctrine of Christ, Nephi testified: "For the gate by which ye should enter is repentance and baptism by water; *and then cometh a remission of your sins by fire and by the Holy Ghost* (2 Nephi 31:17, italics added; see also Moro. 6:4). Future chapters enlarge upon the mission and function of the Holy Ghost. Our purpose here is to show its relevance to the ordinance of baptism.

The baptism of the Holy Ghost renews and makes us born again, new creatures in Christ (Moro. 8:25–26; 2 Cor. 5:17). It places us on the path to eternal life.

And then are ye in this strait and narrow path which leads to eternal life; yea, ye have entered in by the gate; ye have done according to the commandments of the Father and the Son; and ye have received the Holy Ghost, which witnesses of the Father and the Son, unto the fulfilling of the promise which he hath made, that if ye entered in by the way ye should receive. (2 Nephi 31:18)

Those who get on the path to eternal life must follow a straight and narrow course. Those who are baptized are given the gift of the Holy Ghost to guide them along that path to eternal life. Without baptism, one cannot receive the gift necessary to travel along the path that leads to eternal life.

The Challenge

As stated earlier, Christ has fulfilled his part of the covenant. The question pertinent to us today is, What are we doing about our part of the agreement? If we should die tomorrow, will we have lived up to the commitments we made at the waters of baptism? Are we traveling along the path that we entered at baptism, or are we sitting just inside the gate? Are we taking the opportunity to mourn with, comfort, and bear the burdens with our fellow brothers and sisters in the family of Christ? Are we taking the opportunity to stand as a witness to our associates of Christ's goodness and teachings? Are we putting forth our full effort in serving in the capacity to which we have been called? Are we keeping the commandments taught to us by the scriptures and the Lord's servants? As we study the Book of Mormon and come to more fully know of the necessity and purposes of baptism, we should strive more diligently to fulfill the covenant we have or will enter into, and then we will receive the blessings of the Lord promised in the baptismal covenant.

12

LITTLE CHILDREN ALSO HAVE
ETERNAL LIFE

"All little children are alive in Christ, and also all they
that are without the law." (Moro. 8:22)

Although not mentioned in the April 6 revelation, one of the great comforting truths restored through the Book of Mormon is that little children are saved through the Atonement of Christ. There are several references in the Book of Mormon to verify this eternal truth. The Prophet Joseph Smith also gave further insight into this doctrine.

After bearing witness of those who will have part in the first resurrection and thus obtain eternal life (see Mosiah 15:21–24), Abinadi adds what almost seems to be a postscript: "And little children also have eternal life" (v. 25). Because Abinadi does not expound on the doctrine at this time, it suggests that it may have already been a well-known teaching associated with Christ's Atonement. Regardless, the baptism of little children is a doctrine always associated with the apostasy. It was being practiced in Abraham's day at the time God made a covenant with him to restore the gospel (see JST Gen. 17:1–12). It was a common belief with the people of Corinth, which drew written comments from Paul (see 1 Cor. 7:14; D&C 74).

Mormon's epistle on the subject was brought about because of disputations among his missionary son Moroni and others who were serving or associating with him. We know the seeds of apostasy were rampant in this time period. Mormon's letter answers many questions that arise when men reason over the doctrine. Mormon speaks with "authority from God" (Moro. 8:16).

Why Baptism Is Not Required

Mormon gives two reasons why baptism is not required for little children. The first reason came to him "by the power of the Holy Ghost" (Mosiah 8:7):

> *Listen to the words of Christ, your Redeemer, your Lord and your God. Behold I came into the world not to call the righteous but sinners to repentance; the whole need no physician, but they that are sick; wherefore, little children are whole, for they are not capable of committing sin; wherefore the curse of Adam is taken from them in me, that it hath no power over them; and the law of circumcision is done away in me. (Moro. 8:8)*

These words of Christ were probably taught by Jesus when he ministered among the Nephites. This conclusion is based on his having taught similar principles in his Jerusalem ministry (see Mark 2:17; 10:13–16; Matt. 18:1–6; 1 John 1:12). The doctrine of the Atonement covering little children was probably more fully taught during the Jerusalem ministry, but the full truth did not survive the Apostasy.

Little children are not capable of committing sin, because they do not have a full understanding of right and wrong until they reach the age of accountability (see D&C 18:42; 20:71; 29:46–47; 68:25–27). Although they may make mistakes, or transgress laws, there is a difference between sin and transgression, as discussed regarding Adam and Eve partaking of the fruit. The transgressions of little children are covered through the Atonement of Christ as King Benjamin taught: "And even if it were possible that little children could sin they could not be saved; but I say unto you they are blessed; for behold, as in Adam, or by nature, they fall, even so the blood of Christ atoneth for their sins" (Mosiah 3:16).

Mormon provided a second reason: "Little children cannot repent; wherefore, it is awful wickedness to deny the pure mercies of God unto them, for they are all alive in him because of his mercy" (Moro. 8:19). One of the requirements for repentance is to recognize a sin. Since little children are not capable of differentiating between right and wrong, they cannot recognize what is and what is not sin. Once more, the Atonement covers their transgressions because of this inability.

What Infant Baptism Denies

As stated above, the doctrine of infant baptism is a mark of the Apostasy. There are three things that the doctrine denies, as given by Mormon, that are contrary to the gospel of Christ and thus make it apostate doctrine. The first denial is the impartiality of God. God is an impartial, unchanging God and not a respecter of persons. The doctrine of infant baptism denies these characteristics of God. In Mormon's words: "But little children are alive in Christ, even from the foundation of the world; if not so, God is a partial God, and also a changeable God, and a respecter to persons; for how many little children have died without baptism" (Moro. 8:12). Mormon continues his explanation and actually states, as a false premise, what many in the world presently teach, that little children who are not baptized go "to an endless hell" (v. 13). There are other variations of this apostate doctrine taught in the world, but unbaptized little children not going to heaven is a prevalent doctrine taught in the Christian world today.

In addition to denying certain attributes of God, Mormon declares that individuals who teach this doctrine are also denying the basic principles required for individual salvation:

> *14 Behold I say unto you, that he that supposeth that little children need baptism is in the gall of bitterness and in the bonds of iniquity; for he hath neither faith, hope, nor charity; wherefore, should he be cut off while in the thought, he must go down to hell.*

15 For awful is the wickedness to suppose that God saveth one child because of baptism, and the other must perish because he hath no baptism. (Moro. 8:14–15)

The necessity for faith, hope, and charity in the attainment of salvation is taught in both the Book of Mormon and the Bible (see Moro. 7; 1 Cor. 13). In the following verse, Mormon warns those who teach this doctrine: they "shall perish except they repent" (Moro. 8:16).

The third denial of the doctrine of Christ is outlined by Mormon. He also included a warning concerning this denial:

20 And he that saith that little children need baptism denieth the mercies of Christ, and setteth at naught the Atonement of him and the power of his redemption.

21 Wo unto such, for they are in danger of death, hell, and an endless torment. I speak it boldly; God hath commanded me. Listen unto them and give heed, or they stand against you at the judgment–seat of Christ. (Moro. 8:20–21)

This is probably the most significant of all of the denials. The Atonement is the basis of all of the principles of the gospel of Jesus Christ.

Many who have never read the Book of Mormon, or have ignored its teachings against the baptism of little children, will be shocked by the reality of what they have been teaching when they comprehend their error at the judgment seat of Christ.

Blessings Extended to Little Children

The blessings of the Atonement covering little children were determined in the premortal councils of heaven before this world was populated (see Moro. 8:12, quoted above). It is an eternal doctrine, as the arguments mentioned above confirm.

Although Abinadi merely stated that "little children also have *eternal life*" (Mosiah 15:25, italics added), the previous verse

(v. 24) confirms that they will come forth in the first resurrection. But it is to modern revelation and latter-day prophets we turn to amplify the doctrine.

In a vision of the celestial kingdom of God, given to the Prophet Joseph Smith on 21 January 1836, the voice of the Lord declared to him:

> *7 All who have died without a knowledge of this gospel, who would have received it if they had been permitted to tarry, shall be heirs of the celestial kingdom of God;*
>
> *8 Also all that shall die henceforth without a knowledge of it, who would have received it with all their hearts, shall be heirs of that kingdom. (D&C 137:7–8)*

Some have erroneously applied the "heirs" concept to little children being given the opportunity to accept the gospel in the spirit world or to be tested during the millennium. The revelation to Joseph is very clear that the above application is not true. Joseph also beheld that "all children who die before they arrive at the years of accountability are saved in the celestial kingdom of heaven" (D&C 137:10). The Prophet Joseph further taught:

> As concerning the resurrection, I will merely say that all men will come from the grave as they lie down, whether old or young; there will not be "added unto their stature one cubit," neither taken from it; all will be raised by the power of God, having spirit in their bodies, and not blood. Children will be enthroned in the presence of God and the Lamb with bodies of the same stature that they had on earth, having been redeemed by the blood of the Lamb; they will there enjoy the fullness of that light, glory and intelligence, which is prepared in the celestial kingdom. (*TPJS*, 199–200)

President Joseph F. Smith claimed that Joseph Smith taught the doctrine of mothers raising their deceased children in the millennium and "all that could have been obtained and enjoyed by them if they had been permitted to live in the flesh will be provided for them hereafter. They will lose nothing by being taken away from us in this way."[46]

We live in a world of accident and disease. The Church regards the agency of man as essential to life itself.[47] Because of the world situations and the principle of agency, the Lord allows little children to be taken in death. Why are certain ones taken and not others? Joseph Smith answered this question:

> President Smith read the 14th chapter of Revelation, and said—We have again the warning voice sounded in our midst, which shows the uncertainty of human life; and in my leisure moments I have meditated upon the subject, and asked the question, why it is that infants, innocent children, are taken away from us, especially those that seem to be the most intelligent and interesting. The strongest reasons that present themselves to my mind are these: This world is a very wicked world; and it is a proverb that the "world grows weaker and wiser"; if that is the case, the world grows more wicked and corrupt. In the earlier ages of the world a righteous man, and a man of God and of intelligence, had a better chance to do good, to be believed and received than at the present day; but in these days such a man is much opposed and persecuted by most of the inhabitants of the earth, and he has much sorrow to pass through here. The Lord takes many away even in infancy, that they may escape the envy of man, and the sorrows and evils of this present world; they were too pure, too lovely, to live on earth; therefore, if rightly considered, instead of mourning we have reason to rejoice as they are delivered from evil, and we shall soon have

---

46 *Gospel Doctrine,* p. 453. Salt Lake City: Deseret Book.

47 McKay, D. O. (1965). *Conference Report,* October, pp. 7–8.

them again. . . . The doctrine of baptizing children, or sprinkling them, or they must welter in hell, is a doctrine not true, not supported in Holy Writ, and is not consistent with the character of God. All children are redeemed by the blood of Jesus Christ, and the moment that children leave this world, they are taken to the bosom of Abraham. The only difference between the old and young dying is, one lives longer in heaven and eternal light and glory than the other, and is freed a little sooner from this miserable wicked world. Notwithstanding all this glory, we for a moment lose sight of it, and mourn the loss, but we do not mourn as those without hope. (*TPJS,* 196–97)

While many other latter-day prophets have commented on the doctrine of the salvation of little children, the essential doctrines were laid down by Joseph Smith and are sufficient to confirm the Book of Mormon teachings discussed previously.

The Mentally Handicapped

Mormon extended the blessing of little children being alive in Christ to "also all they that are without the law. For the power of redemption cometh on all them that have no law; wherefore, he that is not condemned, or he that is under no condemnation, cannot repent; and unto such baptism availeth nothing" (Moro. 8:22). Since he qualifies these blessings to those who "cannot repent," he must be speaking of these incapable of understanding.[48] The Doctrine and Covenants also reveals the same mercy for those incapable of understanding: "And, again, I say unto you, that whoso having knowledge, have I not commanded to repent? And he that hath no understanding, it remaineth in me to do according as it is written. And now I declare no more unto you at this time. Amen"

---

48 Modern revelation further qualifies that those who are born without an opportunity to accept the gospel are later given that opportunity in the spirit world (see D&C 137; 76:72–75).

(D&C 29:49–50). To deny those who are mentally handicapped of the blessings of eternal life would be the equivalent of denying of God's impartiality. It would also illustrate man's lack of hope, faith, and charity, and deny the merciful Atonement of Jesus Christ just as it does the salvation of little children. The mentally handicapped will receive the same blessings that are promised to little children.

Summary

Mormon gives a fitting conclusion to the doctrine of little children being alive in Christ as he began his letter to his son, Moroni. Referring to the word of the Lord coming to him by the power of the Holy Ghost, he declared:

> *9 Wherefore my beloved son, I know that it is solemn mockery before God, that ye should baptize little children.*
>
> *10 Behold I say unto you that this thing shall ye teach— repentance and baptism unto those who are accountable and capable of committing sin; yea, teach parents that they must repent and be baptized, and humble themselves as their little children, and they shall all be saved with their little children. (Moro. 8:9–10)*

The Savior taught the Nephites that they must become as a little child to inherit the kingdom of God (see 3 Nephi 9:22). Later he taught the same concept, repeating it for emphasis, as a basic principle of his doctrine (see 3 Nephi 11:37–39). Little children also have eternal life as Abinadi taught (see Mosiah 15:25).

The teachings of the Book of Mormon are a great comfort to those who may have lost a child, but they are also a great testimony of the impartiality of God and the mercies of the Atonement to all of mankind.

13

ENDURE IN FAITH

". . . and endure in faith to the end, should be saved."
(D&C 20:25)

As discussed in chapter eleven, there are several principles associated with faith. In that chapter faith as a principle of action was discussed. To endure in faith after baptism seems to be speaking of faith as a principle of power. The *Lectures on Faith* explain this principle:

> 13 As we receive by faith all temporal blessings, so we in like manner receive by faith all spiritual blessings. But faith is not only the principle of action, it is also the principle of power in all intelligent beings, whether in heaven or on earth.
>
> 14 Thus says the author of the epistle to the Hebrews: "Through faith we understand that the worlds were framed by the word of God, so that things which are seen were not made of things which do appear" (11:3).
>
> 15 By this we understand that the principle of power which existed in the bosom of God, by which he framed the worlds, was faith; and that it is by reason of this principle of power existing in the Deity that all

created things exist; so that all things in heaven, on earth, or under the earth exist by reason of faith as it existed in him. (*Lectures on Faith* 1:13–15)

While this quotation refers to the principle of power centered in Deity in the heavens, the Book of Mormon gives many examples of faith as a principle of power used by the prophets, and by those who believed and were baptized, to bring about great miracles in their lives and in the lives of others.

Miracles Accomplished by Faith

A further review of Moroni's list of the Nephites' faith (see Ether 12:6–30) shows many examples of faith as a principle of power. We will supplement his list with other examples from the Book of Mormon.

Moroni's first example declares that it was by faith that Christ "showed himself unto our fathers, after he had risen from the dead" (Ether 12:7). Christ's appearance to the Nephites who had gathered "round about the temple which was in the land Bountiful; and they were marveling and wondering one with another, and were showing one to another the great and marvelous change which had taken place. And they were also conversing about this Jesus Christ, of whom the sign had been given concerning his death" (3 Nephi 11:1–2). The record does not specify what they were saying about Christ, but it was spoken with sufficient faith to bring about the miracle of Christ's appearance to them. They were apparently exercising faith as a principle of power. The description of what those who had gathered were doing exemplifies that they were faithful people who had passed their previous trials of faith as a principle of action. They had apparently been baptized, although under an old covenant, and were subsequently offered the opportunity to be baptized again (see 3 Nephi 7:24–25; 11:21–22). There were many other Nephites who did not see the resurrected Savior, at least on this occasion. Moroni later commented:

7 He showed not himself unto them until after they had faith in him; wherefore, it must needs be that some had faith in him, for he showed himself not unto the world.

8 But because of the faith of men he has shown himself unto the world, and glorified the name of the Father, and prepared a way that thereby others might be partakers of the heavenly gift, that they might hope for those things which they have not seen.

9 Wherefore, ye may also have hope, and be partakers of the gift, if ye will but have faith. (Ether 12:7–9)

Moroni's reference to Jesus having shown himself to the world (v. 7) may be interpreted in various ways, but it certainly refers to his earthly ministry in Palestine. It could also have reference to some unrecorded Nephite appearances. Regardless, the promise of the heavenly gift, referred to by Moroni (v. 8), is the opportunity for all who have faith to come to the waters of baptism (the principle of action), and then qualify themselves to have a personal appearance from Christ. This unites the principle of action and the principle of power. The gathering to the temple was because of faith as a principle of action. The appearance of Christ to those having still more faith was an example of faith as a principle of power.

Another example of great faith listed by Moroni indirectly relates to faith as a principle of power. He states: "Wherefore, by faith was the law of Moses given. But in the gift of his Son hath God prepared a more excellent way; and it is by faith that it hath been fulfilled. For if there be no faith among the children of men, God can do no miracle among them; wherefore, he showed not himself until after their faith" (Ether 12:11–12). The introductory "wherefore" contrasts the calling after the holy order of God (Ether 12:10) with the giving of the law of Moses. Under the law of Moses, only the Aaronic priesthood was given (see D&C 84:25–26). The Priesthood after the order of the Son is the higher priesthood which enables miracles to attend the people. The Prophet Joseph, commenting on Galatians 3:19, taught that the law was added to the gospel (see *TPJS,* 60). The Lord was often so angered over the actions of the children of Israel that he threatened to destroy them all (see Num. 14:11–20; and Jacob 5:49–51). Because Moses pleaded with the Lord, justice was tempered and mercy extended. The faith of Moses brought about the law of Moses. The law of Moses was a "schoolmaster to bring [the children of Israel] unto Christ" (Gal. 3:24). After being prepared by the law of Moses to receive the fulness of the gospel of Jesus Christ, they would be given the higher priesthood, which would enable them to perform miracles through faith as a principle of power. This reasoning seems to be the concept of "by faith was the law of Moses given" (Ether 12:11).

Moroni's declaration that God had prepared a more excellent way "in the gift of his Son," and that "by faith that [law of Moses] hath been fulfilled" (Ether 12:11) is exemplified in the Book of Mormon. Lehi and Nephi were under the law of Moses but obtained the higher priesthood because of their faith. The obtaining of this higher priesthood was clearly associated with faith as a principle of power. Lehi's prayer was answered through a pillar of fire coming down to instruct him (see 1 Nephi 1:5–6). The Lord and angels appear in flaming fire (see *TPJS,* 191; 325; 367). The Lord appeared to Nephi because of his faith (1 Nephi 2:16). Both were shown the future of the nations and kingdoms of the world (1 Nephi 8:11–14). As a result of their faith, the law of Moses became dead unto them, and they were given a more excellent way (see 2 Nephi 25:25).

Appearances of Christ and of angels, a heavenly gift, and other great miracles were attained by other Nephite prophets through faith as a principle of power. The Lord appeared to Jacob (see 2 Nephi 11:3), and by faith the elements of the earth obeyed him (see Jacob 4:6). Nephi, son of Helaman, was given power over his people and over the earth (Hel. 10:4–10). Nephi, son of Nephi, son of Helaman, heard the voice of the Lord, had angels minister unto him daily, and had great miracles, even the raising of the dead, attending his ministry just prior to Jesus' appearance to the Nephites (3 Nephi 7:15–20). These prophets experienced the "more excellent way" (Ether 12:11) because of their faith.

Moroni's next example of faith definitely illustrates faith as a principle of power. Alma and Amulek "caused the prison to tumble to the earth" (Ether 12:13). The power of God came and shook the earth mightily, and all the people within the prison were slain except Alma and Amulek (see Alma 14:27–28). A similar example of the power of faith is shown just prior to the earth shaking as Alma and Amulek broke the cords with which they were bound, receiving strength according to their faith (see Alma 14:26; see also 1 Nephi 4:20–31; 7:16–18; Hel. 5:31).

The next example of faith given by Moroni is also one of power, but is a different type than the others previously cited. It illustrates how the lives of people can be changed by the power of God. Because of the faith of Nephi and Lehi, the sons of Helaman, the Lord poured out his spirit upon the Lamanites, and they were baptized by fire and the Holy Ghost (see Ether 12:14; Hel. 5:43–45). Moroni listed a similar miracle—although it was not as dramatic because it was spread over a fourteen-year period. The lives of thousands of Lamanites were changed by the Spirit of God coming upon them because of the faith of Ammon and his brethren (see Ether 12:15; Alma 26:5–15). The power to change lives by the Spirit can come collectively or individually, but is a real power wrought by faith. Of course, the agency of man must be considered, because some men will harden their hearts and not allow the Spirit to penetrate. Moroni's statement that miracles came both before and after the time of Christ (see Ether 12:17) indicates that miracles, or faith as a principle of power, were operative under the dispensation of Moses, because the Nephites had attained the "more excellent way" (Ether 12:11) of Christ.

Another type of power through faith is listed next by Moroni. The three Nephite disciples obtained a promise that they would not taste death but would remain on earth to bring souls to Christ (see Ether 12:17; 3 Nephi 28:6–11). The power of God came upon them, causing a change to come upon their bodies and sanctifying them in the flesh (3 Nephi 28:37–39). As with others, these three disciples first believed in the Son of God (see Ether 12:18), thus following faith as a principle of action. Through their faith that followed came the power of God to change the nature of their bodies.

Still another type of miracle (through faith as a principle of power) is cited by Moroni: certain individuals were able to penetrate the veil between this earth and the eternal world. While Moroni states that there were many before the time of Christ who could not be kept "from within the veil," he only refers to the brother of Jared, who was so faithful among the Jaredite people (Ether 12:19–21; Ether 3–4). The others referred to by Moroni who could not be kept within the veil would include Ether (see Ether 13:13–14) and Emer (see Ether 9:22) among the Jaredites, and Lehi, Nephi, and Jacob among the Nephites (see 1 Nephi 8:11–14; 2 Nephi 2:4; 6:8–9; 11:2–3). Of course, others such as Moroni who lived after the time of Christ also penetrated the veil (see Morm. 8:34–35).

Another miracle, listed by Moroni, was the promise that these things (the record of the Book of Mormon) would come forth to their brethren, the Lamanites, in the last days (see Ether 12:22). Enos was given this promise (see Enos 1:13–18) but was told that his *fathers* (plural, referring to Jacob and Lehi and perhaps others) had made the same request. Through the miraculous power of God, these plates were preserved and protected for hundreds of years and the promise fulfilled (see D&C 10:46–52). Similar protection and preservation was promised concerning the plates of brass that Nephi brought out of Jerusalem. Concerning these plates, Alma declared,

> *4 Behold, it has been prophesied by our fathers, that they should be kept and handed down from one generation to another, and be kept and preserved by the hand of the Lord until they should go forth unto every nation,*

*kindred, tongue, and people, that they shall know of the
mysteries contained thereon.*

*5 And now behold, if they are kept they must retain their
brightness; yea, and they will retain their brightness; yea,
and also shall all the plates which do contain that which
is holy writ.* (Alma 37:4–5; see also 1 Nephi 5:19)

Verification of this promise is yet to come.

The promise that the record of the Nephites and Jaredites
would come to the Lamanites through the Gentiles raised a
question in Moroni's mind. Having worked with the Jaredite
records, he wondered how he could duplicate their excellence in
his own record. He recognized his weakness in writing compared
to the Jaredites. Without analyzing all of the Lord's answer and
explanation to Moroni, the point here is that through the power
of God other Nephites may have become mighty in writing, like
the Jaredites, because of their faith. To others, the power of the
Lord will make the spoken word great because of their faith (see
Ether 12:23–25). The prophet Nephi taught that "when a man
speaketh by the power of the Holy Ghost the power of the Holy
Ghost carrieth it unto the hearts of the children of men" (2 Nephi
33:1). Those who will humble themselves and recognize their
weakness will, through the power of faith, turn those weaknesses
into strengths (see Ether 12:26–28).

Moroni was comforted by the Lord's answer to him and
remembered and recorded another great miracle produced by the
faith of the brother of Jared, who "said unto the mountain Zerin,
Remove—and it was removed" (Ether 12:30). The historical event
of this great example of faith had not been included in Moroni's
abridgment. Its later inclusion, along with Jacob's testimony
of the mountains obeying their command (see Jacob 4:6), are
second witnesses to the Savior's teaching in his Jerusalem ministry
of faith removing mountains (see Matt. 17:20). Moroni further
acknowledged that the same power of faith which the Nephite
disciples (apostles) had was possessed by the brother of Jared: "For

after they had faith, and did speak in thy name, thou didst show thyself unto them in great power" (Ether 12:31). Moroni seems to be acknowledging that there were other miracles among the Nephites that had not been recorded. From the examples given by Moroni, we see that faith truly is a principle of power and is manifest in divers ways. It enables men to lay hold of every good thing, just as Mormon admonished (see Moro. 7:21, 24).

Obtaining Faith to Perform Miracles

How does one attain this type of faith, and thus have the power of God come into one's life to lay hold of every good thing? Mormon taught that "God knowing all things, being from everlasting to everlasting, behold, he sent angels to minister unto the children of men, to make manifest concerning the coming of Christ; and in Christ there should come every good thing. And God also declared unto prophets, by his own mouth, that Christ should come" (Moro. 7:22–23). Following the coming of Christ, "men also were saved by faith in his name; and by faith they become the sons of God" (Moro. 7:26). Mormon testifies that miracles did not cease, nor did angels cease to minister unto the children of men after the time of Christ (see Moro. 7:27, 29). Accepting the words of angels and prophets concerning Christ in any period of time enables men to obtain faith as a principle of power.

Jacob, brother of Nephi, bore testimony similar to Mormon's. Part of Jacob's testimony has been referred to twice above, but is now quoted more fully to show how faith as a principle of power is attained.

> 6 *Wherefore, we search the prophets, and we have many revelations and the spirit of prophecy; and having all these witnesses we obtain a hope, and our faith becometh unshaken, insomuch that we truly can command in the name of Jesus and the very trees obey us, or the mountains, or the waves of the sea.*

7 Nevertheless, the Lord God showeth us our weakness that we may know that it is by his grace, and his great condescension unto the children of men, that we have power to do these things. (Jacob 4:6–7)

Through scripture study and revelation comes hope, the principle of action; and through positive actions our faith becomes firmer, and we experience the principle of power. Exercising and developing our faith, as a principle of power, will ultimately create an unshakeable power. Jacob also gave his readers some cautions: "despise not the revelations of God . . . seek not to counsel the Lord, but to take counsel from his hand"; and "be reconciled to [God] through the Atonement of Christ" (Jacob 4:8–11). Following these cautions will help us attain faith as a power to experience miracles in our lives. There are other examples of the faith of the Nephites and the Jaredites throughout the Book of Mormon, but the above incidents and principles should clearly illustrate that those who are baptized "and endure in faith to the end, should be saved" (D&C 20:25). Miracles do not save us, but the righteous use of priesthood power through our faith will become a sanctifying influence in our lives to prepare us to be in the Kingdom of God.

14

THE ETERNAL NATURE OF THE GOSPEL

"Not only those who believed after he came in the meridian of time, in the flesh, but all those from the beginning, even as many as were before he came." (D&C 20:26)

The plan of salvation has been the same in all ages of the world. Joseph Smith made this observation: "Now taking it for granted that the scriptures say what they mean, and mean what they say, we have sufficient grounds to go on and prove from the Bible that the gospel has always been the same; the ordinances to fulfil its requirements, the same, and the officers to officiate, the same; and the signs and fruits resulting from the promises, the same" (*TPJS*, 264). The Old Testament confirms the above revelation. For example, in contrasting the law of Moses with the gospel of Jesus Christ, Paul declared to the Galatians that God "preached before the gospel unto Abraham" (Gal. 3:8). In other words, the fullness of the gospel was taught before the law of Moses was added to it. We will examine various principles of the gospel (as they were taught in the Book of Mormon during Old Testament time periods) to show that they existed even before the law of Moses appeared.

Knowledge of Jesus Christ

The Book of Mormon people had a knowledge of Jesus Christ. Somewhere around 500 B.C.,[49] Jacob declared: "For, for this intent have we written these things, that they may know that we knew of Christ, and we had a hope of his glory many hundred years before his coming; and not only we ourselves had a hope of his glory, but also all the holy prophets which were before us" (Jacob 4:4). Later, responding to Sherem's professing to believe in the scriptures, Jacob taught: "Then ye do not understand them; for they truly testify of Christ. Behold, I say unto you that none of the prophets have written, nor prophesied, save they have spoken concerning this Christ" (Jacob 7:11).

The Bible confirms that Moses knew of Christ and esteemed the value of his gospel:

> 24 By faith Moses, when he was come to years, refused to be called the son of Pharaoh's daughter;
>
> 25 Choosing rather to suffer affliction with the people of God, than to enjoy the pleasures of sin for a season;
>
> 26 Esteeming the reproach of Christ greater riches than the treasures in Egypt: for he had respect unto the recompense of the reward.
>
> 27 By faith he forsook Egypt, not fearing the wrath of the king: for he endured, as seeing him who is invisible. (Heb. 11:24–27)

The prophets knew and testified of Christ and understood and taught his doctrine or gospel.

---

49 Nephi died 55 years after they left Jerusalem, about 545 B.C. Jacob and then his son Enos prophesied after Nephi's death (Enos 1:25). There is no record of when Jacob died. Therefore, we give the year 500 B.C. as a general time period.

The Gospel of Jesus Christ

As Nephi concluded his writing on the small plates, sometime before 545 B.C., he wrote concerning the doctrine of Christ: water baptism, repentance, baptism of fire and the Holy Ghost through faith in the Son of God, and enduring to the end (see 2 Nephi 31). All of these principles were a part of the New Testament gospel and are discussed more fully in other chapters. Helaman had taught his sons to:

> . . . remember that it is upon the rock of our Redeemer, who is Christ, the Son of God, that ye must build your foundation; that when the devil shall send forth his mighty winds, yea, his shafts in the whirlwind, yea, when all his hail and his mighty storm shall beat upon you, it shall have no power over you to drag you down to the gulf of misery and endless wo, because of the rock upon which ye are built, which is a sure foundation, a foundation whereon if men build they cannot fall. (Hel. 5:12)

The building upon the rock is readily recognized as the conclusion of the Sermon on the Mount given by Jesus in Galilee during his mortal ministry (see Matt. 7:24–27). The rock upon which the gospel was built in Old or New Testament times was Christ (see 3 Nephi 11:39–40; 1 Cor. 10:4). Christ and his gospel, or plan of salvation, were well known and fundamental teachings among the Book of Mormon prophets in Old Testament times. When the plates of brass are restored as promised (see 1 Nephi 5:18–19; Alma 37:4–5), we will learn that Christ and his plan of salvation were also originally taught in Old Testament times. Moses chapters 6 and 7, in the Pearl of Great Price, restores this knowledge concerning the days of Adam and Enoch.

The Church in the Old Testament

The gospel of Jesus Christ is administered through the priesthood and the Church. The New Testament acknowledges the function of two priesthoods in Old Testament times, although their specific functions have been lost (see Heb. 7:11). The fact that the Church existed in Old Testament times, however, is not generally acknowledged. That Christ's Church existed in Moses' day is testified of by the martyr Stephen: "This is [Moses], that was in the church in the wilderness with the angel which spake to him in the mount Sina, and with our fathers: who received the lively oracles to give unto us" (Acts 7:38). The Book of Mormon confirms what Stephen taught. In about 600 B.C., Nephi spoke to Zoram, Laban's servant, concerning the taking of the plates of brass to Nephi's brethren outside the walls of Jerusalem. Zoram followed Nephi "supposing that [he] spake of the brethren of the church" (1 Nephi 4:26). The supposition confirms the existence of a church at that time.

Jacob, the brother of Nephi, taught his brethren that the Jews would be gathered home to the land of Jerusalem and "be restored to the true church and fold of God" (2 Nephi 9:1–2). The church could not be "restored" if it had not been established before and then taken away.

The Old Testament period Nephites had the Church of Christ and the priesthood to administer the gospel of Jesus Christ. Alma established the church at the waters of Mormon (see Mosiah 18), and there were churches in the land of Zarahemla (see Mosiah 25). The Church is spoken of repeatedly throughout the books of Alma and Helaman.

Christians Before the Times of Christ

Those who were members of the Nephite churches, at least on some occasions, were referred to as *Christians*, a common nickname today of all who believe in Christ. As General Moroni rallied his people to fight against the Lamanites:

> *13 . . . he prayed mightily unto his God for the blessings of liberty to rest upon his brethren, so long as there should a band of Christians remain to possess the land—*

14 For thus were all the true believers of Christ, who belonged to the church of God, called by those who did not belong to the church.

15 And those who did belong to the church were faithful; yea, all those who were true believers in Christ took upon them, gladly, the name of Christ, or Christians as they were called, because of their belief in Christ who should come. (Alma 46:13–15)

Since many other Nephites took upon themselves the name of Christ as they were baptized, it is reasonable to assume that *"Christians"* was a formal title, as well. The name *"Christians"* was used to describe the church in Antioch in the days of Paul: "the disciples were called Christians first in Antioch" (Acts 11:26). This designation has led critics to yell "plagiarism" when they read in the Book of Mormon that in the days of the great general, Moroni, the believers in Christ were called Christians.

When all the evidence is collected, showing the great knowledge of Christ that was held among the people who lived before he came to earth, the charge of plagiarism must be changed to one of awe and respect for the universal plan of salvation introduced before the world was and carried out consistently as long as men did not reject the truth of the gospel. That the name "Christian" is said to have been used first in Antioch can be expected when it is recognized that, at that time, the knowledge of the unborn Christ had been rejected and the knowledge of the plan of salvation had been lost.

Baptism, the Gate of Heaven

"Heaven" is the term used to describe the abode of God. "Gates" are entry ways. To enter the gate of heaven is equivalent to being saved in God's kingdom. Again, the Book of Mormon shows that entry into God's kingdom has been through Christ in every age of man. Mormon gave this editorial comment about the Nephites in 43 B.C.:

27 Thus we may see that the Lord is merciful unto all who will, in the sincerity of their hearts, call upon his holy name.

28 Yea, thus we see that the gate of heaven is open unto all, even to those who will believe on the name of Jesus Christ, who is the Son of God.

29 Yea, we see that whosoever will may lay hold upon the word of God, which is quick and powerful, which shall divide asunder all the cunning and the snares and the wiles of the devil, and lead the man of Christ in a straight and narrow course across that everlasting gulf of misery which is prepared to engulf the wicked—

30 And land their souls, yea, their immortal souls, at the right hand of God in the kingdom of heaven, to sit down with Abraham, and Isaac, and with Jacob, and with all our holy fathers, to go no more out. (Hel. 3:27–30)

Those who entered this gate of heaven, held open for them by Christ, were to sit down in the kingdom with Abraham, Isaac, and Jacob. It is obvious, if God is the same yesterday, today, and forever, as the scriptures testify (see Heb. 13:8), that Abraham, Isaac, and Jacob must have entered into heaven through the same procedure that Mormon refers to in 43 B.C. These tens of thousands of converts spoken of by Mormon (see Hel. 3:26) not only believed in Christ, but had entered into the Church by baptism to receive the blessings poured out upon them (see Hel. 3:24–25).

It should be noted that while baptism is the gate by which one enters the path to eternal life (see 2 Nephi 31:9), it does not place the baptized into heaven. As discussed in chapter 11, after entering the path, one must press forward with a steadfastness in Christ to attain eternal life (see 2 Nephi 31:17–20). Nonetheless, baptism is a requirement to enter the kingdom of heaven in whatever age of the world man may live.

The Holy Ghost

That the Holy Ghost did not function before the time of Christ is commonly taught in the Christian world. Since the same plan of salvation has continually been and still is in effect, the Holy Ghost should carry out the same function before and after the time of Christ. Nephi bears testimony early in the Book of Mormon record:

> *18 For he is the same yesterday, today, and forever; and the way is prepared for all men from the foundation of the world, if it so be that they repent and come unto him.*
>
> *19 For he that diligently seeketh shall find; and the mysteries of God shall be unfolded unto them, by the power of the Holy Ghost, as well in these times as in times of old, and as well of old as in times to come; wherefore, the course of the Lord is one eternal round. (1 Nephi 10:18–19)*

The Holy Ghost is a witness, or testator, of the other two members of the Godhead (see 3 Nephi 11:32; *TPJS*, 190). The function of the Holy Ghost among the Nephites was identical to the function of the Holy Ghost to the Jerusalem disciples. Jesus testified:

> *26 But the Comforter, which is the Holy Ghost, whom the Father will send in my name, he shall teach you all things, and bring all things to your remembrance, whatsoever I have said unto you. (John 14:26)*
>
> *12 I have yet many things to say unto you, but ye cannot bear them now.*
>
> *13 Howbeit when he, the Spirit of truth, is come, he will guide you in to all truth; for he shall not speak of himself; but whatsoever he shall hear, that shall he speak: and he will shew you things to come.*

14 He shall glorify me: for he shall receive of mine, and shall shew it unto you. (John 16:12–14)

The Apostle Peter taught that the Holy Ghost functioned in Old Testament times: "Men and brethren, this scripture must needs have been fulfilled, which the Holy Ghost by the mouth of David spake before concerning Judas, which was a guide to them that took Jesus" (Acts 1:16).

The Book of Mormon teachings about the Holy Ghost in the Old Testament times again shows the consistency of the gospel plan.

Men Became Sons of Christ

Paul emphasized to the New Testament Saints that a spiritual adoption, or rebirth, was a necessary experience for them. This spiritual adoption gave them a new Father, "For as many as are led by the Spirit of God, they are the sons of God. For ye have not received the spirit of bondage again to fear; but ye have received the Spirit of adoption, whereby we cry, Abba, Father" (Rom. 8:14–15; see also Gal. 6:1–7).

In the Hebrew, "abba" designates "father," specifically one's own father. Those who are spiritually begotten thus cry "abba" in their hearts. They come to know a new father in Jesus Christ. He is their father of eternal life. This same spiritual experience took place and was taught in the Book of Mormon before the meridian of time. King Benjamin's great sermon was attended by the manifestation of the Spirit to such an extent that the listeners experienced a mighty change in their hearts, having no disposition to do evil (see Mosiah 5:1–2). They said:

> *And we are willing to enter into a covenant with our God to do his will, and to be obedient to his commandments in all things that he shall command us, all the remainder of our days, that we may not bring upon ourselves a never-ending torment, as has been spoken by the angel,*

that we may not drink out of the cup of the wrath of God.
(Mosiah 5:5)

Following their covenant, King Benjamin explained: "And now, because of the covenant which ye have made ye shall be called the children of Christ, his sons, and his daughters; for behold, this day he hath spiritually begotten you; for ye say that your hearts are changed through faith on his name; therefore, ye are born of him and have become his sons and his daughters" (Mosiah 5:7).

In their born-again state they also had a new father, as Paul had written to the Romans. Again the Book of Mormon teaches an eternal principle of the gospel.

The Gathering of Israel

As Jesus journeyed to Jerusalem in the last week of his life, he lamented: "O Jerusalem, Jerusalem, thou that killest the prophets, and stonest them which are sent unto thee, how often would I have gathered thy children together, even as a hen gathereth her chickens under her wings, and ye would not!" (Matt. 23:37). Note that Jesus said how oft would *I* have gathered you, showing once more his involvement in Old Testament times. The same concept of Christ's willingness to gather Israel was taught to the Nephites by Christ. Furthermore, he extended the teaching:

4 O ye people of these great cities which have fallen, who are descendants of Jacob, yea, who are of the house of Israel, how oft have I gathered you as a hen gathereth her chickens under her wings, and have nourished you.

5 And again, how oft would I have gathered you as a hen gathereth her chickens under her wings, yea, O ye people of the house of Israel, who have fallen; yea, O ye people of the house of Israel, ye that dwell at Jerusalem, as ye that have fallen; yea, how oft would I have gathered you as a hen gathereth her chickens, and ye would not.

6 O ye house of Israel whom I have spared, how oft will I gather you as a hen gathereth her chickens under her wings, if ye will repent and return unto me with full purpose of heart.

7 But if not, O house of Israel, the places of your dwellings shall become desolate until the time of the fulfilling of the covenant to your fathers. (3 Nephi 10:4–7)

Christ was involved in the gathering of Israel and was ever willing to gather them throughout the Old Testament time period. Israel as a covenant people originated with Abraham. Since the Nephites were a branch of the house of Israel, their gathering to America, and within America, was a part of the plan of salvation.

Summary

There are other principles of the gospel taught in the Book of Mormon that are taught in the Old and New Testament, but the above are sufficient to establish that the gospel is eternal. The plan of salvation was presented in the grand council of heaven (see Abraham 3:24–28). The opportunity to follow that plan extended from Adam to the last days, although Christ came in the meridian of time to fulfill his part of the plan—to perform the Atonement. The only time the opportunity to follow this plan was not given was because of apostasy and rejection as indicated by Jesus above. One of those rejections was by the children of Israel coming out of Egypt. However, because it was not a total rejection, the Lord added the law of Moses to the gospel.

The Law of Moses

The Law of Moses was practiced for some time between twelve to fourteen hundred years before the coming of Christ.[50]

---

50 The traditional date is about 1400 B.C., but many scholars have moved the date to about 1200 B.C. Whichever date is accepted, it still represents less than half of the Old Testament period.

The fuller gospel had been revealed to men like Adam, Enoch, Noah, Abraham, and Abraham's successors during the previous twenty-eight to twenty-six hundred years before the law of Moses was revealed . . . *even as many as were before [Christ] came*" (*D&C 20:26;* italics added).

The law of Moses is usually equated with blood sacrifice, the Ten Commandments, and the concept of "an eye for an eye, and a tooth for a tooth" (Matt. 5:38; see also Ex. 21:24). However, blood sacrifices and the Ten Commandments are not unique to the law of Moses, and the principle of "an eye for an eye" is frequently misunderstood. Adam offered blood sacrifices before the law of Moses was given (see Moses 5:5–7; Gen. 4:4). The Ten Commandments are eternal laws given to every dispensation (see D&C 42:18–24; Gen. 9:6; 39:9; Moses 5:5). The "eye for an eye" concept was a liability law to compensate the injured (see Ex. 21:22–36).

Paul said that the law of Moses "was added because of transgressions" (Gal. 3:19). Commenting on Paul's statement, Joseph Smith asked, "What, we ask, was this law added to, if it was not added to the Gospel? It must be plain that it was added to the Gospel, since we learn that they had the Gospel preached to them" (*TPJS,* 60).[51] The Book of Mormon helps us better understand the above statements and gives us more information about the purpose and function of the law. "And notwithstanding we believe in Christ, we keep the law of Moses, and look forward with steadfastness unto Christ, until the law shall be fulfilled" (2 Nephi 25:24).

Who Gave the Law

When Jesus appeared to the Nephites, he told them "that the law is fulfilled that was given unto Moses. Behold, I am he that gave the law, and I am he who covenanted with my people Israel; therefore, the law in me is fulfilled, for I have come to fulfil the law; therefore it hath an end" (3 Nephi 15:4–5). Since Christ gave

---

51 Joseph had previously quoted Galations 3:8 and Hebrews 4:2 to show that the gospel had been preached to Israel in Old Testament times.

the law, we must conclude that it was a *good* law, for as Mormon taught: "But behold, that which is of God inviteth and enticeth to do good continually; wherefore, every thing which inviteth and enticeth to do good, and to love God, and to serve him, is inspired of God" (Moro. 7:13; see also James 1:17–18). The purpose of the law further substantiates that it was a good law.

Why Was the Law Given

Although it was a good law, it was not a law sufficient to bring salvation. The prophet Abinadi taught the wicked priests of Noah that the law did not bring salvation (see Mosiah 13:27–28) and what was the true purpose of the law:

> 29 And now I say unto you that it was expedient that there should be a law given to the children of Israel, yea, even a very strict law; for they were a stiffnecked people, quick to do iniquity, and slow to remember the Lord their God;
>
> 30 Therefore there was a law given them, yea, a law of performances and of ordinances, a law which they were to observe strictly from day to day, to keep them in remembrance of God and their duty towards him. (Mosiah 13:29–30)

Through the lesser law, the people were to be again prepared to receive the gospel, or the higher law of Christ. As quoted above: "the law was our schoolmaster to bring us unto Christ" (Gal. 3:24).

The Book of Mormon illustrates how this was accomplished among the Nephites. Because Lehi and Ishmael and their families responded to the Lord's call to come out of the wickedness of Jerusalem before it was destroyed, they were offered and received the higher law of Christ. Nephi explained:

> 23 For we labor diligently to write, to persuade our children, and also our brethren, to believe in Christ, and

to be reconciled to God; for we know that it is by grace that we are saved, after all we can do.

24 And, notwithstanding we believe in Christ, we keep the law of Moses, and look forward with steadfastness unto Christ, until the law shall be fulfilled.

25 For, for this end was the law given; wherefore the law hath become dead unto us, and we are made alive in Christ because of our faith; yet we keep the law because of the commandments.

26 And we talk of Christ, we rejoice in Christ, we preach of Christ, we prophesy of Christ, and we write according to our prophecies, that our children may know to what source they may look for a remission of their sins.

27 Wherefore, we speak concerning the law that our children may know the deadness of the law; and they, by knowing the deadness of the law, may look forward unto that life which is in Christ, and know for what end the law was given. And after the law is fulfilled in Christ, that they need not harden their hearts against him when the law ought to be done away. (2 Nephi 25:23–27)

The extent to which the Nephites continued to keep the law is enlarged upon later in Alma:

15 Yea, and they did keep the law of Moses; for it was expedient that they should keep the law of Moses as yet, for it was not all fulfilled. But notwithstanding the law of Moses, they did look forward to the coming of Christ, considering that the law of Moses was a type of his coming, and believing that they must keep those outward performances until the time that he should be revealed unto them.

16 Now they did not suppose that salvation came by the law of Moses; but the law of Moses did serve to strengthen their faith in Christ; and thus they did retain a hope through faith, unto eternal salvation, relying upon the spirit of prophecy, which spake of those things to come. (Alma 25:15–16)

An explanation of the "outward ordinances" (v. 15) that were kept is not given but would probably have included the ordinances that pointed the people's minds to Christ. The performances and ordinances observed daily were probably the minutia that were eliminated under the higher law. They were probably what Paul referred to in writing to the Hebrews: "Which *consisted* only in meats and drinks, and divers washings, and carnal ordinances, imposed on them until the time of reformation" (JST Heb. 9:10, italics added).[52] The "meats and drinks" were probably health and dietary laws, and the "divers washings, and carnal ordinances" were probably daily reminders of Christ given because of the stiffneckedness of the people. Under the higher law, ordinances are performed weekly instead of daily because, assumedly, the people are not as hardhearted or stiffnecked as the people who were given the law.

Carnal commandments are also mentioned in the revelation to the Prophet Joseph Smith concerning the Melchizedek priesthood being taken out of Israel, and the Aaronic priesthood continuing: "Which gospel is the gospel of repentance and baptism, and the remission of sins, and the law of carnal commandments, which the Lord in his wrath caused to continue with the house of Aaron among the children of Israel until John, whom God raised up, being filled with the Holy Ghost from his mother's womb" (D&C 84:27). That the Aaronic priesthood continued shows that it functioned before the law. Its purpose was that of a preparatory priesthood, given before the higher Melchizedek priesthood. While

---

52 The only change in the JST is the second word "stood" that is changed to "consisted."

the Aaronic priesthood was the prevalent authority among the people, the Prophet Joseph Smith declared: "All the prophets had the Melchizedek Priesthood and were ordained by God himself" (*TPJS*, 181).

Although there is no account of Lehi holding the priesthood, it is evident from the Book of Mormon that he did. He was not of the tribe of Levi, and therefore would not have had the Aaronic priesthood under the law of Moses. He probably was one of those who were "ordained by God himself," either before or after he left for America. Nephi had apparently received the priesthood from his father and/or under heavenly direction. Nephi had consecrated his younger brothers to be priests and teachers over his people (2 Nephi 5:26; Jacob 1:18). The Nephites functioned "after the order of the Son of God," or the higher priesthood (see Alma 13:7; 4:20; 5:44, 54; 6:8; 43:2). President Joseph Fielding Smith quoted some of the above verses and made this declaration:

> The Nephites were descendants of Joseph. Lehi discovered this when reading the brass plates. He was a descendant of Manasseh, and Ishmael, who accompanied him with his family, was of the tribe of Ephraim. Therefore there were no Levites who accompanied Lehi to the Western Hemisphere. Under these conditions the Nephites officiated by virtue of the Melchizedek Priesthood from the days of Lehi to the days of the appearance of our Savior among them. It is true that Nephi "consecrated Jacob and Joseph" that they should be priests and teachers over the land of the Nephites, but the fact that plural terms *priests* and *teachers* were used indicates that this was not a reference to the definite office in the priesthood in either case, but it was a general assignment to teach, direct, and admonish the people. Otherwise the terms *priest* and *teacher* would have been given. . . .
>
> From these and numerous other passages we learn that it was by the authority of the Melchizedek

Priesthood that the Nephites administered from the
time they left Jerusalem until the time of the coming
of Jesus Christ. By the power of this priesthood they
baptized, confirmed, and ordained. During these years
they also observed the law of Moses. They offered
sacrifice and performed the duties which in Israel had
been assigned to the priests and Levites. They observed
in every detail the requirements of the law. When the
Savior came to them, he fulfilled the carnal law and
did away with the sacrifice by the shedding of blood
of animals. He informed the Nephites that in him the
law of Moses was fulfilled.[53]

Although they had the Melchizedek priesthood, they still
observed the law of Moses, as will be shown later.

The Law Typifies Christ

A second reason for keeping the law was given by Abinadi:
"But behold, I say unto you, that all these things were types of
things to come" (Mosiah 13:31). As stated above, the law of Moses
was administered daily and probably in more detail than under the
fuller gospel plan. Nephi testified: "Behold, my soul delighteth in
proving unto my people the truth of the coming of Christ; for, for
this end hath the law of Moses been given; and all things which
have been given of God from the beginning of the world, unto
man, are the typifying of him" (2 Nephi 11:4). We read another
testimony of this purpose in Jarom:

> *Wherefore, the prophets, and the priests, and the teachers,*
> *did labor diligently, exhorting with all long-suffering the*
> *people to diligence; teaching the law of Moses, and the*
> *intent for which it was given; persuading them to look*
> *forward unto the Messiah, and believe in him to come as*
> *though he already was. And after this manner did they*
> *teach them. (Jarom 1:11)*

---

53 *Answers to Gospel Questions,* 1:124–126.

An example of Moses typifying Christ is taught in the book of Helaman. In speaking of the great power given to Moses and the words which he spoke concerning the Messiah, we read:

14 Yea, did he not bear record that the Son of God should come? And as he lifted up the brazen serpent in the wilderness, even so shall he be lifted up who should come.

15 And as many as should look upon that serpent should live, even so as many as should look upon the Son of God with faith, having a contrite spirit, might live, even unto that life which is eternal. (Hel. 8:14–15; see also Alma 33:19; 1 Nephi 17:40–42; and John 3:14)

Abinadi testified to the priests of Noah of the performances and ordinances of the law of Moses being "types of things to come" (Mosiah 13:31). He concluded:

13 And now, ought ye not to tremble and repent of your sins, and remember that only in and through Christ ye can be saved?

14 Therefore, if ye teach the law of Moses, also teach that it is a shadow of those things which are to come—

15 Teach them that redemption cometh through Christ the Lord, who is the very Eternal Father. Amen. (Mosiah 16:13–15)

All that was added to the gospel was to further remind the people of Christ, but it still was insufficient, as Abinadi said: "And now, did they understand the law? I say unto you, Nay, they did not all understand the law; and this because of the hardness of their hearts; for they understood not that there could not any man be saved except it were through the redemption of God" (Mosiah 13:32). Abinadi's concluding remarks to the priests of Noah (quoted above) further verify that Christ was the center of the law of Moses. All things bear record of Christ (Moses 6:63), but the law of Moses was to be a daily reminder of him.

The Law Fulfilled

Although some of the Nephites thought the law was fulfilled at the birth of Christ (see 3 Nephi 1:24–25), it was not fulfilled until the Atonement and the sacrifice of Christ were made. The law had been pointing to these glorious events. They were the ultimate of all sacrifices. To this Amulek bore testimony:

13 Therefore, it is expedient that there should be a great and last sacrifice, and then shall there be, or it is expedient there should be, a stop to the shedding of blood; then shall the law of Moses be fulfilled; yea, it shall be all fulfilled, every jot and tittle, and none shall have passed away.

14 And behold, this is the whole meaning of the law, every whit pointing to that great and last sacrifice; and that great and last sacrifice will be the son of God, yea, infinite and eternal.

15 And thus he shall bring salvation to all those who shall believe on his name; this being the intent of this last sacrifice, to bring about the bowels of mercy, which overpowereth justice, and bringeth about means unto men that they may have faith unto repentance. (Alma 34:13–15)

In the great sermon to the Nephites, as previously explained, Jesus testified that "one jot nor one tittle hath not passed away from the law, but in me hath all been fulfilled" (3 Nephi 12:18). His testimony illustrated the completeness of the fulfillment of the law.

A note of caution should be added. Some have supposed that the Old Testament was fulfilled with Christ's fulfilling of the law. To the Nephites he explained, "I do not destroy the prophets, for as many as have not been fulfilled in me, verily I say unto you, shall all be fulfilled" (3 Nephi 15:6). The prophets of the Old Testament foretold of the latter-day restoration. Those prophecies are being fulfilled today (see 3 Nephi 20:11–12).

Summary

The law of Moses was added to the gospel because of the people being hardhearted and stiffnecked. Today we sometimes need similar laws added for similar reasons. If we lived as the gospel teaches, no such laws would be needed. But many others do not understand the gospel, even as the children of Israel did not understand the law of Moses. In addition, failure to see Christ as the central figure of the gospel sometimes results in an emphasis on programs or activities. Regarding this Elder Bruce R. McConkie has said:

> Our tendency—it is an almost universal practice among most church leaders—is to get so involved with the operation of the institutional Church that we never gain faith like the ancients, simply because we do not involve ourselves in the basic gospel matters that were the center of their lives.
>
> We are so wound up in programs and statistics and trends, in properties, lands, and mammon, and in achieving goals that will highlight the excellence of our work, that we "have omitted the weightier matters of the law." And as Jesus would have said: "These [weightier things] ought ye to have done, and not to leave the other undone" (Matthew 23:23).
>
> Let us be reminded of the great basic verities upon which all church programs and all church organization rest.
>
> We are not saved by church programs as such, by church organizations alone, or even by the Church itself. It is the gospel that saves. The gospel is "the power of God unto salvation."[54]

The law of Moses was fulfilled in Christ. We should follow the example of the Nephites as recorded in the Book of Mormon, and believe in Christ and the higher ordinances of his gospel.

---

54 (1982). Regional Representative Seminar, April 2; see Rom. 1:16.

15

BELIEVE IN THE PROPHETS

". . . who believed in the words of the holy prophets, who spake as they were inspired by the gift of the Holy Ghost, who truly testified of [Christ] in all things, should have eternal life." (D&C 20:26)

The Book of Mormon begins by relating that in the first year of the reign of Zedekiah, king of Judah, "there came many prophets, prophesying unto the people that they must repent, or the great city Jerusalem must be destroyed" (1 Nephi 1:4). Lehi believed the prophets and was led out of Jerusalem before it was destroyed (see 2 Nephi 1:3–4). Upon arriving in the land he had been promised, he foretold of others "who should be led out of other countries by the hand of the Lord." He also prophesied "according to the workings of the Spirit which is in me, that there shall none come into this land save they shall be brought by the hand of the Lord" (2 Nephi 1:6–7). The prophets in Jerusalem, and Lehi, had been "inspired by the gift of the Holy Ghost" (D&C 20:26).

Nephi later taught, in commenting on the prophecies of Isaiah: "And as one generation hath been destroyed among the Jews because of iniquity, even so have they been destroyed from generation to generation according to their iniquities; and never hath any of them been destroyed save it were foretold them by the prophets of the Lord" (2 Nephi 25:9). Nephi went on to prophesy of future destructions, scatterings, and gatherings of the Jews from and to Jerusalem (see 2 Nephi 25:10–19). A study of the times foretold by Nephi would show that there were, as Nephi said, prophets who forewarned of those Jerusalem destructions. The same pattern is seen among the peoples of the Book of Mormon (see Enos 1:22–24; Jarom 1:10–11; Ether 9:28; 11:1). Nephi's declaration is sustained in both the Nephite and Jaredite records.

The Righteous Shall Not Perish

Nephi taught a principle that the Lord follows: "And he raiseth up a righteous nation, and destroyeth the nations of the wicked. And he leadeth away the righteous into precious lands, and the wicked he destroyeth, and curseth the land unto them for their sakes" (1 Nephi 17:37–38). There are other examples of the righteous Nephites being led out from the wicked after the families of Lehi and Ishmael had settled in the promised land. Nephi was warned of the Lord after the death of his father that he "should depart from [his wicked brethren] and flee into the wilderness, and all those who would go with [him]" (2 Nephi 5:5; see also Jacob 3:3–4; Omni 1:14–16). The books of Mosiah, Alma, and Helaman show various migrations of righteous people between the lands of Zarahemla and Nephi. We will not discuss these here, but as you read these books note that the righteous were led out by a prophet according to the principle given us by Nephi. There were similar expeditions among the Jaredites. The preservation of the righteous Nephites and the destruction of the wicked is illustrated most vividly at the time of the crucifixion of Jesus. Mormon identified those who were spared:

> *11 And thus far were the scriptures fulfilled which had been spoken by the prophets.*
>
> *12 And it was the more righteous part of the people who were saved, and it was they who received the prophets and stoned them not; and it was they who had not shed the blood of the saints, who were spared. . . .*

14 And now, whoso readeth, let him understand; he that hath the scriptures, let him search them, and see and behold if all these deaths and destructions by fire, and by smoke, and by tempests, and by whirlwinds, and by the opening of the earth to receive them, and all these things are not unto the fulfilling of the prophecies of many of the holy prophets. (3 Nephi 10:11–12, 14)

Mormon repeatedly acknowledges the role of the prophets preceding this terrible destruction (see 3 Nephi 6:20–24; 7:14–20).

The ultimate preservation of the righteous and the destruction of the wicked will come at the Second Coming. A prophet quoted by Nephi, probably Zenos or Isaiah, declared:

16 For the time soon cometh that the fulness of the wrath of God shall be poured out upon all the children of men; for he will not suffer that the wicked shall destroy the righteous.

17 Wherefore, he will preserve the righteous by his power, even if it so be that the fulness of his wrath must come, and the righteous be preserved, even unto the destruction of their enemies by fire. Wherefore, the righteous need not fear; for thus saith the prophet, they shall be saved, even if it so be as by fire. (1 Nephi 22:16–17)

The Lord will preserve the righteous who hearken to the prophets.

The Prophets Establish Peace

Another role of the prophets is to establish peace in the land. Peace is the result of the gospel being taught, accepted, and lived. There are examples of this among both the Nephites and the Jaredites.

As Mormon bridged the gap between the small plates and the large plates, he recorded the work of King Benjamin and the prophets in the Words of Mormon:

16 And after there had been false prophets, and false preachers and teachers among the people, and all these having been punished according to their crimes; and after there having been much contention and many dissensions away unto the Lamanites, behold, it came to pass that King Benjamin, with the assistance of the holy prophets who were among his people—

17 For behold, King Benjamin was a holy man, and he did reign over his people in righteousness; and there were many holy men in the land, and they did speak the word of God with power and with authority; and they did use much sharpness because of the stiffneckedness of the people—

18 Wherefore, with the help of these, King Benjamin, by laboring with all the might of his body and the faculty of his whole soul, and also the prophets, did once more establish peace in the land. (W of M 1:16–18)

The same principle was followed among the Jaredites:

23 And also in the reign of Shule there came prophets among the people, who were sent from the Lord, prophesying that the wickedness and idolatry of the people was bringing a curse upon the land, and they should be destroyed if they did not repent.

24 And it came to pass that the people did revile against the prophets, and did mock them. And it came to pass that king Shule did execute judgment against all those who did revile against the prophets.

26 And he did execute a law throughout all the land, which gave power unto the prophets that they should go whithersoever they would; and by this cause the people were brought unto repentance.

27 And because the people did repent of their iniquities and idolatries the Lord did spare them, and they began to prosper again in the land. (Ether 7:23–26)

The prophets always work within the law of the land as illustrated above (see Articles of Faith 12; D&C 98:4–10; 134).

The Lord Protects His Prophets

Prophets of the Lord are almost always persecuted to one degree or another (see 3 Nephi 12:12). Some are even slain, thus sealing their testimony with their blood. The Lord will protect his prophets, however, until their missions are completed. King Noah sent his priests to slay Abinadi, but as they attempted to lay hands on him he said:

3 Touch me not, for God shall smite you if ye lay your hands upon me, for I have not delivered the message which the Lord sent me to deliver; neither have I told you that which ye requested that I should tell; therefore, God will not suffer that I shall be destroyed at this time.

4 But I must fulfil the commandments wherewith God has commanded me; and because I have told you the truth ye are angry with me. And again, because I have spoken the word of God ye have judged me that I am mad.

5 Now it came to pass after Abinadi had spoken these words that the people of king Noah durst not lay their hands on him, for the Spirit of the Lord was upon him; and his face shone with exceeding luster, even as Moses' did while in the mount of Sinai, while speaking with the Lord.

6 And he spake with power and authority from God. (Mosiah 13:3–6)

Thus Abinadi demanded their attention. He went on to deliver one of the great sermons recorded in the Book of Mormon. Because he would not recount his words, he was burned at the stake (Mosiah 17:13–20).[55] Abinadi is the scriptural proof that God protects his prophets until their mission is complete but will allow their testimony to be sealed in blood. Joseph Smith was given the same assurance as Abinadi and so declared several times: "I shall not be sacrificed until my time comes; then I shall be offered freely" (*TPJS,* 274). On another occasion, he said: "I defy all the world to destroy the work of God; and I prophesy they never will have power to kill me till my work is accomplished, and I am ready to die" (*TPJS,* 328; see also pp. 258 and 361). Although a prophet's earthly life is taken, he is received into the rest of the Lord (see Alma 60:13). The rest of the Lord "is the fulness of his glory" (D&C 84:24).

There are several other Book of Mormon examples (see 1 Nephi 2:14; 17:48, 52–54; Alma 14:13; Hel. 5:23–25; Hel. 16:2; and 3 Nephi 7:18). The Book of Mormon repeatedly bears testimony that the Lord protects his prophets until their mission is completed.

The words of the prophets are always fulfilled and are— ultimately—always verified. Lehi was shown in vision that Jerusalem had been destroyed (2 Nephi 1:4) as the prophets had warned (see 1 Nephi 1:4). The destruction of Jerusalem was later verified by the arrival of the Mulekites in America (see Hel. 8:21–22). Therefore the Nephites had a spiritual and a physical witness of the fulfillment of the prophets. At the time of the birth of Christ, the unbelievers set a date to put to death all who believed in the signs prophesied by Samuel the Lamanite. However, these signs came, "yea, all things, every whit, according to the words of the

---

55 The principle of sealing one's testimony with death is taught in Hebrews 9:15–17. There are many Old Testament prophets who exemplified this principle (see Matt. 23:35). The Prophet Joseph Smith sealed "his testimony with his blood, that he might be honored and the wicked might be condemned" (D&C 136:39).

prophets" (3 Nephi 1:20). Those who believed in the words of the prophets ultimately found them fulfilled. Those who continually follow the prophets in our day will obtain eternal life, as the April 6 revelation declares. The Book of Mormon prophets "spake as they were inspired by the gift of the Holy Ghost" (D&C 20:26).

The Holy Prophets Testified of Christ

Jacob, the brother of Nephi, gave the purpose of his and Nephi's writing: "For this intent have we written these things, that they may know that we knew of Christ, and we had a hope of his glory many hundred years before his coming; and not only we ourselves had a hope of his glory, but also all the holy prophets which were before us" (Jacob 4:4). His testimony of "all the holy prophets which were before us" must refer to all of those who lived from Adam to the time of their leaving Jerusalem in 600 B.C. This conclusion is made from his later response to Sherem the anti-Christ's claim that he believed in the scriptures: "And I said unto him: Then ye do not understand them; for they truly testify of Christ. Behold, I say unto you that none of the prophets have written, nor prophesied, save they have spoken concerning this Christ" (Jacob 7:11). This later testimony includes not only the prophets who wrote, but all who have spoken. Jesus, when he visited the Nephites, made a similar statement: "Verily I say unto you, yea, and all the prophets from Samuel and those that follow after, as many as have spoken, have testified of me"[56] (3 Nephi 20:24; see Acts 3:24). With a general affirmation that all of the prophets testified of Christ, let us consider the specific testimonies of the prophets recorded in the Book of Mormon concerning Christ.

---

56 Samuel was considered the first prophet following the time period of the Judges. Since Jesus had been speaking of his being the prophet spoken of by Moses, he is apparently speaking of the prophets following Moses.

The Testimonies from the Plates of Brass

Lehi bore testimony that the plates of brass contained "the prophecies of the holy prophets, from the beginning, even down to . . . many prophecies . . . spoken by the mouth of Jeremiah" (1 Nephi 5:13). As Nephi wrote upon his smaller plates, he quoted many prophecies of Christ from Isaiah (see 1 Nephi 20–21; 2 Nephi 12–24), and three other prophets now lost from the Old Testament that must have been taken from the plates of brass.

> *The God of Abraham, and of Isaac, and the God of Jacob, yieldeth himself, according to the words of the angel, as a man, into the hands of wicked men, to be lifted up, according to the words of Zenock, and to be crucified, according to the words of Neum, and to be buried in a sepulchre, according to the words of Zenos, which he spake concerning the three days of darkness, which should be a sign given of his death unto those who should inhabit the isles of the sea, more especially given unto those who are of the house of Israel. (1 Nephi 19:10)*

These three prophesies of Christ were recorded upon the plates of brass. Nephi went on quoting Zenos' prophecy (see 1 Nephi 19:11–17; see also Alma 33:11–17). Lehi also quoted, from the plates of brass, a prophecy of Joseph who was sold into Egypt regarding the Messiah being manifest in the latter days (see 2 Nephi 3:5–21; 4:1–2). Jacob testified of Abraham "being obedient unto the commands of God in offering up his son Isaac which is a similitude of God and his Only Begotten Son" (Jacob 4:5), and of God speaking truths to the prophets of old (see Jacob 4:13). He apparently learned these things from the plates of brass. He also declared that the scriptures foretold of the Jews rejecting the stone (Christ) that would "become the great, and the last, and the only sure foundation, upon which the Jews can build" (Jacob 4:16). To establish the fulfillment of Christ being that stone, he quoted the words of Zenos, the allegory of the house of Israel (see Jacob 5).

That the allegory was taken from the plates of brass is supported by Paul's writings to the Romans (see Rom. 11:16–24).

Still later in the Book of Mormon we have another series of prophets quoted because of their prophecies of the Messiah. Nephi, son of Helaman, asked if the people had not read[57] of the power given to Moses and referred to Moses speaking concerning the coming of the Messiah (see Hel. 8:11–15). He then declared:

16 And now behold, Moses did not only testify of these things, but also all the holy prophets, from his days even to the days of Abraham.

17 Yea, and behold, Abraham saw of his coming, and was filled with gladness and did rejoice.

18 Yea, and behold I say unto you, that Abraham not only knew of these things, but there were many before the days of Abraham who were called by the order of God; yea, even after the order of his Son; and this that it should be shown unto the people, a great many thousand years before his coming, that even redemption should come unto them.

19 And now I would that ye should know, that even since the days of Abraham there have been many prophets that have testified these things; yea, behold, the prophet Zenos did testify boldly; for the which he was slain.

20 And behold, also Zenock, and also Ezias, and also Isaiah, and Jeremiah, (Jeremiah being that same prophet who testified of the destruction of Jerusalem) and now

---

57 Nephi is undoubtedly referring to having read from copies made from the plates of brass. That there were copies made is evident from the fact that Ammon and Aaron, sons of Mosiah, each read about Adam and the creation to one of the Lamanite kings at the same time, yet each were in a different area of the land. See Alma 18:36 and 22:12.

we know that Jerusalem was destroyed according to the words of Jeremiah. O then why not the Son of God come, according to his prophecy? (Hel. 8:16–20)

Nephi, son of Helaman, names seven prophets who had testified of the Messiah: Moses, Abraham, Zenos, Zenoch, Ezias, Isaiah, and Jeremiah, as well as all the prophets both before and after Abraham. Thus the Book of Mormon quotes nine specific prophets from the plates of brass who testified of Christ (the seven above plus Joseph and Neum). It also testifies of many prophets before Abraham, and all those after Abraham. Only five of the nine specified are presently in the Old Testament. The total number of prophets who testified of Christ are not known to us but would have been many.

The Nephite Prophets on the Small Plates of Nephi

The Nephite prophets foretold of Christ in many ways and by various names. Lehi saw him descending out of heaven, and Christ ministered to him. He described him as one whose "luster was above that of the sun at noon-day" (1 Nephi 1:9) and referred to him as the Lord, the Messiah, or the Son of God (see 1 Nephi 1:18–19; 10:4–17).

The Lord visited Nephi, son of Lehi, and spoke to him (see 1 Nephi 2:16, 19; 2 Nephi 11:2). He referred to him as the God of Abraham, Isaac, and Jacob (see 1 Nephi 6:4), the Messiah, and knew "his name shall be Jesus Christ, the Son of God" (see 2 Nephi 25:18–20). He was shown Christ's earthly ministry to the Jews and his appearance to the Nephites after his resurrection (see 1 Nephi 11–12). He testified of his doctrine and mission among the children of men (see 2 Nephi 31–33).

Jacob also saw Christ (see 2 Nephi 2:3–4; 11:3). An angel told Jacob the name of Christ and of his coming among the Jews (see 2 Nephi 10:3). Jacob's purpose in writing upon the plates was to persuade man to "believe in Christ, and view his death, and suffer his cross and bear the shame of the world" (Jacob 1:8).

Enos was forgiven of his sins because of his faith in Christ (see Enos 1:5–8). From that point in his life he declared "the truth which is in Christ" and knew he would "soon go to the place of my rest, which is with my Redeemer" (Enos 1:26–27). Jarom did not name the prophets but recorded that they were "persuading [the people] to look forward unto the Messiah, and believe in him to come as though he already was" (Jarom 1:11).

There were five men who recorded upon the plates called the Book of Omni. The first four of these writers' records were very brief, covering over a hundred-year time period in less than one page in our present text. Two of the four mentioned only that the promise of the Lord was verified, that "Inasmuch as ye will not keep my commandments ye shall not prosper in the land" (Omni 1:6). The last recorder, Amaleki, told of the Lord warning the righteous to leave the land of Nephi and of the discovery of a people who had a large stone that was interpreted and told of a people coming "from the tower, at the time the Lord confounded the language of the people" (Omni 1:22). This brief writing verifies that the Lord was involved at the time the nations of the earth were dispersed and the languages became different. Amaleki concluded his record by "exhorting all men to come unto God, the Holy One of Israel" and testified that Christ "is the Holy One of Israel" (Omni 1:25–26).

Mormon was so impressed with the small plates, "which contained this small account of the prophets from Jacob down to the reign of this King Benjamin, and also many of the words of Nephi . . . because of the prophecies of the coming of Christ," that he chose to finish his record upon them and to include them with the remainder of his abridgment. The Spirit whispered to him to do this, and his prayer was that his brethren would "once again come to the knowledge of God, yea, the redemption of Christ" (W of M 1:3–8). As Mormon finished his record upon these small plates, he recorded that King Benjamin was able to drive out the Lamanites because of the strength of the Lord; to put down the false Christs; and, with the help of the prophets, establish peace (see W of M 1:12–18).

Thus the small plates of Nephi record the testimony of six Nephite prophets, plus Mormon and other unnamed prophets who testified of Christ. Their testimonies are powerful and extensive, covering Christ's birth, ministry, mission, and doctrine. These six Nephite prophets, plus the mighty testimonies of the biblical prophets Isaiah, Jeremiah, and Zenos, and others from the plates of brass, should persuade all men to "believe in Christ, and view his death, and suffer his cross and bear the shame of the world," as Jacob desired (Jacob 1:8).

The Nephite Prophets on the Large Plates

The abridgment of the large plates of Nephi, that are in our present-day Book of Mormon, begins with the last recorded sermon of King Benjamin (see Mosiah 2:9–3:27). This powerful sermon is divided into two parts and is centered around Christ, although he is not so named until he quotes the words of an angel who had appeared unto him (see Mosiah 3:2). The words quoted were so powerful that all of the king's subjects fell to the earth (see Mosiah 4:1. They foretell the coming of Christ to the earth, his ministry, Atonement, crucifixion, resurrection, and judgment. Although the second part of the king's sermon is focused toward mankind, their relationship to Christ is the prevalent theme.

The reader next encounters another king, Limhi by name. He testified of the God of Abraham, Isaac, and Jacob who brought Israel through the Red Sea and that Christ should take upon him the image of man (see Mosiah 7:19, 27). Ammon, a man from the land of Zarahemla, taught king Limhi about king Mosiah, who was a prophet and revelator (see Mosiah 8:13–18). Ammon was not a prophet, but king Mosiah knew of Christ and testified of him in a later speech recorded in the last chapter of the book named for him (see Mosiah 29).

Abinadi was sent among the subjects of wicked King Noah and delivered extensive testimony of Jesus Christ. He testified that the Lord their God was the person of whom the law of Moses was a type and shadow and was the Messiah who was to come among the children of men (see Mosiah 13:29–35). As a commentary upon Isaiah, he testified further of Christ's role as the Father and the Son—one eternal God—and his power to break the bands of death and bring about the resurrection (see Mosiah 14–15). He testified further "that only in and through Christ ye can be saved . . . who is the very Eternal Father" (Mosiah 16:13–15). Abinadi was put to death because of his testimony of Christ (see Mosiah 17). Because of Abinadi's testimony, Alma was converted and established the Church of Christ among the apostate Nephites of king Noah's time.

The people of Alma, and another group under Ammon, were led back to Zarahemla. In their accounts there is further testimony of Christ, such as the covenant to grant eternal life to Alma and Alma's rebirth experience (see Mosiah 26:14–32; 27:25–31). Also, as mentioned previously, king Mosiah speaks of the relationship of God [Christ] and the government. Thus the book of Mosiah has the testimony of six prophets counting Isaiah, who testified of Christ, and not counting Ammon, who was an emissary of Christ to lead the people to Zarahemla.

Alma, the son of Alma, is the first prophet (in the book called after his name) to testify of Christ. His words spoken to the people of Zarahemla (see Alma 5), and his words to the people of Gideon (see Alma 7), are both centered in Christ. He is later joined by Amulek, and their testimonies of Christ to the people of Ammonihah are also recorded (see Alma 9–13). Chapters seventeen through twenty-six are an account of the mission of the sons of Mosiah to the Lamanites. The testimonies of Ammon and Aaron concerning Christ are recorded (see Alma 18:24–35; 22:8–14), and the other sons of Mosiah and those accompanying them certainly bore testimony of him, as well.

The testimonies of Alma and Amulek to the Zoramites are centered in Christ and are included in chapters thirty through thirty-four. Chapters thirty-six through forty-two are the words of Alma to his three sons (Helaman, Shiblon, and Coriantumr) and expound the doctrine of Christ. The final testimony of Alma is recorded in Alma 45 as he turned over the records to Helaman.

Throughout the war chapters (see Alma 43–62), General Moroni's testimony of Christ is given directly (see Alma 46:23–27) and indirectly by Mormon as he abridged the record (see Alma 46–48). General Moroni's testimony included a prophecy of Jacob, the father of the twelve tribes of Israel, that God would preserve a remnant of his son Joseph (see Alma 46:23–26). Although there are no other recorded testimonies in these war chapters, Helaman's faith in God and his 2,060 Lamanite warriors is repeatedly mentioned. Thus there are five prophets, counting General Moroni as a prophet, whose strong testimonies are recorded in the book of Alma, plus the words of the Patriarch Jacob, and the faith in God of Helaman and his sons.

The book of Helaman bears witness of Helaman and his people having faith in Christ (see Hel. 3:35) but does not record any of the people's words. Helaman's words to his two sons reflect his great faith in Christ (see Hel. 5:6–12). These two sons, Nephi and Lehi, went throughout the land preaching with great power, but their words were not recorded. We do have the admonition of Aminadab, a Nephite by birth, to have faith in Christ (see Hel. 5:35–41). The words of Nephi, the son of Helaman who succeeded his father as chief judge, are recorded later, and he does testify of Christ (see Hel. 7:13–29; 8:11–28). Following these words, the words of Christ, the Lord God Almighty, spoken to Nephi are recorded (see Hel. 10:4–11). The prophecy of Samuel the Lamanite is lengthy and Christ-centered (see Hel. 13–15).

The book of Helaman has only three prophets whose testimonies of Christ are recorded. These are Helaman, Nephi son of Helaman, and Samuel the Lamanite. Certainly Lehi, Nephi's brother, and others did testify of him.

The words of Christ to Nephi, son of Nephi, are recorded (3 Nephi 1:13–14), and it is stated that Lachoneus uttered great and marvelous words and prophecies, but his words were not recorded. Mormon inserted a testimony of Christ as he abridged the record, but he will be considered as a prophet following the time of Christ. Therefore, there are no other testimonies of Christ by prophets recorded in the early chapters of 3 Nephi, although there were many spoken, and the unabridged records will certainly reflect these. However, there are fourteen prophets whose testimonies of Christ are recorded on the large plates of Nephi in the time period before the coming of Christ. There are several others who did bear testimony, but due to the abridgment of these plates, their testimonies of Christ are not included.

The Nephite Prophets After the Time of Christ

Third Nephi, from chapters nine through twenty-eight, is a brief account of the Savior's ministry among the Nephites. Although he chose twelve apostles and sent them out to preach to the people, their testimonies are not recorded. The book of 4 Nephi is a four-page summary of 286 years of the Nephite record and contains no words of the prophets. Therefore, the only testimonies of Jesus Christ by prophets recorded after the time of Christ are Mormon's (see Morm. 5:8–24; 6:17–22; 7:2–10) and Moroni's (see Moroni 10). These two prophets' testimonies are glorious and powerful.

The Jaredite Prophets

The book of Ether is also an extremely brief account. Many of the words in the book are the words or testimony of the abridger, Moroni (see Ether 2:9–12; 4:4–5:6; 8:20–26; 12:6–41). There are several accounts of many prophets testifying to the Jaredite people (see Ether 7:23–26; 9:28; 11:1, 12, 20), but only two Jaredite prophets have their testimonies of Christ recorded. These two prophets are the brother of Jared and Ether. The brother of Jared saw the premortal Christ and conversed with him (see Ether 3:2–28). Ether prophesied many great and marvelous things but, although he saw the days of Christ, only his prophecies of the establishment of Zion societies are recorded (see Ether 12:1–5; 13:2–12). Emer also saw the Redeemer, but none of his words were recorded (see Ether 9:22).

Summary

There are twenty-four prophets whose testimonies of Christ are recorded in the Book of Mormon. In addition there are numerous other statements about other prophets who also testified. When the unabridged record becomes available, their testimonies will be known. All the prophets in the Book of Mormon testified of Christ, and many of these testimonies are recorded. The book is indeed another testament of Jesus Christ.

16

GIFTS AND CALLINGS OF GOD

Those "who should believe in the gifts and callings of God by the Holy Ghost" should have eternal life." (D&C 20:26–27)

The Book of Mormon gives a list of the gifts of the Spirit, which is very similar to those written by Paul (see 1 Cor. 12) and those revealed to Joseph Smith (see D&C 46). The gifts enumerated by Moroni are a good summary of the teachings of the Book of Mormon on the subject of spiritual gifts. The Prophet Joseph Smith wrote an editorial in the early newspaper *Times and Seasons* giving guidance to the Saints regarding the various gifts of the Spirit. His words are a fitting introduction to a review of the gifts mentioned in the Book of Mormon.

> Various and conflicting are the opinions of men in regard to the gift of the Holy Ghost. Some people have been in the habit of calling every supernatural manifestation the effects of the Spirit of God, whilst there are others that think there is no manifestation connected with it at all; and that it is nothing but a mere impulse of the mind, or an inward feeling, impression, or secret testimony or evidence, which men possess, and that there is no such thing as an outward manifestation.

It is not to be wondered at that men should be ignorant, in a great measure, of the principles of salvation, and more especially of the nature, office, power, influence, gifts, and blessings of the gift of the Holy Ghost; when we consider that the human family have been enveloped in gross darkness and ignorance for many centuries past, without revelation, or any just criterion [by which] to arrive at a knowledge of the things of God, which can only be known by the Spirit of God. Hence it not infrequently occurs, that when the Elders of this Church preach to the inhabitants of the world, that if they obey the Gospel they shall receive the gift of the Holy Ghost, that the people expect to see some wonderful manifestation, some great display of power, or some extraordinary miracle performed; and it is often the case that young members of this Church for want of better information, carry along with them their old notions of things, and sometimes fall into egregious errors. We have lately had some information concerning a few members that are in this dilemma, and for their information make a few remarks upon the subject. (*TPJS,* 242)

After recording his promise to the reader to "ask God, the Eternal Father, in the name of Christ, if [the Book of Mormon] is not true" (Moro. 10:4), Moroni gives some conditional exhortation for knowing the truthfulness of the Book of Mormon. One of these exhortations was to "deny not the gifts of God" (Moro. 10:8). He gave this warning because it is through "the gifts of God" that the truthfulness of the Book of Mormon is manifest; and salvation in the kingdom of God, in the dispensation of the fulness of times, is dependent upon one's accepting and following the teachings of the Book of Mormon. Moroni further exhorts us to know that these manifestations are not all the same: "They are many; and they come from the same God. [Furthermore], there are different ways that these gifts are administered; but it is the same God who worketh all in all [i.e., each one is for the same purpose]; and they are given by the manifestations of the Spirit of God unto men, to profit them" (Moro. 10:8). Moroni then lists nine separate gifts of the Spirit. Since there are a variety of people and situations in the world, Moroni seems to exhort the readers to acknowledge whatever gift the Lord may choose to manifest to them. One should not expect to have a duplicate experience of a friend, a neighbor, or of an occasional sensational episode that is published or spread by word of mouth. While the Lord does give externally observable manifestations of the Holy Ghost, most often the Spirit works in a quiet and internal fashion. We need to recognize that the Lord will choose the gift that is best for us; but through that gift, he will make known to us that the Book of Mormon is true.

The nine gifts of the Spirit written by Moroni were not meant to be all-inclusive. They are, however, representative of ways that we can know all truth. Before listing the nine gifts of the Spirit, Moroni testified that "by the power of the Holy Ghost ye may know the truth of all things" (Moro. 10:5). Moroni also testified that the reader "may know that [Christ] is by the power of the Holy Ghost" (Moro. 10:7). This is also a gift of the Spirit. The first gift revealed to Joseph Smith the Prophet was "to know that Jesus is the Son of God" (D&C 46:13). Therefore, there are ten gifts spoken of by Moroni as he concluded the Book of Mormon record. We will note in this chapter examples from the Book of Mormon that illustrate the ten gifts of the Spirit listed by Moroni.

Know That Jesus Is the Son of God

There are two ways to know that Jesus is the Christ: "To some it is given by the Holy Ghost to know that Jesus Christ is the Son of God, and that he was crucified for the sins of the world. To others it is given to believe on their words, that they also might have eternal life if they continue faithful" (D&C 46:13–14). The first way is a direct gift, given by the Holy Ghost. The second way is to believe on the testimony, or the words, of those who know by that gift. Both of these ways are illustrated in the account of Abish, the Lamanite woman, who had "been converted unto the Lord for many years, on account of a remarkable vision of her father" (Alma 19:16). Her father had a direct gift of the Spirit given to him, and she had believed on his words and also came to know of the Christ. The Lord apparently gave these manifestations in preparation for the successful missionary work of the sons of Mosiah among the Lamanites.

Another example of coming to know Jesus Christ through these two ways is Lehi and Nephi. We do not know if Lehi obtained his testimony of Christ before the initial experience recorded in the Book of Mormon, but there he saw one whose "luster was above that of the sun at noon-day," followed by twelve others, "and the first came and stood before" Lehi (1 Nephi 1:9–11). Certainly he then knew of Christ by the power of the Holy Ghost. After telling his family and others of this marvelous experience, his son Nephi prayed unto the Lord, having great desires to know of the mysteries of God. The Lord visited Nephi "and did soften [his] heart that [he] did believe all the words which had been spoken by [his] father" (1 Nephi 2:16).

Paul taught the Corinthian Saints that "No man can say that Jesus is the Lord, but by the Holy Ghost" (1 Cor. 12:3). The Prophet Joseph said this passage "should be translated 'no man can *know* that Jesus is the Lord, but by the Holy Ghost'" (*TPJS*, 223; italics added). There are other examples in the Book of Mormon, but the two examples above illustrate the gift to know that Jesus is the Christ.

Teach the Word of Wisdom

The first of the nine gifts listed by Moroni, after exhorting us not to deny the gifts of God, follows: "To one is given by the Spirit of God, that he may teach the word of wisdom" (Moro. 10:9). Wisdom is generally interpreted to be the application of knowledge.

However, Alma taught his son Shiblon that he had taught him of Christ "that ye may learn wisdom, that ye may learn of me that there is no other way or means whereby man can be saved, only in and through Christ" (Alma 38:9). Perhaps Moroni listed it first, intending to reflect Alma's teaching of wisdom being a knowledge of salvation through Christ. This wisdom is the epitome of the gift of the Spirit, but it certainly applies to all of the principles of the gospel. Alma went on to encourage his son to "continue to teach; and I would that ye would be diligent and temperate in all things" (Alma 38:10), implying that he should seek the spirit in all of his teaching. Some people are given a gift to analyze and interpret the scriptures in a manner so that "he that preacheth and he that receiveth, understand one another, and both are edified and rejoice together" (D&C 50:22). Emma Smith was called by the Lord "to expound scriptures, and to exhort the [women of the] church, according as it shall be given thee by my Spirit" (D&C 25:7). This is a latter-day example of this gift.

The Prophet Joseph taught that "the word of wisdom, and the word of knowledge, are as much gifts as any other, yet if a person possessed both of these gifts, or received them by the imposition of hands, who would know it?" (*TPJS,* 246). The two gifts mentioned are not externally observable.

Teach the Word of Knowledge

The second of the nine gifts, enumerated by Moroni, was that to some it was given a gift "that he may teach the word of knowledge by the same Spirit" (Moro. 10:10). This gift of teaching is exemplified in the Book of Mormon by the sons of Mosiah. These sons "had waxed strong in the knowledge of the truth; for they were men of a sound understanding and they had searched the scriptures diligently, that they might know the word of God" (Alma 17:2). In teaching the Lamanite king Lamoni, Ammon "began at the creation of the world, and also the creation of Adam, and told him all the things concerning the fall of man, and rehearsed and laid before him the records and the holy scriptures of the people, which had been spoken by the prophets, even down to the time that their father, Lehi, left Jerusalem" (Alma 18:36). Aaron taught the father of king Lamoni in the same manner: "Aaron did expound unto him the scriptures from the creation of Adam, laying the fall of man before him, and their carnal state and also the plan of redemption, which was prepared from the foundation of the world, through Christ, for all whosoever would believe on his name" (Alma 22:13; see also vv. 12 and 14). These two sons of king Mosiah certainly had a gift of knowledge of the scriptures and taught them by the Spirit, as their results verify (Alma 26:3–22).

Exceeding Great Faith

The gift of "exceedingly great faith" was next cited by Moroni (Moro. 10:11). The Book of Mormon records numerous examples of faith that are varied in nature and principle. As Moroni abridged the record of the Jaredites, he listed several examples of what had been accomplished among the Nephites through their faith (Ether 12:6–19). We will not repeat them here but urge you to review them. Faith, in its many manifestations, is given as a gift of the Spirit to some that it may profit the rest of us. The gift of faith is a catalyst to all the other gifts. Joseph Smith said that "a man who has none of the gifts has no faith; and he deceives himself, if he supposes he has" (*TPJS,* 270).

Gifts of Healing

"The gifts of healing by the same Spirit" (Moro. 10:11) is stated in the plural by Moroni. This plural rendering may be because of the many different infirmities that can be healed by this gift, or it may be because of the healings coming either immediately or through a more prolonged period of the natural body processes. These processes might be speeded up through this gift of healing. Another possible reason for the plural *gifts* is because of the spiritual healings as well as the physical ones. An example of an immediate healing is Alma blessing Zeezrom:

3 And also Zeezrom lay sick at Sidom, with a burning fever, which was caused by the great tribulations of his mind on account of his wickedness, for he supposed that Alma and Amulek were no more; and he supposed that they had been slain because of his iniquity. And this great sin, and his many other sins, did harrow up his mind until it did become exceedingly sore, having no deliverance; therefore he began to be scorched with a burning heat.

4 Now, when he heard that Alma and Amulek were in the land of Sidom, his heart began to take courage; and he sent a message immediately unto them, desiring them to come unto him.

5 And it came to pass that they went immediately, obeying the message which he had sent unto them; and they went in unto the house unto Zeezrom; and they found him upon his bed, sick, being very low with a burning fever; and his mind also was exceedingly sore because of his iniquities; and when he saw them he stretched forth his hand, and besought them that they would heal him.

6 And it came to pass that Alma said unto him, taking him by the hand: Believest thou in the power of Christ unto salvation?

7 And he answered and said: Yea, I believe all the words that thou hast taught.

8 And Alma said: If thou believest in the redemption of Christ thou canst be healed.

9 And he said: Yea, I believe according to thy words.

10 And then Alma cried unto the Lord, saying: O Lord our God, have mercy on this man, and heal him according to his faith which is in Christ.

11 And when Alma had said these words, Zeezrom leaped upon his feet, and began to walk; and this was done to the astonishment of all the people; and the knowledge of this went forth throughout all the land of Sidom. (Alma 15:3–11)

The Book of Mormon does not speak of any healings that took place over an extended time period, but it does speak of many who "were healed of their sicknesses and their infirmities, [and] did truly manifest unto the people that they had been wrought upon by the Spirit of God, and had been healed" (3 Nephi 7:22; see also 4 Nephi 1:5). That some of these were not immediate is suggested from the Lord's directions to the sick given in the law of the Church: "And whosoever among you are sick, and have not faith to be healed, but believe, shall be nourished with all tenderness, with herbs and mild food, and that not by the hand of the enemy" (D&C 42:43). That the Book of Mormon people followed similar practices is shown from the account of the people under Helaman, son of Alma:

And there were some who died with fevers, which at some seasons of the year were very frequent in the land—but not so much so with fevers, because of the excellent qualities of the many plants and roots which God had prepared to remove the cause of diseases, to which men were subject by the nature of the climate. (Alma 46:40)

The Spirit may direct people to use these plants and roots, or other remedies, and through their faith be healed.

Work Mighty Miracles

Another gift of the Spirit mentioned by Moroni is that a person "may work mighty miracles" (Moro. 10:12). Alma and

Amulek were imprisoned; and Alma, through his faith, asked for deliverance:

> *27 And the earth shook mightily, and the walls of the prison were rent in twain, so that they fell to the earth; and the chief judge, and the lawyers, and priests, and teachers, who smote upon Alma and Amulek, were slain by the fall thereof.*
>
> *28 And Alma and Amulek came forth out of the prison, and they were not hurt; for the Lord had granted unto them power, according to their faith which was in Christ. And they straightway came forth out of the prison; and they were loosed from their bands; and the prison had fallen to the earth, and every soul within the walls thereof, save it were Alma and Amulek, was slain; and they straightway came forth into the city. (Alma 14:27–28)*

Nephi and Lehi, sons of Helaman, had a similar experience in prison, but the walls did not fall (see Hel. 5:21–44). Moroni listed "the change upon the Lamanites" as one of the great miracles that was accomplished by faith (Ether 12:14). President Harold B. Lee called the healing of the soul "one of the greatest miracles."[58]

Prophesy Concerning All Things

The gift to "prophesy concerning all things" is next enumerated by Moroni (Moro. 10:13). "All things" may be interpreted to mean foretelling all things from the beginning to the end, or it may mean to prophesy concerning anything that the Lord wants the Spirit to make manifest to a person. Both interpretations are exemplified in the Book of Mormon. Nephi, son of Lehi, saw and prophesied of the future of the Jews (see 1 Nephi 11), the Nephites and Lamanites (see 1 Nephi 12), and of the Gentiles to the end of

---

58 Williams, C. J. (1996). *The Teachings of Harold B. Lee*, p. 120. Salt Lake City: Bookcraft.

the world (see 1 Nephi 13–14). He did not write his prophecies of
the very end of the world, because the Apostle of the Lamb (John)
was commissioned to write this account (1 Nephi 14:18–27 and
the book of Revelation). The angel who showed Nephi these things
declared: "And also others who have been, to them hath he shown
all things, and they have written them; and they are sealed up to
come forth in their purity, according to the truth which is in the
Lamb, in the own due time of the Lord, unto the house of Israel"
(1 Nephi 14:26). The brother of Jared was one of those who saw
and wrote of the happenings of man to the end of the world (see
Ether 3:25). Others were Adam (see D&C 107:56), Enoch (see
Moses 7:67), Abraham (see Abraham 3), and Moses (see Moses
1:27–29). The Lord spoke to Isaiah saying that he declares "the
end from the beginning" (Isaiah 46:10). Isaiah very probably was
shown these things also. In our own dispensation Joseph Smith was
shown many terrible things of the future (see JD 2:147). Through
the Spirit a man can prophesy of things from the beginning to the
end.

The Book of Mormon also records prophecies of what men
will say and do in a coming situation. Nephi foretold what the
brother of the chief judge would say and do as he was confronted
with the charge of having slain the chief judge (see Hel. 8:27–28;
9:25–37). Alma foretold what would happen to the Nephites "in
four hundred years from the time that Jesus Christ shall manifest
himself unto them" (Alma 45:9–16). Samuel the Lamanite foretold
the signs and conditions that would come in five years when Christ
would be born, and of his death following his ministry (see Hel.
13–15). The gift of the Spirit can tell of all things to come.

Angels and Ministering of Spirits

The next gift of the Spirit listed by Moroni is "the beholding
of angels and ministering spirits" (Moro. 10:14). After the Spirit of
the Lord spoke unto Nephi "as a man speaketh with another" (1
Nephi 11:11), an angel came down and guided Nephi through his

vision of Jerusalem, the Nephites, and the Gentile nations (1 Nephi 11:14; 14:29). An angel told Jacob the name of Christ (see 2 Nephi 10:3). An angel awoke King Benjamin and told him concerning the coming of Christ (see Mosiah 3:2–27). An angel appeared to Alma and the sons of Mosiah and called them to repentance (see Mosiah 27:11–17). Jacob bore testimony that he "truly had seen angels, and they had ministered unto [him]" (Jacob 7:5). Nephi, son of Nephi, had such great faith "on the Lord Jesus Christ that angels did minister unto him daily" (3 Nephi 7:18). The Book of Mormon also teaches the office and ministry of angels (Moro. 7:31),[59] but our purpose here is only to confirm the ministering of angels as a gift of the Spirit.

A problem often arises in relation to the ministry of angels and how to discern between angels of God and angels of the devil. This is technically another gift of the Spirit, "the discerning of spirits" (D&C 46:23). Since it is not listed by Moroni, we will indicate it as part of the gift of ministering of angels as a means to discern between the devil and his angels and the messengers from God (see D&C 129).

The Book of Mormon gives us another key for discerning of the devil's angels from messengers of God. Paul taught that the devil may appear as an angel of light (see 2 Cor. 11:14). Jacob, brother of Lehi, gave an important qualification of appearances of the devil. He taught that Satan "transformeth himself *nigh* unto an angel of light" (2 Nephi 9:9, italics added). There is a discernable difference between the countenance of Satan and an angel of God. Those who have not seen the glory of an angel would be more easily deceived. When Satan appeared to Moses following the appearance of Christ, claiming to be the Son of God, Moses asked, "Where is thy glory" (Moses 1:13). Only heavenly messengers have a glory that attends them; therefore, it is important to understand the distinction between the *spirits of the just* as "heavenly messengers" and *resurrected beings,* or angels, as "heavenly messengers." The

---

59 See Nyman, M. S. (1991). *The Most Correct Book,* chapter 6. Salt Lake City: Bookcraft.

Prophet Joseph taught: "Spirits can only be revealed in flaming fire and glory. Angels have advanced further, their light and glory being tabernacled; and hence they appear in bodily shape. The spirits of just men are made ministering servants to those who are sealed unto life eternal, and it is through them that the sealing power comes down" (*TPJS*, 325).

There is also a difference in the feelings experienced or accompanying an angel of God and an angel of the devil. The angel of God brings joy, peace, and light. The spirit of the devil brings darkness and fear. The Lord revealed the key to the Church when they were receiving spirits they could not understand: "And that which doth not edify is not of God, and is darkness. That which is of God is light; and he that receiveth light, and continueth in God, receiveth more light; and that light groweth brighter and brighter until the perfect day" (D&C 50:23–24). Those who live close to the Spirit will have the gift of discernment. An angel of the devil appeared to Korihor and deceived him (see Alma 30:53). There were undoubtedly many more instances of the devil appearing among the Nephites as evidenced by the many warnings and admonitions given to them in the Book of Mormon. Joseph Smith also gave extensive warnings in regards to the discerning of false spirits (see *TPJS*, 206–7; 213–15).

Tongues and the Interpretation of Languages

The last two gifts of the Spirit mentioned by Moroni are related: "all kinds of tongues," and "the interpretation of languages and of divers kinds of tongues" (Moro. 10:15–16). Joseph the Prophet declared, "The gift of tongues is the smallest gift perhaps of the whole, and yet it is the one that is most sought after" (*TPJS*, 246). The fact that it is the smallest gift is perhaps why there is only one specific incident in the Book of Mormon where speaking in tongues may have happened. When one of the queens of the Lamanites, the wife of king Lamoni, was revived from having been overpowered by the Spirit (see Alma 19:13), she was "filled with joy, speaking many words which were not understood" (Alma 19:30). There is no record of her words being interpreted, which leaves a question in our minds. Were her words not understood by anyone or just by the majority that were present? The fact that the queen was filled with joy suggests that it was the Spirit that moved her to speak, and therefore she did speak in tongues. The absence of accounts of speaking with tongues among the Nephites may be because, as the Prophet Joseph said, "Tongues were given for the purpose of preaching among those whose language is not understood; as on the day of Pentecost, etc., and it is not necessary for tongues to be taught to the Church particularly" (*TPJS*, 148–49). On the other hand, Amalaki exhorts all men to believe "in the gift of speaking with tongues, and in the gift of interpreting languages" (Omni 1:25). The Lamanite queen account was among a people of another language, but most of the Book of Mormon record is not. The knowledge of the gift in the days of Amalaki may have been due to the discovery of the large stone giving an account of Coriantumr, the last of the Jaredites (see Omni 1:21). However, Alma warned the people of Ammoniah that it was far more tolerable for the Lamanites not to believe than for them because they had been highly favored of the Lord. They had experienced many gifts including "the gift of speaking with tongues" (Alma 9:21). Therefore, we know that the gift was had among the Nephites.

The interpretation of languages and of divers kinds of tongues is actually rarely mentioned in the Book of Mormon. Mosiah (the first) interpreted the engravings upon the stone giving an account of Coriantumr, and he did it "by the gift and power of God" (Omni 1:20). The Prophet Joseph also admonished the Saints: "Do not speak in tongues except there be an interpreter present; the ultimate design of tongues is to speak to foreigners" (*TPJS*, 247).

Aminadi interpreted "the writing which was upon the wall of the temple, which was written by the finger of God" (Alma 10:2). Once again, the abridged record did not include this amazing account, but it does verify that the gift of interpreting languages was had among the Nephites. In finishing his father's record, Moroni warned against saying that there were no "speaking with tongues, and the interpretation of tongues" (Morm. 9:7; see also 3 Nephi 29:6). He was speaking of the day when the Book of Mormon would come forth. The extent of their being among the Nephites is not known, but they are gifts of the Spirit, and the two gifts go together as the Prophet Joseph Smith said.

The ending of Moroni's exhortation regarding the gifts of God is a fitting conclusion to this chapter: "And all these gifts come by the Spirit of Christ; and they come unto every man severally, according as he will. And I would exhort you, my beloved brethren, that ye remember that every good gift cometh of Christ" (Moro. 10:17–18).

Conclusion

A man who has none of the gifts has no faith; and he deceives himself, if he supposes he has. (TPJS, 270)

And all these gifts come by the Spirit of Christ; and they come unto every man severally, according as he will. And I would exhort you, my beloved brethren, that ye remember that every good gift cometh of Christ. (Moroni 10:17–18)

17

THE HOLY GHOST

*"the Holy Ghost, which beareth record of the Father and of the Son
. . . which Father, Son, and Holy Ghost are one God, infinite and
eternal, without end. Amen." (D&C 20:27–28)*

The first Article of Faith of The Church of Jesus Christ of Latter-day Saints is, "We believe in God the Eternal Father, and in his Son, Jesus Christ, and in the Holy Ghost." Although the three members of the Godhead are unified, each has a separate role. The Prophet Joseph Smith said: "Everlasting covenant was made between three personages before the organization of this earth, and relates to their dispensation of things to men on the earth; these personages, according to Abraham's record, are called God the first, the Creator; God the second, the Redeemer; and God the third, the witness or Testator" (*TPJS,* 190). The primary role of the Testator is to bear "record of the Father and of the Son" (D&C 20:27; see also John 15:26). However, as stated above, we learn from the Savior's ministry to the Nephites that all of these members of the Godhead bear record of each other. Jesus taught: "I bear record of the Father, and the Father beareth record of me, and the Holy Ghost beareth record of the Father and me" (3 Nephi 11:32).

Christ Bears Record of the Father

When Jesus appeared among the Nephites, he said he would declare unto them his doctrine. He then qualified his doctrine as "the doctrine which the Father hath given unto me, and *I bear record of the Father*" (3 Nephi 11:31–32; italics added; see also v. 35). As Jesus ministered to the Nephites, he repeatedly told them that he was teaching what the father had commanded him to teach (see 3 Nephi 15:16, 18–19; 17:2; 18:14). Following his three-day ministry to the Nephites, he appeared to his disciples and declared: "Behold I have given unto you my gospel, and this is the gospel which I have given unto you—that I came into the world to do the will of my Father, because my Father sent me" (3 Nephi 27:13). Therefore the Book of Mormon bears witness that the doctrine that he taught, or the gospel of Christ, came from the Father. Jesus taught the same concept to the Jews in his earthly ministry:

> *14 Now about the midst of the feast [of Tabernacles] Jesus went up into the temple, and taught.*
>
> *15 And the Jews marvelled, saying, How knoweth this man letters, having never learned?*
>
> *16 Jesus answered them, and said, My doctrine is not mine, but his that sent me.*
>
> *17 If any man will do his will, he shall know of the doctrine, whether it be of God, or whether I speak of myself. (John 7:14–17)*

The Book of Mormon and the Bible bear witness of the Father as the source of Christ's doctrine.

Nephi, son of Lehi, also prophesied of the doctrine of Christ (see 2 Nephi 31:1–2). He foretold of the baptism of the Lamb of God to fulfill all righteousness and explained that the fulfilling of all righteousness in being baptized by water was to show "unto the children of men that, according to the flesh he humbleth himself before the Father, and witnesseth unto the Father that he would be obedient unto him in keeping his commandments" (2 Nephi 31:7). Nephi then posed the question, "Wherefore, my beloved brethren, can we follow Jesus save we shall be willing to keep the commandments of the Father?" (2 Nephi 31:10). To the Nephites, Jesus bore "record that the Father commandeth all men, everywhere, to repent and believe in me" (3 Nephi 11:32). The example was set by Jesus for all mankind to keep the Father's commandments.

Another dimension of Christ carrying out the Father's plan of salvation is his overseeing of the work upon the earth. The angel who appeared to King Benjamin said:

> *3 Awake, and hear the words which I shall tell thee; for behold, I am come to declare unto you the glad tidings of great joy.*
>
> *4 For the Lord hath heard thy prayers, and hath judged of thy righteousness, and hath sent me to declare unto thee that thou mayest rejoice; and that thou mayest declare unto thy people, that they may also be filled with joy.*
>
> *5 For behold, the time cometh, and is not far distant, that with power, the Lord Omnipotent who reigneth, who was, and is from all eternity to all eternity, shall come down from heaven among the children of men. (Mosiah 3:3–5)*

From previous instructions of Nephi and Jacob, we can assume that King Benjamin had prayed to the Father (see 2 Nephi 32:9; Jacob 4:5). However, it was Christ the Lord Omnipotent who answered King Benjamin's prayer (see Mosiah 3:4, 17–23). Christ reigns in heaven as the administrator of the gospel and in that role bears witness of the Father's plan, "the glad tidings" (Mosiah 3:3) that tell us the way to return to his presence. As we pray to the Father, we do so in the name of Christ; and as the mediator of the gospel plan, Christ may also answer those prayers through angels or the Holy Ghost giving revelation to outline the path to eternal life. But, they "minister according to the word of his command" (Moro. 7:30).

The Father Bears Record of the Son

Sometime following the great destruction on the American continent, twenty-five hundred Nephites were gathered at the temple in the land Bountiful (see 3 Nephi 11:1; 17:25). As they were conversing about Jesus Christ, "they heard a voice as if it came out of heaven." This voice was repeated three times until they understood it (see 3 Nephi 11:2–6). It was the voice of the Father saying: "Behold my Beloved Son, in whom I am well pleased, in whom I have glorified my name—hear ye him" (3 Nephi 11:7). The Father has similarly introduced his Son on other occasions: (1) at the baptism of Christ in the Jordan River (see Matt. 3:17); (2) on the Mount of Transfiguration to Peter, James, and John (see Matt. 17:5); and (3) to Joseph Smith in the Sacred Grove in New York (see JS–H 1:17). There were certainly other occasions that have not been recorded. The Father's admonition to "hear ye him" is an acknowledgment that Christ has been delegated the authority to fulfill the plan of salvation and direct all of the Father's affairs regarding this earth. The significance of this doctrine is shown in Joseph Smith's translation of the Bible: "And no man hath seen God at any time, except he hath borne record of the Son; for except it is through him no man can be saved" (JST John 1:19). The Father has given the Son complete authority and responsibility for the salvation of the earth's inhabitants; and whenever the Father appears to man, he verifies the position of his Son.

Nephi, son of Lehi, quoted the Father as saying, "repent ye, and be baptized in the name of my Beloved Son" (2 Nephi 31:11). He also heard the voice of the Son, saying: "He that is baptized in my name, to him will the Father give the Holy Ghost, like unto me; wherefore, follow me, and do the things which ye have seen me do" (2 Nephi 31:12). After being instructed further on the ordinance of baptism, Christ's teachings were confirmed to Nephi by "a voice from the Father, saying: Yea, the words of my Beloved are true and faithful. He that endureth to the end, the same shall be saved" (2 Nephi 31:15). The Father bore witness of the Son to Nephi because Nephi believed in the Son. Again, the Bible teaches the same doctrine. Jesus acknowledged John the Baptist as the burning and shining light who had witnessed for him (see John 5:32–35) and then declared:

> *36 But I have greater witness than that of John: for the works which the Father hath given me to finish, the same works that I do, bear witness of me, that the Father hath sent me.*

> *37 And the Father himself, which hath sent me, hath borne witness of me. Ye have neither heard his voice at any time, nor seen his shape.*

> *38 And ye have not his word abiding in you: for whom he hath sent, him ye believe not. (John 5:36–38)*

Unlike Nephi, the Jews had not received the Father's witness because of their unbelief.

The Holy Ghost Bears Record of the Father and Christ

After giving the commandment to the Nephites to be baptized, Jesus testified: "Whoso believeth in me believeth in the Father also; and unto him will the Father bear record of me, for he will visit him with fire and with the Holy Ghost . . . and the Holy Ghost will bear record unto him [that believeth] of the Father and me" (3 Nephi 11:35–36). The Holy Ghost bears record of the Father in different ways. The Nephites could not understand the voice of the Father until the third time, when they were in tune with the Spirit (3 Nephi 11:2–6). The Lamanites, who were witnesses of Nephi and Lehi being encircled as if by fire, also heard a voice from heaven three distinct times (see Hel. 5:25–33): "It was not a voice of thunder, neither was it a voice of great tumultuous noise, but behold, it was a still voice of perfect mildness, as it had been a whisper, and it did pierce even to the very soul" (Hel. 5:30; compare 1 Kings 19:11–12). Some of the words of the voice were recorded and some were "marvelous words which cannot be uttered by man" (Hel. 5:33). As these amazed Lamanites continued to call unto the voice, they too were encircled as if in the midst of flaming fire:

> *44 And they were filled with that joy which is unspeakable and full of glory.*
>
> *45 And behold, the Holy Spirit of God did come down from heaven, and did enter into their hearts, and they were filled as if with fire, and they could speak forth marvelous words.*
>
> *46 And it came to pass that there came a voice unto them, yea, a pleasant voice, as if it were a whisper, saying:*
>
> *47 Peace, peace be unto you, because of your faith in my Well Beloved, who was from the foundation of the world. (Hel. 5:44–47)*

Therefore the voice of the Father is understood through the Holy Spirit of God.

To the Nephites, Jesus quoted the Father as saying to Abraham, "In thy seed shall all the kindreds of the earth be blessed—unto the pouring out of the Holy Ghost through me upon the Gentiles" (3 Nephi 20:27). Thus the Holy Ghost bears record of the Father by blessing the Gentiles through Christ, which will eventually bring about his covenant to gather the house of Israel and at the same time give the Gentiles an opportunity to be numbered with the house of Israel (see 3 Nephi 30).

The Holy Ghost also bears record of Christ in other ways. As discussed above, Nephi had been shown the ministry of Jesus and prophesied that when Christ "was baptized with water the Holy Ghost (would descend) upon him in the form [sign] of a dove" (2 Nephi 31:8). The New Testament records the fulfillment of Nephi's prophecy (see Matt. 3:16; Mark 1:10; Luke 3:22; John 1:32). The "form" of the dove meaning the "sign" of the dove was learned, or was verified to Joseph Smith, in the writings of Abraham (see facsimile #2, explanation of figure 7). The disciples of Jesus knew of the authenticity of Jesus as the Christ, or the Messiah, by this sign of the Holy Ghost.

When Jesus appeared to the Nephites in A.D. 34, he invited them to come forth and:

> *14 ...thrust your hands into my side, and also that ye may feel the prints of the nails in my hands and in my feet, that ye may know that I am the God of Israel, and the God of the whole earth, and have been slain for the sins of the world.*
>
> *15 And it came to pass that the multitude went forth, and thrust their hands into his side, and did feel the prints of the nails in his hands and in his feet; and this they did do, going forth one by one until they had all gone forth, and did see with their eyes and did feel with their hands, and did know of a surety and did bear record, that it was he, of whom it was written by the prophets, that should come. (3 Nephi 11:14–15)*

To know of a surety must have been by a witness of the Holy Ghost. Brigham Young taught:

> I have proven to my satisfaction, according to the best knowledge I can gather, that man can be deceived by the sight of the natural eye, he can be deceived by the hearing of the ear, and by the touch of the hand; that he can be deceived in all of what are called the natural senses. But there is one thing in which he cannot be deceived. What is that? It is the operations of the Holy Ghost, the Spirit and power of God upon the creature. It teaches him of heavenly things; it directs him in the way of life; it affords him the key by which he can test the devices of man; and which recommends the things of God.[60]

---

60 *Journal of Discourses*, 18:230.

As quoted previously, "no man can *know* that Jesus is the Lord, but by the Holy Ghost" (1 Cor. 12:3; *TPJS*, 223, italics added). According to the Gospel of John, one of the missions of the Holy Ghost is to bear witness of Christ: "But when the Comforter is come, whom I will send unto you from the Father, even the Spirit of truth, which proceedeth from the Father, he shall testify of me" (John 15:26).

When Jesus granted the three Nephite apostles their desire to remain on the earth and bring souls unto him, he spoke of the oneness of him and his Father and then proclaimed: "And the Holy Ghost beareth record of the Father and me; and the Father giveth the Holy Ghost unto the children of men, because of me" (3 Nephi 28:11). This promise is further evidence of the Holy Ghost's role as a "witness or testator" (*TPJS*, 190). Once more the Bible (John 15:26 above) and the Book of Mormon (3 Nephi 28:11 above) act as two witnesses of gospel principles.

Nephi, son of Lehi, bore testimony that the Holy Ghost "witnesses of the Father and the Son, unto the fulfilling of the promise which he hath made, that if ye entered in by the way [the gate and path to eternal life] ye should receive [the Holy Ghost]" (2 Nephi 31:18). The three members of the Godhead are all involved in the plan of salvation, testifying of each other in bringing "to pass the immortality and eternal life of man" (Moses 1:39).

The Father, Son, and Holy Ghost Are One God

Prior to 1820, the doctrine of the trinity was almost universally accepted in the Christian world. This doctrine basically teaches that the Godhead is three entities engulfed into one. When Joseph Smith emerged from his experience in the Sacred Grove, he knew of a surety that the traditional doctrine of the trinity was not true. He had been visited by two heavenly personages, one of whom had introduced the other: "This is my Beloved Son" (JS–H 2:17). This experience was the basis for Joseph Smith's teaching the correct doctrine of the Godhead, and subsequent experiences and revelations further substantiated his knowledge. He later declared: "I have always declared God to be a distinct personage, Jesus Christ a separate and distinct personage from God the Father, and that the Holy Ghost was a distinct personage and a Spirit: and these three constitute three distinct personages and three Gods" (*TPJS*, 370).

The doctrine of the Godhead introduced by Joseph Smith was so upsetting to the Christian world that it led to his martyrdom in 1844 at the young age of thirty-eight. Is it just a coincidence, or is it a parallel of the Book of Mormon prophet Abinadi? Abinadi was slain because he taught:

> ... *that Christ was the God, the Father of all things, and said that he should take upon him the image of man, and it should be the image after which man was created in the beginning; or in other words, he said that man was created after the image of God, and that God should come down among the children of men, and take upon him flesh and blood, and go forth upon the face of the earth.* (Mosiah 7:27)

While the doctrinal truth that the Godhead includes three separate personages, two having bodies of flesh and bones and the third a personage of spirit (see D&C 130:22), has been proclaimed by the elders of the Church since Joseph Smith's day, the question has often arisen about the Book of Mormon teachings on this subject. Why doesn't this sacred volume of scripture contain a more concise statement on this doctrine? Not only does it lack a clear, concise explanation of the subject, but there are also statements within the Book of Mormon that seem to lend support to the traditional concept of the trinity that is taught in the Christian world. This question has usually been quickly passed off by admitting that the Book of Mormon is not a good scripture from which to teach the Godhead. The issue is further complicated by the testimony of the three witnesses to the Book of Mormon. On the surface, their testimony appears to be an endorsement of a triune God.

A careful examination of the Book of Mormon passages which speak of the three members of the Godhead show that they do teach the correct concept of the Godhead but emphasize their unity. The key to the statement of the witnesses and to the passages in the Book of Mormon about the three members of the Godhead is the verb usage. The verb "is" is a singular verb, while the verb "are" is plural. Both verbs are used in the Book of Mormon in conjunction with the Father, the Son, and the Holy Ghost. The context of the passage reflects why the singular or the plural verb is used and at the same time teaches important truths about the Godhead.

The Oneness of the Godhead

The testimony of the witnesses concludes with a declaration that the Father, the Son, and the Holy Ghost *is* one God. Why is the singular verb used? The entire testimony of the witnesses is concerning the latter-day work being the work of God the Father and His Son, the Lord Jesus Christ. They further testify that they know of a surety of the truthfulness of this work. This sure knowledge came through a witness of the Holy Ghost, who is God the Testator. The following excerpts from "The Testimony of Three Witnesses" illustrate the above concepts.

> Be It Known unto all nations, kindreds, tongues, and people, unto whom this work shall come: That we, through the grace of God the Father, and our Lord Jesus Christ, have seen the plates which contain this record. . . . And we also know that they have been translated by the gift and power of God, for his voice hath declared it unto us; wherefore we know of a surety that the work is true. And we also testify that we have seen the engravings which are upon the plates; and they have been shown unto us by the power of God, and not of man. . . . and we know that it is by the grace of God the Father, and our Lord Jesus Christ, that we behold and bear record that these things are true. And

it is marvelous in our eyes. Nevertheless, the voice of the Lord commanded us that we should bear record of it. . . . And the honor be to the Father, and the Son, and to the Holy Ghost, which *is* one God. Amen.

The singular verb used with all three members of the Godhead is appropriate in the context of the testimony. All three members are involved in the plan of salvation, revealed through the Book of Mormon, for the inhabitants of this world. The Godhead is one in perfect unity for the administering of this plan and work in such complete harmony and agreement that their efforts become *one* effort. The plan of salvation presented in the premortal council of heaven was a singular plan. The plan was the plan of the Father; the Son offered himself and was chosen to carry out this plan:

> *1 And I, the Lord God, spake unto Moses, saying: That Satan, whom thou hast commanded in the name of mine Only Begotten, is the same which was from the beginning, and he came before me, saying—Behold, here am I, send me, I will be thy son, and I will redeem all mankind, that one soul shall not be lost, and surely I will do it; wherefore give me thine honor.*

> *2 But, behold, my Beloved Son, which was my Beloved and Chosen from the beginning, said unto me—Father, thy will be done, and the glory be thine forever.*

> *3 Wherefore, because that Satan rebelled against me, and sought to destroy the agency of man, which I, the Lord God, had given him, and also, that I should give unto him mine own power; by the power of mine Only Begotten, I caused that he should be cast down. (Moses 4:1–3)*

Jesus repeatedly verified that He was on earth only to carry out the will of the Father. "I can of my own self do nothing: as I hear, I judge: and my judgment is just; because I seek not mine own will, but the will of the Father which hath sent me" (John 5:30; see also John 6:38; 7:16–17). Together, the three individuals are carrying out the one singular plan and are in complete harmony, unity, and purpose. Therefore, when the plan is spoken of, the singular verb is appropriate.

Oneness of Doctrine

Other passages within the Book of Mormon are also consistent in their context with the use of the singular verb. Nephi, in concluding his record, writes concerning the doctrine of Christ (see 2 Nephi 31). After a lengthy and beautiful explanation of the doctrine, Nephi emphasizes that there is only one way or doctrine whereby man can be saved.

> *And now, behold, my beloved brethren, this is the way; and there is none other way nor name given under heaven whereby man can be saved in the kingdom of God. And now, behold, this is the doctrine of Christ, and the only and true doctrine of the Father, and of the Son, and of the Holy Ghost, which is one God, without end. Amen. (2 Nephi 31:21)*

Note again that the singular verb is used. There is only one doctrine; and those who would suggest an alternate plan, or doctrine, have not learned it through the messenger of the Godhead, the Holy Ghost. As one studies the unity of doctrine represented in the Godhead, he should seek that Messenger in his own life in order to comply with this singular doctrine.

Oneness of Judgment

In another Book of Mormon passage, Amulek bore testimony that in the resurrection "every thing shall be restored to its perfect frame, as it is now, or in the body, and shall be brought and be arraigned before the bar of Christ the Son, and God the

Father, and the Holy Spirit, which *is* one Eternal God, to be judged according to their works, whether they be good or whether they be evil" (Alma 11:44). The Father, the Son, and the Holy Ghost again represent a oneness of the Godhead in the judgment; a complete oneness represented with a singular verb.

The context of the three passages analyzed above exemplifies a complete oneness of the Godhead from eternity [before mortality] to eternity [after mortality]. Before this mortal probation, they were unified in declaring the plan of salvation. During our mortal probation, they are unified in the following of the doctrine of Christ. After this mortal probation of mankind, they shall be unified in bringing about the resurrection and judgment. In the context of the above verses, the Father, the Son, and the Holy Ghost is one God.

Three Separate Personages

Although there is a oneness in the three members of the Godhead, they are separate individuals as shown in the beginning of this chapter. This is also recognized in the Book of Mormon. Ammon and Aaron taught from the scriptures that man was created in the image of God (see Alma 18:34; 22:12). As quoted earlier, Abinadi was slain for teaching that Christ took upon him the image of man (see Mosiah 7:27). Christ taught the brother of Jared that man was created after the image of Christ's spirit (see Ether 3:15–16). The Spirit of the Lord who appeared to Nephi was in the form of a man (see 1 Nephi 11:11).[61] Therefore, the Book of Mormon recognizes the individuality of Christ and implies the separate entities of the other two members of the Godhead. All three members are in the same form as mortal men.

---

61 Some interpret the Spirit of the Lord to be the premortal spirit of Christ. Others believe it to be the Holy Ghost as a spirit personage. We will not discuss the arguments here. The point that we seek to establish is not altered by who the spirit personage is. However, the author's opinion, based on the context and other passages of the Book of Mormon, is that the personage was the Holy Ghost.

Other Book of Mormon passages designating the three individual members of the Godhead use the plural verb. When Christ gave instructions concerning those who were desirous to be baptized in His name, he gave these instructions:

> 23 *Verily I say unto you, that whoso repenteth of his sins through your words, and desireth to be baptized in my name, on this wise shall ye baptize them—Behold, ye shall go down and stand in the water, and in my name shall ye baptize them.*
>
> 24 *And now behold, these are the words which ye shall say, calling them by name, saying:*
>
> 25 *Having authority given me of Jesus Christ, I baptize you in the name of the Father, and of the Son, and of the Holy Ghost. Amen.*
>
> 26 *And then shall ye immerse them in the water, and come forth again out of the water.*
>
> 27 *And after this manner shall ye baptize in my name; for behold, verily I say unto you, that the Father, and the Son, and the Holy Ghost are one; and I am in the Father, and the Father in me, and the Father and I are one."* (3 *Nephi 11:27)*

All three members of the Godhead are mentioned in the baptismal prayer. Christ explained that the three of them *are* one. All three personages are involved in this baptism; and since they are separate individuals, the plural verb is used. The latter part of this statement does not include the Holy Ghost. This was probably given as a verification that the authority given to the disciples to baptize was from Christ but under the direction of the Father.

The scriptures teach us that the fulness of joy is only attainable as a resurrected being: "For man is spirit. The elements are eternal, and spirit and element, inseparably connected, receive a fulness of joy; And when separated, man cannot receive a fulness of joy" (D&C 93:33–34). And from the Book of Mormon: "But, behold, the righteous, the saints of the Holy One of Israel, they who have believed in the Holy One of Israel, they who have endured the crosses of the world, and despised the shame of it, they shall inherit the kingdom of God, which was prepared for them from the foundation of the world, and their joy shall be full forever" (2 Nephi 9:18).

Both the Father and the Son have attained a fulness of joy in their resurrected, perfected state. Because they are two separate individuals, their state of oneness is described with a plural verb: "And for this cause ye shall have fulness of joy; and ye shall sit down in the kingdom of my Father; yea, your joy shall be full, even as the Father hath given me fulness of joy; and ye shall be even as I am, and I am even as the Father; and the Father and I *are* one" (3 Nephi 28:10).

The plural verb is used again with the Godhead in describing the oneness of separate beings who live in the presence of God in a state of happiness:

> And he hath brought to pass the redemption of the world, whereby he that is found guiltless before him at the judgment day hath it given unto him to dwell in the presence of God in his kingdom, to sing ceaseless praises with the choirs above, unto the Father, and unto the Son, and unto the Holy Ghost, which are one God, in a state of happiness which hath no end. (Morm. 7:7)

The members of the Godhead have developed to such a state of righteousness that it has become a part of their nature. It is the character "which is in our great and Eternal Head" (Hel. 13:38). Their perfect natures were recognized by the brother of Jared as being in the Lord Jesus Christ: "Yea, Lord, I know that thou speakest the truth, for thou art a God of truth, and canst not lie" (Ether 3:11–12). All three members of the Godhead have attained perfection in righteousness, and thus all three of their names are appropriately mentioned by using the plural verb.

In summary, the Book of Mormon teaches us the complete oneness of the plan of salvation, doctrine, and judgment of the members of the Godhead. Because there is only one acceptable plan, doctrine, and judgment, a singular verb is appropriate. In carrying out the ordinances and administration of these singular aspects of the plan, all three members of the Godhead are involved, and so a plural verb is appropriate in naming these three members of the Godhead.

As we keep the commandments of God, we too can enjoy the state of happiness described by King Benjamin:

> *And moreover, I would desire that ye should consider on the blessed and happy state of those that keep the commandments of God. For behold, they are blessed in all things, both temporal and spiritual; and if they hold out faithful to the end they are received into heaven, that thereby they may dwell with God in a state of never-ending happiness. O remember, remember that these things are true; for the Lord God hath spoken it. (Mosiah 2:41)*

We will then become one with Christ and the Father. As Christ has said, "Be one; and if ye are not one ye are not mine" (D&C 38:27).

18

ALL MEN MUST REPENT

"And we know that all men must repent and believe on the name of Jesus Christ." (D&C 20:29)

Repentance, to some degree, is an accepted principle among all peoples and religions. In the Judeo-Christian world, it is a prominent theme. In the Old Testament we read of the need for all to repent: "For there is not a just man upon the earth, that doeth good, and sinneth not" (Ecc. 7:20). Various aspects of repentance are also taught: "he shall restore that which he took violently away" (Lev. 6:4); "he shall recompense his trespass with the principle thereof" (Num. 5:7); "make confession unto the Lord God of our fathers" (Ezra 10:11); "I will be sorry for my sin" (Ps. 38:18); "whoso confesseth and forsaketh [sins] shall have mercy" (Prov. 28:13); and "Jacob shall repent of his wickedness" (JST Amos 7:6). In the New Testament, Paul teaches the necessity of repentance to the Romans: "For all have sinned and come short of the glory of God" (Rom. 3:23). The message of John the Baptist was "Repent ye: for the kingdom of heaven is at hand" (Matt. 3:1–2).

Repentance is also a prominent theme in the Book of Mormon. The Book of Mormon teachings on repentance are too extensive to include all of them, but we will emphasize the major concepts and how to adhere to the principle. Lehi taught that, following the fall of Adam and Eve:

. . . the days of the children of men were prolonged, according to the will of God, that they might repent while in the flesh; wherefore, their state became a state of probation, and their time was lengthened, according to the commandments which the Lord God gave unto the children of men. For he gave commandment that all men must repent; for he showed unto all men that they were lost, because of the transgression of their parents. (2 Nephi 2:21)

As previously discussed, men are born innocent but born into an environment of sin; and, "by nature, they fall" (Mosiah 3:16). Because of the fall their "natures have become evil continually" (Ether 3:2), and thus the Holy One of Israel "commandeth all men that they must repent, and be baptized in his name. . . . And if they will not repent, and believe in his name, and be baptized in his name, and endure to the end, they must be damned" (2 Nephi 9:23–24).

Mormon taught that "the first fruits of repentance is baptism" (Moro. 8:25). Since the "first" fruits is baptism, there must be other fruits of repentance. This concept is further supported by Alma's words to the people of Zarahemla. After calling the people to repentance concerning many issues, he said: "I speak by way of command unto you that belong to the church; and unto those who do not belong to the church I speak by way of invitation, saying: Come and be baptized unto repentance, that ye also may be partakers of the fruit of the tree of life" (Alma 5:62). Those who have been baptized still need the principle of repentance. The scriptures help us understand why repentance is a principle of the gospel. In defining the gospel, Jesus said: "And no unclean thing can enter into his kingdom; therefore nothing entereth into his rest save it be those who have washed their garments in my blood, because of their faith, and the repentance of *all* their sins, and their faithfulness unto the end" (3 Nephi 27:19, italics added). As a principle of the gospel, there is a sequence in following it. The steps of repentance are outlined with some variation in Church literature. We will follow a sequence commonly used in the Church and taught in the Book of Mormon.

Recognition and Sorrow for Sin

All people are born into the world with the Spirit of Christ "that [they] may know good from evil" (Moro. 7:16). Therefore, there is no excuse for not recognizing that certain actions are not in harmony with the will of our Heavenly Father. Furthermore, for those who "feast upon the words of Christ," whether baptized or not, "the words of Christ [scripture] will tell [him] all things what [he] should do" (2 Nephi 32:3). For those who are baptized "and receive the Holy Ghost, it will show unto [them] all things that [they] should do" (2 Nephi 32:5). The leaders of the Church are under an obligation to warn and admonish those for whom they have a stewardship. Jacob writes that making these warnings and admonitions is part of magnifying our office unto the Lord.

And we did magnify our office unto the Lord, taking upon us the responsibility, answering the sins of the people upon our own heads if we did not teach them the word of God with all diligence; wherefore, by laboring with our might their blood might not come upon our garments; otherwise their blood would come upon our garments, and we would not be found spotless at the last day. (Jacob 1:19; compare Ezekiel 33:1–9)

That Jacob followed his own counsel is shown earlier in the Book of Mormon. He warned:

45 O, my beloved brethren, turn away from your sins; shake off the chains of him that would bind you fast; come unto that God who is the rock of your salvation.

46 Prepare your souls for that glorious day when justice shall be administered unto the righteous, even the day of judgment, that ye may not shrink with awful fear; that ye may not remember your awful guilt in perfectness, and be constrained to exclaim: Holy, holy are thy judgments, O Lord God Almighty—but I know my guilt; I transgressed thy law, and my transgressions are mine; and the devil hath obtained me, that I am a prey to his awful misery.

47 But behold, my brethren, is it expedient that I should awake you to an awful reality of these things? Would I harrow up your souls if your minds were pure? Would I be plain unto you according to the plainness of the truth if ye were freed from sin?

48 Behold, if ye were holy I would speak unto you of holiness; but as ye are not holy, and ye look upon me as a teacher, it must needs be expedient that I teach you the consequences of sin. (2 Nephi 9:45–48)

Jacob also teaches us of the responsibility of leaders to be compassionate and yet direct in their admonitions. Note his approach to warning his people of the grievous sins of pride and unchastity:

2 Now, my beloved brethren, I, Jacob, according to the responsibility which I am under to God, to magnify mine office with soberness, and that I might rid my garments of your sins, I come up into the temple this day that I might declare unto you the word of God.

3 And ye yourselves know that I have hitherto been diligent in the office of my calling; but I this day am weighed down with much more desire and anxiety for the welfare of your souls than I have hitherto been.

4 For behold, as yet, ye have been obedient unto the word of the Lord, which I have given unto you.

5 But behold, hearken ye unto me, and know that by the help of the all-powerful Creator of heaven and earth I can tell you concerning your thoughts, how that ye are beginning to labor in sin, which sin appeareth very abominable unto me, yea, and abominable unto God.

6 Yea, it grieveth my soul and causeth me to shrink with shame before the presence of my Maker, that I must testify unto you concerning the wickedness of your hearts.

7 And also it grieveth me that I must use so much boldness of speech concerning you, before your wives and your children, many of whose feelings are exceedingly tender and chaste and delicate before God, which thing is pleasing unto God;

8 And it supposeth me that they have come up hither to hear the pleasing word of God, yea, the word which healeth the wounded soul.

9 Wherefore, it burdeneth my soul that I should be constrained, because of the strict commandment which I have received from God, to admonish you according to your crimes, to enlarge the wounds of those who are already wounded, instead of consoling and healing their wounds; and those who have not been wounded, instead of feasting upon the pleasing word of God have daggers placed to pierce their souls and wound their delicate minds.

10 But, notwithstanding the greatness of the task, I must do according to the strict commands of God, and tell you concerning your wickedness and abominations, in the presence of the pure in heart, and the broken heart, and under the glance of the piercing eye of the Almighty God.

11 Wherefore, I must tell you the truth according to the plainness of the word of God. For behold, as I inquired of the Lord, thus came the word unto me, saying: Jacob, get thou up into the temple on the morrow, and declare the word which I shall give thee unto this people. (Jacob 2:2–11)

Through the scriptures and the living prophets people are led to recognize and, if in tune with the Spirit, be sorrowful for sin. However, if people ignore these sources of recognizing sin, they may become hardened in their hearts and past feeling, as happened to Laman and Lemuel (see 1 Nephi 7:8–12; 17:45).

Another danger is their being sorry for their sins, but not unto Godly sorrow. Ungodly sorrow can happen individually or collectively. Mormon recognized this condition among the Nephite society a few years prior to their final destruction:

10 And it came to pass that the Nephites began to repent of their iniquity, and began to cry even as had been prophesied by Samuel the prophet; for behold no man could keep that which was his own, for the thieves, and the robbers, and the murderers, and the magic art, and the witchcraft which was in the land.

11 Thus there began to be a mourning and a lamentation in all the land because of these things, and more especially among the people of Nephi.

12 And it came to pass that when I, Mormon, saw their lamentation and their mourning and their sorrow before the Lord, my heart did begin to rejoice within me, knowing the mercies and the long-suffering of the Lord, therefore supposing that he would be merciful unto them that they would again become a righteous people.

13 But behold this my joy was vain, for their sorrowing was not unto repentance, because of the goodness of God;

but it was rather the sorrowing of the damned, because the Lord would not always suffer them to take happiness in sin.

14 And they did not come unto Jesus with broken hearts and contrite spirits, but they did curse God, and wish to die. Nevertheless they would struggle with the sword for their lives. (Morm. 2:10–14; see also 2 Cor. 7:10)

Being sorry because of embarrassment, or restriction that has resulted from our actions, is not Godly sorrow. We must be sorry because we have offended God, or have caused unhappiness to some of his children: "wickedness never was happiness" (Alma 41:10).

Abandonment of Sin

The Prophet Joseph Smith taught that "Repentance is a thing that cannot be trifled with every day. Daily transgression and daily repentance is not that which is pleasing in the sight of God" (*TPJS,* 148). The Book of Mormon teaches this same concept. King Benjamin taught his subjects that they should "believe that ye must repent of your sins and forsake them" (Mosiah 4:10). Alma told his son Corianton that he "should repent and forsake [his] sins" (Alma 39:9). As Amulek contended with Zeezrom, the crafty lawyer asked if the Son of God shall "save his people in their sins." Amulek answered, "I say unto you he shall not, for it is impossible for him to deny his words." Then Zeezrom attempted to twist Amulek's words and Amulek replied, "Behold thou hast lied, for thou sayest that I spake as though I had authority to command God, because I said he shall not save his people in their sins" (Alma 11:34–36). Years later, Helaman quoted Amulek to his sons Nephi and Lehi:

10 And remember also the words which Amulek spake unto Zeezrom, in the city of Ammonihah; for he said unto him that the Lord surely should come to redeem his people, but that he should not come to redeem them in their sins, but to redeem them from their sins.

11 And he hath power given unto him from the Father to redeem them from their sins because of repentance; therefore he hath sent his angels to declare the tidings of the conditions of repentance, which bringeth unto the power of the Redeemer, unto the salvation of their souls. (Hel. 5:10–11)

The plan of salvation promises that Christ will pay for our sins if we will abandon them.

One of the major purposes of the Church is to help people to repent. The Prophet Joseph Smith observed:

> Christ said he came to call sinners to repentance, to save them. Christ was condemned by the self-righteous Jews because He took sinners into His society; He took them upon the principle that they repented of their sins. It is the object of this society to reform persons, not to take those that are corrupt and foster them in their wickedness; but if they repent, we are bound to take them, and by kindness sanctify and cleanse them from all unrighteousness by our influence in watching over them. Nothing will have such influence over people as the fear of being disfellowshipped by so goodly a society as this. . . .
>
> Nothing is so much calculated to lead people to forsake sin as to take them by the hand, and watch over them with tenderness. When persons manifest the least kindness and love to me, O what power it has over my mind, while the opposite course has tendency to harrow up all the harsh feelings and depress the human mind. (*TPJS*, 240)

As someone proclaimed, the Church is not a graveyard for Saints but a hospital for sinners.

As the Lord revealed to Joseph Smith, "By this ye may know if a man repenteth of his sins—behold, he will confess them and forsake them" (D&C 58:43). This introduces us to a third step in the process of repentance.

Confession of Sin

When Alma sought the Lord's counsel in judging the people for their crimes, the Lord answered: "Therefore I say unto you, Go; and whosoever transgresseth against me, him shall ye judge according to the sins which he has committed; and if he confess his sins before thee and me, and repenteth in the sincerity of his heart, him shall ye forgive, and I will forgive him also. Yea, and as often as my people repent will I forgive them their trespasses against me" (Mosiah 26:29–30). From this passage we learn that there are two personages before whom we must confess: the Lord's servant [thee] and the Lord [me]. Of course the Lord has the ultimate jurisdiction of forgiving sin, but the Lord's servants—judges in Israel—also have the authority and responsibility to judge one's worthiness for membership and/or service in the kingdom. This is evidenced in Alma's actions following the Lord's instructions: "And whosoever repented of their sins and did confess them, them he did number among the people of the church; And those that would not confess their sins and repent of their iniquity, the same were not numbered among the people of the church, and their names were blotted out" (Mosiah 26:35–36). President Spencer W. Kimball outlined the responsibility of the Lord's servants:

> The confession of sin is an important element in repentance. Many offenders have seemed to feel that a few prayers to the Lord were sufficient and they have thus justified themselves in hiding their sins. The Proverbs tell us: "He that covereth his sins shall not prosper: but whoso confesseth and forsaketh them

shall have mercy (Proverbs 28:13; quotes also D&C 58:43 above).

Especially grave errors such as sexual sins shall be confessed to the bishop as well as to the Lord. There are two remissions that one might wish to have: first, the forgiveness from the Lord, and second, the forgiveness of the Lord's church through its leaders. As soon as one has an inner conviction of his sins, he should go to the Lord in "mighty prayer," as did Enos, and never cease his supplications until he shall, like Enos, receive the assurance that his sins have been forgiven by the Lord. It is unthinkable that God absolves serious sins upon a few requests. He is likely to wait until there has been long-sustained repentance as evidenced by a willingness to comply with all his other requirements. So far as the Church is concerned, no priest nor elder is authorized by virtue of that calling to perform this act for the Church. The Lord has a consistent, orderly plan. Every soul in the organized stakes is given a bishop who, by the very nature of his calling and his ordination, is a "judge in Israel." In the missions a branch president fills that responsibility. The bishop may be one's best earthly friend. He will hear the problems, judge the seriousness thereof, determine the degree of adjustment, and decide if it warrants an eventual forgiveness. He does this as the earthly representative of God, who is the master physician, the master psychologist, the master psychiatrist. If repentance is sufficient, he may waive penalties, which is tantamount to forgiveness so far as the church organization is concerned. The bishop claims no authority to absolve sins, but he does share the burden, waive penalties, relieve tension and strain, and he may assure a continuation of church activity. He will keep the whole matter most confidential.

Some missionaries have foolishly carried with them their secret, unadjusted guilt into the field and have suffered seriously in the effort to get and retain the spirit of the mission. The conflict in the soul is most frustrating. But he who totally repents, voluntarily confesses, and clears his difficulty so far as possible, triumphs in his work and enjoys sweet peace.[62]

As noted by President J. Reuben Clark, "I would like to point out that to me there is a great difference between confession and admission, after transgression is proved. I doubt much the efficacy of an admission as a confession."[63] Admissions are often just an acknowledgment that we were caught in our sins. Confessions are an admission of guilt, made to enable the Lord's servants to outline the requirements for forgiveness, and not for embarrassment of the sinner. Confessions should always be treated with strictest confidentiality.

Forgiveness of Sins

Part of the Lord's prayer was: "And forgive us our debts, as we forgive our debtors" (3 Nephi 13:11). Alma had taught his servants the same principle:

31 And ye shall also forgive one another your trespasses; for verily I say unto you, he that forgiveth not his neighbor's trespasses when he says that he repents, the same hath brought himself under condemnation.

32 Now I say unto you, Go; and whosoever will not repent of his sins the same shall not be numbered among my people; and this shall be observed from this time forward. (Mosiah 26:31–32)

---

62 Kimball, S. W. (1972). *Faith Precedes the Miracle,* pp. 181–182. Salt Lake City: Deseret Book.

63 Clark, J. R. (1950). *Conference Report,* April, p. 166.

In modern revelation, the Lord has said, "I the Lord will forgive whom I will forgive, but of you it is required to forgive all men" (D&C 64:10).

Restitution for Sin

Some sins are more serious than others because it is impossible or difficult to make restitution to those offended, or to somehow dispel the harm that has been done. The Book of Mormon illustrates this principle well. The sons of King Mosiah had gone about secretly, "seeking to destroy the Church, and to lead astray the people of the Lord" (Mosiah 27:10). Following their conversion:

> 35 . . . they traveled throughout all the land of Zarahemla, and among all the people who were under the reign of king Mosiah, zealously striving to repair all the injuries which they had done to the church, confessing all their sins, and publishing all the things which they had seen, and explaining the prophecies and the scriptures to all who desired to hear them.
>
> 36 And thus they were instruments in the hands of God in bringing many to the knowledge of the truth, yea, to the knowledge of their Redeemer. (Mosiah 27:35–36)

Alma encouraged his son Corianton to "return unto [the Zoramites] and acknowledge your faults and that wrong which ye have done" (Alma 39:13). Such action by Corianton would be at least the beginning of making restitution. Nephi and Lehi, sons of Helaman, were so effective in confounding the Nephite dissenters who were among the Lamanites "that they came forth and did confess their sins and were baptized unto repentance, and immediately returned to the Nephites to endeavor to repair unto them the wrongs which they had done" (Hel. 5:17). For those sins for which there can be no restitution made, fornication or the loss of virtue for example, we can indirectly make restitution by helping others to prevent the same sins in their lives. This must be done discreetly, and without personal confession, lest it cause rationalization for those whom we are seeking to help. Making restitution is an important element of repentance.

A Time to Repent

A well-known scripture in the Book of Mormon is Alma 34:30–35:

> 30 And now, my brethren, I would that, after ye have received so many witnesses, seeing that the holy scriptures testify of these things, ye come forth and bring fruit unto repentance.

> 31 Yea, I would that ye would come forth and harden not your hearts any longer; for behold, now is the time and the day of your salvation; and therefore, if ye will repent and harden not your hearts, immediately shall the great plan of redemption be brought about unto you.

> 32 For behold, this life is the time for men to prepare to meet God; yea, behold the day of this life is the day for men to perform their labors.

> 33 And now, as I said unto you before, as ye have had so many witnesses, therefore, I beseech of you that ye do not procrastinate the day of your repentance until the end; for after this day of life, which is given us to prepare for eternity, behold, if we do not improve our time while in this life, then cometh the night of darkness wherein there can be no labor performed.

> 34 Ye cannot say, when ye are brought to that awful crisis, that I will repent, that I will return to my God. Nay, ye cannot say this; for that same spirit which doth possess your bodies at the time that ye go out of this life, that

same spirit will have power to possess your body in that eternal world.

35 For behold, if ye have procrastinated the day of your repentance even until death, behold, ye have become subjected to the spirit of the devil, and he doth seal you his; therefore, the Spirit of the Lord hath withdrawn from you, and hath no place in you, and the devil hath all power over you; and this is the final state of the wicked. (Alma 34:30–35)

That we should not procrastinate the day of our repentance is the major message, but we sometimes miss another important message.

The "same spirit" that will have power to possess our bodies in the eternal world, if we do not repent, is the spirit of the devil. When we have the opportunity for the Spirit of Christ to come into our lives and neglect to receive it, the spirit of the devil will abide with us into the hereafter. Therefore, this day—now—is truly the day to repent that we may become righteous through the Spirit of the Lord and have that Spirit dwell in our hearts. Alma continues: "And this I know, because the Lord hath said he dwelleth not in unholy temples, but in the hearts of the righteous doth he dwell; yea, and he has also said that the righteous shall sit down in his kingdom, to go no more out; but their garments should be made white through the blood of the Lamb" (Alma 34:36).

The Book of Mormon thus warns against the popular doctrine of the world: deathbed repentance. Joseph Smith further substantiates this Book of Mormon teaching:

> We should take warning and not wait for the death-bed to repent, as we see the infant taken away by death, so may the youth and middle-aged, as well as the infant be suddenly called into eternity. Let this, then, prove as a warning to all not to procrastinate repentance, or wait till a death-bed, for it is the will of

God that man should repent and serve Him in health, and in the strength and power of his mind, in order to secure his blessing, and not wait until he is called to die. (*TPJS*, 197)

Elder Melvin J. Ballard gave this thoughtful observation:

> It is my judgment that any man or woman can do more to conform to the laws of God in one year in this life than they could in ten years when they are dead. The spirit only can repent and change, and then the battle has to go forward with the flesh afterwards. It is much easier to overcome and serve the Lord when both flesh and spirit are combined as one. This is the time when men are more pliable and susceptible. When clay is pliable, it is much easier to change than when it gets hard and sets.
>
> This life is the time to repent. That is why I presume it will take a thousand years after the first resurrection until the last group will be prepared to come forth. It will take them a thousand years to do what it would have taken, but three score years and ten to accomplish in this life.[64]

Summary

With an understanding of repentance, we should learn that it is easier to prevent sin than to repent. Thus Alma's admonition to Corianton to "not risk one more offense against your God upon those points of doctrine, which ye have hitherto risked to commit sin" (Alma 41:9) is appropriate to end this discussion, along with a further admonition of Alma. To Corianton he cautioned, "And now, my son, I desire that ye should let these things trouble you no more, and only let your sins trouble you, with that trouble which

---

64 Hinckley, B.S. (1949). *Sermons and missionary services of Melvin J. Ballard*, p. 241. Salt Lake City: Deseret Book.

shall bring you down unto repentance" (Alma 42:29). It is reported that Mark Twain was once asked which of all the scriptures bothered him the most. His answer was, "the ones I understand." May we understand the commandments of God, live them, and repent of our sins.

19

WORSHIP THE FATHER

All men must "worship the father in [Christ's] name."

(D&C 20:29)

The basic form of worship is prayer. Amulek equated Zenos' teachings on prayer with worship (see Alma 33:3). We "worship the Father in [Christ's] name" individually and collectively as a church. The Book of Mormon has a constant theme of prayer running from the first chapter, where Lehi prays "with all his heart, in behalf of his people" (1 Nephi 1:5), through the last chapter, where Moroni exhorts the reader to "ask God, the Eternal Father, in the name of Christ" if the Book of Mormon is not true (Moro. 10:4). This chapter will not cover all the examples of prayer in the Book of Mormon but will focus on principles of prayer that the book teaches.

To Whom Do We Pray?

We pray to the Father, which recognizes him as our Father and also acknowledges that he has the power to bring about our requests. It is an acknowledgment that he is our God, a glorious supreme being.

There are several passages in the Book of Mormon to confirm the proper salutation of prayer. Nephi, son of Lehi, tells us, "ye shall pray unto the Father in the name of Christ" (2 Nephi 32:9). Jacob, the brother of Nephi, described his people by saying that "they believed in Christ and worshiped the Father in his name" (Jacob 4:5). Thus, the Nephites during the Old Testament time period were praying to the Father in the name of Christ. In the equivalent New Testament era of the Book of Mormon, they were instructed to pray in the same manner. When Jesus appeared to the Nephites, he taught them, "ye must always pray unto the Father in my name" (3 Nephi 18:19). That the righteous Nephites were still following this pattern, about four hundred years later, is shown by Moroni's exhortation to the future reader of the Book of Mormon to "ask God, the Eternal Father, the name of Christ" (Moro. 10:4).

Occasionally a question arises concerning the Nephites' praying to Jesus when he appeared to them (see 3 Nephi 19:18). The question is answered as one continues to read. Jesus departed from those who were praying to him and prayed to the Father, himself. In his prayer, undoubtedly for the Nephites' benefit, and now for ours as we read the account, he explained that "they pray unto me because I am with them" (3 Nephi 19:22). Because Jesus is also a God, a resurrected glorified being, it is only natural for righteous men and women who are in his presence to pray unto him. This concept is shown in the dedicatory prayer of the Kirtland Temple. In this prayer, given by revelation, the Prophet Joseph Smith frequently addresses Jehovah, or Jesus Christ (D&C 109:34, 42, 56) but formally addresses the prayer to the Holy Father (see D&C 109:4) and makes further requests of him (vv. 14, 22, 24, 29, 47). Since it was the dedication of the house of the Lord [Jesus Christ], he was certainly present, and that is probably the reason Joseph prayed directly to him. When Jehovah is addressed, it seems to be for requests that come under his role as the Son. The requests made to Jehovah would probably be answered by him. This is suggested by the angel who appeared to King Benjamin, who declared that "the Lord [Christ, the Lord Omnipotent, Mosiah 3:17] hath heard thy prayers, . . . and hath sent me to declare unto thee" (Mosiah

3:4). Although Christ may answer our prayer, it is the Father to whom we are instructed to pray.

How Do We Pray?

The Book of Mormon teaches us to pray by or in the Spirit. Nephi admonishes us, "If ye would hearken unto the Spirit which teacheth a man to pray ye would know that ye must pray; for the evil spirit teacheth not a man to pray, but teacheth him that he must not pray" (2 Nephi 32:8). The Spirit teaches us to pray by guiding us in our prayers. When the Nephites prayed to Jesus "they did still continue, without ceasing, to pray unto him; and they did not multiply many words, for it was *given unto them* what they should pray, and they were filled with desire" (3 Nephi 19:24, italics added). As previously discussed, the New Testament teaches the same concept of praying in the Spirit (see Rom. 8:26; Eph. 6:18; and Jude 1:20). The latter part of the Roman's scripture, given a plainer translation by Joseph Smith, is repeated here for emphasis: "The Spirit maketh intercession for us with *striving* which cannot be expressed" (*TPJS*, 278). Through the Spirit we can communicate Spirit to Spirit: "He that asketh in Spirit shall receive in Spirit" (D&C 46:28). Furthermore, the Spirit would eliminate vain repetitions in our prayers (3 Nephi 13:7).

As we learn to use the Spirit in our prayers, we can receive more and more of the things for which we ask. This is illustrated in the Book of Mormon. The disciples were told: "And whatsoever ye shall ask the Father in my name, which is right, believing that ye shall receive, behold it shall be given unto you" (3 Nephi 18:20). In contrast, the Nephite Twelve were told by Jesus that "whatsoever things ye shall ask the Father in my name shall be given unto you" (3 Nephi 27:28). This promise was apparently given to them because they had learned, or would learn, to pray by the Spirit. The Twelve in Jerusalem were given the same promise (see John 15:16). Nephi, son of Helaman, was told "all things shall be done unto thee according to thy word, for thou shalt not ask that which is contrary to my will" (Hel. 10:5). Those who pray in the Spirit may have the same assurance.

How Often Should We Pray?

Jesus taught the Nephite multitude that they should pray "as I have prayed among you" and that they "must watch and pray always lest ye enter into temptation; for Satan desireth to have you, that he may sift you as wheat" (3 Nephi 18:16, 18). Note that Jesus associated not praying with Satan, just as Nephi did (see 2 Nephi 32:8). Nephi went on to emphasize the constant use of prayer, as did Jesus to the Nephite disciples: "But behold, I say unto you that ye must pray always, and not faint; that ye must not perform any thing unto the Lord save in the first place ye shall pray unto the Father in the name of Christ, that he will consecrate thy performance unto thee, that thy performance may be for the welfare of thy soul" (2 Nephi 32:9). However, to pray always does not mean to be always praying verbally, but that we should always have a prayer in our heart. Amulek probably said this best: "Yea, and when you do not cry unto the Lord, let your hearts be full, drawn out in prayer unto him continually for your welfare, and also for the welfare of those who are around you" (Alma 34:27).

Although we should always have a prayer in our heart, there are instructions in the Book of Mormon for the times of more formal prayer. Amulek taught the Zoramites to "Cry unto him in your houses, yea, over all your household, both morning, mid-day, and evening" (Alma 34:21). Alma taught his son Helaman in a similar way:

> *36 Yea, and cry unto God for all thy support; yea, let all thy doings be unto the Lord, and whithersoever thou goest let it be in the Lord; yea, let all thy thoughts be directed unto the Lord; yea, let the affections of thy heart be placed upon the Lord forever.*

37 Counsel with the Lord in all thy doings, and he will direct thee for good; yea, when thou liest down at night lie down unto the Lord, that he may watch over you in your sleep; and when thou risest in the morning let thy heart be full of thanks unto God; and if ye do these things, ye shall be lifted up in the last day. (Alma 37:36–37)

In summary, we should pray formally two or three times a day but always have a prayer in our heart.

Where Should We Pray?

Alma quoted the prophet Zenos, whose instructions are now lost from the Old Testament, concerning prayer or worship (see Alma 33:3). Zenos acknowledged that the Lord had answered his prayers "in the wilderness"; "in my field"; in "my house"; in "my closet"; and "in the midst of thy congregations" (Alma 33:4–9). In other words, the Lord will hear our prayers wherever and whenever they are uttered. However, there are more sacred areas we should establish as places for worship or prayer on a daily basis. Jesus taught: "But thou, when thou prayest, enter into thy closet, and when thou hast shut thy door, pray to thy Father who is in secret; and thy Father, who seeth in secret, shall reward thee openly" (3 Nephi 13:6; compare Matt. 6:6). Other translations of the Sermon on the Mount given in Galilee (which is almost identical to the Nephite sermon) render the phrase "enter into thy closet" slightly differently. Some examples are: "thine inner chamber"; "thy secret chamber"; "go into your own room"; or "go into a room by yourself."[65] From these translations, it seems evident that Jesus is teaching his disciples to establish a place where they can feel close to their Father in Heaven and communicate with him without being interrupted.

---

65 Vaughan, C., Ed. (1967). *The New Testament from 26 Translations*, p. 21. Grand Rapids: Zonderven.

For What Should We Pray?

The Spirit will direct our prayers, not by dictation of words, but by giving us ideas in our minds. Of course there are things for which we repeatedly pray that are not vain repetitions. The Savior gave us a pattern for these things in what is known as the Lord's Prayer (see 3 Nephi 13:9–13). As given in the Book of Mormon account, we should pray for the Father's will to be done on earth. This would include a prayer for the work of the Church to go forward and a blessing for those who are carrying out that work (i.e., the general authorities, the stake presidents, bishops, missionaries, and others). We should pray for forgiveness and the ability to forgive others. This relates to our relationships with others. We should ask for protection and guidance from temptations, harms, and evil. We should pray for truth and wisdom. The Prophet Joseph said, "The best way to obtain truth and wisdom is not to ask it from books, but to go to God in prayer, and obtain divine teaching" (*TPJS,* 191). Thus, we seek learning by faith (see D&C 88:118). As we pray for various things, we end by recognizing the source of the granting of these blessings, or the protection we seek, through Jesus Christ.

Some raise a question of why there are differences in the Nephite and the Galilean rendering of the Lord's Prayer. First of all, it was not meant to be a set prayer as it has become. Jesus introduced the prayer by saying, "After this manner therefore pray ye" (3 Nephi 13:9; Matt. 6:9), indicating a pattern of prayer, not a prayer that is to be memorized and recited. Perhaps he purposely altered the prayer to illustrate it was not a set prayer. The two notable differences, (1) "Thy kingdom come" and (2) "give us this day our daily bread," are not stated to the Nephites. When Jesus gave the instructions in Galilee, the kingdom had not been established; but when they were given to the Nephites, it had. This is perhaps why the request for the kingdom to come is not included in the Nephite prayer. The request for daily bread may have been because of conditions that did and would exist in Palestine. Twice Christ miraculously provided bread for the multitude (Matt. 14:15–21; 15:32–37). He accused some of only seeking "free lunches" because of these miracles, and then taught them that he was the bread of life (see John 6:22–35). Among the Nephites, the concept of bread was never taught except as part of the sacrament. Perhaps the Nephites did not need to be reminded of the concept of bread being a gift from God, as did the Galileans. There are probably other reasons.

There are other things for which we should pray, according to the Book of Mormon. Amulek enumerates many things to be included in our prayers (see Alma 34:18–25). The list includes requests for blessings on our physical possessions, blessings for self, and protection from the devil and our enemies. These things can be rather easily correlated with the Lord's prayer.

Other examples of prayer and worship are the individual prayers recorded in the Book of Mormon. The prayer of Enos gives us an example of someone praying for the welfare of his soul (Enos 1:2–8); and through the Spirit coming upon him, his concern turned to his brethren the Nephites (Enos 1:9–10). His concern then turned to his enemies the Lamanites (Enos 1:11–18). The example of Enos shows how to attain the higher level of Christ's gospel and "love your enemies, bless them that curse you, do good to them that hate you, and pray for them who despitefully use you and persecute you" (3 Nephi 12:44). To pray for the welfare of others is a recognition that God and Christ have a power beyond our own to bless them.

The prayer of Alma for the Zoramites is another example to follow. He asked the Lord for understanding and compassion on the suffering caused by the wickedness of the people and then asked for strength to endure those afflictions. He prayed for success for himself and his fellow laborers among the apostate Zoramites and acknowledged before the Lord that their souls were precious; therefore, he sought wisdom and power to bring their souls to the Lord (see Alma 31:26–35). This is an example of praying for the will of the Lord to be done.

There are also examples of how not to pray. Jesus said: "And when thou prayest thou shalt not do as the hypocrites, for they love to pray, standing in the synagogues and in the corners of the streets, that they may be seen of men. Verily I say unto you, they have their reward" (3 Nephi 13:5; see also Matt. 6:5). The prayer of the apostate Zoramites on their Rameumpton illustrates this teaching of Jesus. They offered the same, vain, repetitious prayer, in the same place; and then "returned to their homes, never speaking of their God again until they had assembled themselves together again" (Alma 31:13–23). Their prayer showed thoughtless egotism.

Of course proper fasting increases our prayer's effectiveness and thus our worship of the Father. When we pray, the answers will come, although perhaps not in the manner that we expect. As stated before, it most often comes through the still small voice to our mind (see Enos 1:10; 1 Kings 19:11–12). The Prophet Joseph gave this admonition to the brethren:

> The Lord cannot always be known by the thunder of His voice, by the display of His Glory or by the manifestation of His power, and those that are the most anxious to see these things, are the least prepared to meet them, and were the Lord to manifest His powers as He did to the children of Israel, such characters would be the first to say, "Let not the Lord speak any more, lest we His people die."
>
> We would say to the brethren, seek to know God in your closets, call upon him in the fields. Follow the directions of the Book of Mormon, and pray over, and for your families, your cattle, your flocks, your herds, your corn, and all things that you possess; ask the blessing of God upon all your labors, and everything that you engage in. Be virtuous and pure; be men of integrity and truth; keep the commandments of God; and then you will be able more perfectly to understand the difference between right and wrong—between the

things of God and the things of men; and your path will be like that of the just, which shineth brighter and brighter unto the perfect day. (*TPJS*, 247)

There are many other principles of prayer taught in the Book of Mormon, and many of these are shown in the other principles discussed in other chapters. The formula for improvement of our prayers is given in the pages of the Book of Mormon. We must obtain the Spirit to guide us and teach us how to pray. As we pray we are worshiping the father in the name of Christ.

The Sacrament

One of the purposes of government, as taught in the Book of Mormon, is "to grant unto [the people] their sacred privileges to worship the Lord their God" (Alma 50:39). The people should have the privilege (agency) to worship under a free government. Another of the basic forms of worship provided by the Church, and taught in the Book of Mormon, is through the ordinance of partaking of the sacrament.

A Commandment

On the first day of his divine ministry among the Nephites, "Jesus commanded his disciples that they should bring forth some bread and wine unto him":

2 And while they were gone for bread and wine, he commanded the multitude that they should sit themselves down upon the earth.

3 And when the disciples had come with bread and wine, he took of the bread and brake and blessed it; and he gave unto the disciples and commanded that they should eat.

4 And when they had eaten and were filled, he commanded that they should give unto the multitude. (3 Nephi 18:2–4)

Thus the ordinance of the sacrament was initiated by Jesus as he began his ministry among the Nephites.

In abridging the Nephite record, Mormon recorded "that the Lord truly did teach the people, for the space of three days; and after that he did show himself unto them oft, and did break bread oft, and bless it, and give unto them" (3 Nephi 26:13). Moroni tells us that following his ministry, the Church "did meet together oft to partake of bread and wine, in remembrance of the Lord Jesus" (Moro. 6:6).

Under the law of Moses, because the people were stiffnecked and "quick to do iniquity, and slow to remember the Lord their God," ordinances were observed "strictly from day to day, to keep them in remembrance of God and their duty towards him" (Mosiah 13:29–30). The sacrament introduced by Jesus replaced many of these ordinances; but because the people more readily believed in and followed the teachings of their Redeemer, it was not administered daily. How often the Book of Mormon does not say, but from the practice followed today we assume it was on a weekly basis. The gospel is the same yesterday, today and forever. The Book of Mormon does instruct us on how to administer the sacrament.

One Ordained to Minister

Jesus instructed the Nephite disciples: "Behold there shall one be ordained among you, and to him will I give power that he shall break bread and bless it and give it unto the people of my church, unto all those who shall believe and be baptized in my name. And this shall ye always observe to do, even as I have done, even as I have broken bread and blessed it and given it unto you" (3 Nephi 18:5–6). The one ordained may be interpreted as one holding the keys for the whole Church, the president of the Church (D&C 132:7); or it may be the bishop, or branch president, responsible for the sacrament in each ward or branch of the Church; or it may be interpreted as a statement of authority, that the sacrament ordinance is to be performed by someone holding the priesthood.

Moroni, speaking of the time of Jesus' ministry, tells of "The manner of their *elders and priests* administering the flesh and blood of Christ unto the church; and they administered it according to the commandments of Christ; wherefore we know the manner to be true; and the elder or priest did minister it—And they did kneel down with the church, and pray to the Father [worship] in the name of Christ" (Moro. 4:1–2, italics added). Moroni's description seems to favor the later interpretation, the sacrament being administered by a holder of the priesthood. Nonetheless, in the Church today, the bishop is the one responsible for overseeing the ordinance of the sacrament in the congregation, and the president of the Church does hold the keys for the whole Church; thus, all three of the above interpretations are valid. That the elder or priest "did kneel down with the church" would probably give a more accurate reading, "did kneel down in behalf of the church." This interpretation is taken from the practice of the Church today. As the elder or priest kneels, he represents all of the congregation. When we say "Amen," we are acknowledging that the prayer was also in our behalf.

The wording for the sacrament prayers was given to the Nephites by the Savior; they are among the few set prayers in the Church (Moro. 4:3; 5:2). The same prayers are recorded in the Doctrine and Covenants for the latter-day Church (see D&C 20:77–79). These prayers reveal the purpose of our partaking and, in essence, are a summary of what Jesus taught the Nephites about the sacrament.

In Remembrance and Testimony

In the Christian world today, there are various beliefs about the partaking of the sacrament. Some believe the blessing of the emblems brings a literal change upon the bread and wine—either before or after they are partaken. Others believe that partaking brings the "real presence" of Christ to them. Still another belief is that the ordinance is done in remembrance of Christ and his mission. The Book of Mormon verifies the concept of remembering Christ and clarifies what we should remember as we partake.

As Jesus broke the bread and blessed it, he taught: "And this shall ye do in remembrance of my body, which I have shown unto you. And it shall be a testimony unto the Father that ye do always remember me. And if ye do always remember me ye shall have my Spirit to be with you" (3 Nephi 18:7). The body Christ showed to the Nephites was his resurrected body. Therefore, as we partake of the bread, we should remember that he laid down his body for us and took it up again to break the bands of death and gain victory over the grave (see Mosiah 16:17–18).

The resurrection of Christ brought about the eventual resurrection of all mankind (see Alma 40:4–5), but there is a varying quality of the resurrection. Some will be resurrected as celestial beings, some as terrestrial beings, some as telestial beings, and even the sons of perdition will be resurrected (see D&C 88:27–32). The sacramental prayer is a covenant made between the partakers and God the Eternal Father "that they are willing to take upon them the name of [Christ], and always remember him, and keep his commandments which he hath given them" (Moro. 4:3). Therefore, as the sacrament is being administered to the congregation, individuals have the opportunity to think of the past week (or time since they last partook), and review in their minds whether or not they have kept the commandments. This reflection enables them to recommit themselves, witness [testify] to the Father that they will overcome their shortcomings, and endeavor to do better during the forthcoming time period in their quest to become celestial people.

After Jesus had given the disciples and the multitude the bread, he likewise instructed them concerning the wine. He again taught the purpose of partaking:

> *10 Blessed are ye for this thing which ye have done, for this is fulfilling my commandments, and this doth witness unto the Father that ye are willing to do that which I have commanded you.*

11 And this shall ye always do to those who repent and are baptized in my name; and ye shall do it in remembrance of my blood, which I have shed for you, that ye may witness unto the Father that ye do always remember me. And if ye do always remember me ye shall have my Spirit to be with you. (3 Nephi 18:10–11)

Christ shed his blood for us as he suffered in the Garden of Gethsemane, paying the demands of justice for our sins through his mercy. Therefore, if we will repent of our sins, the payment that he has made will become efficacious to us. As the wine [water] is being administered to the congregation, we have an opportunity to reflect upon those sins that we have committed, both long-term and in the past week. As we drink of it, we witness [testify] to the Father in thanksgiving and recommitment to continue to do our best to keep the commandments—as the blessing states. This weekly opportunity enables us to remember our baptismal covenants, to rededicate ourselves to fulfill these commitments, and to be true disciples of Jesus Christ.

The Promise of the Spirit

Both of the sacrament prayers give a promised blessing to those who righteously partake "that they may have [God's] Spirit to be with them" (Moro. 4:3; 5:2).[66] Concerning Jesus' instituting the ordinance of partaking of the bread, the Book of Mormon states, "And when [the disciples] had eaten and were filled, he commanded that they should give unto the multitude. And when the multitude had eaten and were filled" (3 Nephi 18:4–5), but does not state how or with what they were filled. On the second day of his ministry, he administered the ordinance to both the disciples and the multitude again. On this occasion, the bread and wine were miraculously provided for them, because neither the disciples nor the multitude had brought the elements of the sacrament (see 3 Nephi 20:3–7).

---

66 The promise quoted here is from the prayer offered over the bread. The prayer on the water is identical except the word "always" is not used.

But, also on the second day, the text gives a further explanation of the purpose, or blessing, of the spirit promised to those who partook worthily and also tells us with what the multitude were filled following their partaking of the bread and wine:

> *8 And he said unto them: He that eateth this bread eateth of my body to his soul; and he that drinketh of this wine drinketh of my blood to his soul; and his soul shall never hunger nor thirst, but shall be filled.*
>
> *9 Now, when the multitude had all eaten and drunk, behold, they were filled with the Spirit; and they did cry out with one voice, and gave glory to Jesus, whom they both saw and heard. (3 Nephi 20:8–9)*

Worthily partaking of the sacrament brings the personal effects of Christ's resurrection and Atonement to each individual. These blessings are, of course, future; but the promise of being filled with the Spirit may be fulfilled at that time or in the near future and therefore are not as distant as the resurrection and judgment. The constant companionship of the Holy Ghost, as promised to the faithful priesthood holders (D&C 121:46), becomes more realistic to every member of the Church through the partaking of the sacrament.

Do Not Partake Unworthily

Jesus commanded his disciples "that ye shall not suffer [allow] any one knowingly to partake of my flesh and blood unworthily, when ye shall minister it; For whoso eateth and drinketh my flesh and blood unworthily eateth and drinketh damnation to his soul; therefore if ye know that a man is unworthy to eat and drink of my flesh and blood ye shall forbid him" (3 Nephi 18:28–29). Paul gave a similar injunction to the Saints in Corinth (see 1 Cor. 11:27–34). Moroni, as he finished his father's record, repeated the warning not to partake of the sacrament unworthily (see Morm. 9:29).

To bring damnation to our soul has, of course, eternal consequences, but it also has effects upon us while in this life. Paul told the Corinthians: "For this cause many are weak and sickly among you, and many sleep" (1 Cor. 11:30). President John Taylor interpreted Paul's warning as a reason that the Saints had sickness among them (see *JD* 20:360). As stated above, it is the bishop's responsibility to determine who should not partake. However, each person is to examine his or her own worthiness and, if in doubt of his or her worthiness, should discuss it with the bishop. Nevertheless, those who are unworthy are still welcome to meet with the Saints. Jesus instructed his disciples: "Nevertheless, ye shall not cast him out from among you, but ye shall minister unto him and shall pray for him unto the Father, in my name; and if it so be that he repenteth and is baptized in my name, then shall ye receive him, and shall minister unto him of my flesh and blood" (3 Nephi 18:30). To continue to partake of the sacrament—willfully and unworthily—might bring further Church disciplinary action, particularly if the unworthy are affecting negatively the lives of those who are worthy. However, the unworthy are still invited to come to the Church meetings:

> *31 But if he repent not he shall not be numbered among my people, that he may not destroy my people, for behold I know my sheep, and they are numbered.*
>
> *32 Nevertheless, ye shall not cast him out of your synagogues, or your places of worship, for unto such shall ye continue to minister; for ye know not but what they will return and repent, and come unto me with full purpose of heart, and I shall heal them; and ye shall be the means of bringing salvation unto them. (3 Nephi 18:31–32)*

Those who knowingly partake unworthily, or administer it to others without having authority, are on the road to or in a state of apostasy (see 4 Nephi 1:27).

The ordinance of the sacrament was given to strengthen us and will be a great blessing to those who worthily repent. We should take seriously the admonition of Jesus and his apostles as given to us in the Book of Mormon. As we worship the Father through the ordinance of the sacrament, we should meditate on our relationship with him.

There are many ways to worship the Father in the name of Christ (see Moro. 6:9). The Book of Mormon does not directly teach us about worshiping through song, speech, or other ways, although they may be suggested indirectly. Therefore, we will not discuss the subject of worship further in this work. We do, however, learn much from the Book of Mormon about worshiping the Father in the name of Christ.

20

ENDURE IN FAITH

*"All men must . . . endure in faith on his name to the end,
or they cannot be saved in the kingdom of God." (D&C 20:29)*

The third principle of faith, drawn from the *Lectures on Faith* and discussed in chapter thirteen, is faith as a principle of life and salvation. To obtain life unto salvation is to have one's calling and election made sure, or receiving the more sure word of prophecy spoken of by the Apostle Peter (see 2 Pet. 1:10, 19). Modern revelation gives us further insight: "The more sure word of prophecy means a man's knowing that he is sealed up unto eternal life, by revelation and the spirit of prophecy, through the power of the Holy Priesthood. It is impossible for a man to be saved in ignorance" (D&C 131:5–6). Through faith in Christ we attain the more sure word of prophecy.

An assurance of eternal life comes after a lifetime of hungering and thirsting after righteousness and exercising our faith in Christ. The Second Comforter is then given. Joseph Smith the Prophet spoke of the two comforters mentioned in the Gospel of John.[67]

---

67 For a fuller explanation of having one's calling and election made sure, see Elder Bruce R. McConkie's analysis of 2 Peter chapter one. McConkie, B. R. (1973). *Doctrinal New Testament Commentary,* 3:323–355. Salt Lake City: Bookcraft.

The other Comforter spoken of is a subject of great interest, and perhaps understood by few of this generation. After a person has faith in Christ, repents of his sins, and is baptized for the remission of his sins and receives the Holy Ghost, (by the laying on of hands), which is the first Comforter, then let him continue to humble himself before God, hungering and thirsting after righteousness, and living by every word of God, and the Lord will soon say unto him, Son, thou shalt be exalted. When the Lord has thoroughly proved him, and finds that the man is determined to serve Him at all hazards, then the man will find his calling and his election made sure, then it will be his privilege to receive the other Comforter, which the Lord hath promised the Saints, as is recorded in the testimony of St. John, in the 14th chapter, from the 12th to the 27th verses. (*TPJS*, 150)

In this chapter we are equating enduring in faith to the end with the third principle of faith. The Book of Mormon gives several examples of "faith unto life and salvation."

Faith to Suffer Death, Goods Spoiled

The *Lectures on Faith* state that any person "must have an actual knowledge that the course he is pursuing is according to the will of God to enable him to have that confidence in God . . . to endure all their afflictions and persecutions" (6:2). Father Lehi was willing to depart "into the wilderness. And he left his house, and the land of his inheritance, and his gold, and his silver, and his precious things, and took nothing with him, save it were his family, and provisions, and tents, and departed into the wilderness" (1 Nephi 2:4) The Lord had spoken unto him in a dream and commanded that he should take his family and depart. The dream was revealed to him because he had been faithful in the previous commandments the Lord had given him (1 Nephi 2:1–2).

The converted Lamanites, who became known as "the people of Ammon" (Alma 27:26), when they "were brought to believe and to know the truth, they were firm, and would suffer even unto death rather than commit sin" (Alma 24:19). When their fellow, unconverted Lamanites came up to the land of Nephi with the intent to destroy those who had been converted, the converts

> *21 . . . went out to meet them, and prostrated themselves before them to the earth, and began to call on the name of the Lord; and thus they were in this attitude when the Lamanites began to fall upon them, and began to slay them with the sword.*
>
> *22 And thus without meeting any resistance, they did slay a thousand and five of them; and we know that they are blessed, for they have gone to dwell with their God. (Alma 24:21–22)*

When the warring Lamanites saw those being killed praising God as they perished,

> *23 . . . there were many whose hearts had swollen in them for those of their brethren who had fallen under the sword, for they repented of the things which they had done.*
>
> *24 And it came to pass that they threw down their weapons of war, and they would not take them again, for they were stung for the murders which they had committed; and they came down even as their brethren, relying upon the mercies of those whose arms were lifted to slay them. (Alma 24:24–25)*

Those who joined the people of God because of the faith unto life and salvation of these converted Lamanites were "more than the number who had been slain" (Alma 24:26). The people of Ammon were willing to sacrifice their very lives because of their faith.

Sacrifice of All Things

The *Lectures on Faith* go on to say that "a religion that does not require the sacrifice of all things never has power sufficient to produce the faith necessary unto life and salvation" (6:7). The sacrifice of the converted Lamanites is a great contrast to many in the world today who try to make following their religion easier by attempting to make it more convenient or minimize the requirements for salvation, rather than teach and live the law of sacrifice.

When Alma and Amulek went among the people of Ammonihah (the Nephites who had apostatized), they were rejected. The unbelievers "brought [the believers'] wives and children together, and whosoever believed or had been taught to believe in the word of God they caused that they should be cast into the fire; and they also brought forth their records which contained the holy scriptures, and cast them into the fire also, that they might be burned and destroyed by fire" (Alma 14:8). Alma and Amulek were brought "to the place of martyrdom, that they might witness the destruction of those who were consumed by fire" (Alma 14:9). Seeing the pains of the women and children being consumed by fire, Amulek proposed to Alma that they:

10 . . . stretch forth our hands, and exercise the power of God which is in us, and save them from the flames.

11 But Alma said unto him: The Spirit constraineth me that I must not stretch forth mine hand; for behold the Lord receiveth them up unto himself, in glory; and he doth suffer that they may do this thing, or that the people may do this thing unto them, according to the hardness of their hearts, that the judgments which he shall exercise upon them in his wrath may be just; and the blood of the innocent shall stand as witness against them, yea, and cry mightily against them at the last day.

*12 Now Amulek said unto Alma: Behold, perhaps they
will burn us also.*

*13 And Alma said: Be it according to the will of the Lord.
But, behold, our work is not finished; therefore they burn
us not. (Alma 14:10–13)*

The Lord received those faithful martyrs unto himself in glory. Their salvation was apparently made sure.

Alma and Amulek were then imprisoned and smitten, mocked, denied food and water, stripped of their clothes, and bound with strong cords. After much suffering, Alma exercised his power of faith, and the Lord miraculously delivered him and Amulek (see Alma 14:14–29). This is a great example of faith unto life and salvation exemplified by Alma and Amulek among the people of Ammonihah.

Another type of faith unto life and salvation in the Book of Mormon comes from the Lamanite king Lamoni and his father. When Ammon, one of king Mosiah's sons, came among the Lamanites to do missionary work, he miraculously preserved the flocks and servants of the king. After perceiving by the Spirit the thoughts of the king, the king said to Ammon: "And now, if thou wilt tell me concerning these things, whatsoever thou desirest I will give unto thee; and if it were needed, I would guard thee with my armies; but I know that thou art more powerful than all they; nevertheless, whatsoever thou desirest of me I will grant it unto thee" (Alma 18:21). The king's willingness to follow Ammon led to the conversion of his wife and servants and the opening of missionary work among the Lamanites (see Alma 18:22–19:36). Following this great experience, Ammon went to Middoni, following again the will of the Lord, to free his brethren from prison (see Alma 20:1–5). King Lamoni went with Ammon to render assistance, and en route they met the king's father. King Lamoni refused to follow his father's command to kill Ammon because he was a Nephite, exemplifying the converted king's willingness to follow the will of the Lord (see Alma 20:8–15). Ammon then prevented the father of King Lamoni from killing his son; and because of the father's fear of Ammon, he offered Ammon whatever he asked, "even to half of the kingdom" (Alma 20:16–23). Ammon sought only the freedom of his brethren who were in prison, a request which the father of Lamoni had power to grant, and also that king Lamoni might retain his kingdom. The older king was so astonished over Ammon's love for the king's son that he was desirous to learn more (see Alma 20:24–27). Later he was taught by Aaron, another son of King Mosiah. Expressing his desire for eternal life to Aaron, Aaron admonished him to repent and call on the name of God in faith. In his prayer, he promised to "give away all my sins to know thee, and that I may be raised from the dead, and be saved at the last day" (Alma 22:18). Note the contrast of the desires of the king when he feared for his physical life before Ammon and when he desired to obtain eternal life before Aaron. Certainly he was willing to sacrifice all things to achieve salvation.

Know the Will of the Lord

The *Lectures on Faith* teach:

> When a man has offered in sacrifice all that he has for the truth's sake, not even withholding his life, and believing before God that he has been called to make this sacrifice because he seeks to do His will, he does know, most assuredly, that God does and will accept his sacrifice and offering and that he has not sought nor will he seek His face in vain. Under these circumstances, then, he can obtain the faith necessary for him to lay hold on eternal life. (6:7)

The slaying of Laban by Nephi exemplifies this teaching in a convincing way.

As Nephi was led by the Spirit towards the house of Laban in Jerusalem, he found Laban in a drunken stupor. Seeing Laban's "exceedingly fine" sword, he drew it from its sheath and "was constrained by the Spirit that [he] should kill Laban; but [he] said in [his] heart: Never at any time have I shed the blood of man. And [he] shrunk and would that [he] might not slay him" (1 Nephi 4:10). The Spirit told Nephi twice more to slay him, adding this reasoning to Nephi: "Behold the Lord slayeth the wicked to bring forth his righteous purposes. It is better that one man should perish than that a nation should dwindle and perish in unbelief" (1 Nephi 4:13). This verse is very well known to members of the Church and is the usual answer given to those who question why Nephi would take another's life. However, what the Spirit told Nephi the second time he was commanded to slay Laban is more important than the reason just cited: "And the Spirit said unto me again: Behold the Lord hath delivered him into thy hands. Yea, and I also knew that he had sought to take away mine own life; yea, and he would not hearken unto the commandments of the Lord; and he also had taken away our property" (1 Nephi 4:11). An analysis of this verse shows that Laban had offended Nephi three times prior to this time. He had threatened to kill Laman the first time he had gone into his house and sought to obtain the plates of brass. After Nephi and brothers had offered to buy the plates, Laban had sent his servants to slay them (see 1 Nephi 3:13, 25). This was the first offense. Apparently Laman, or another of the brothers, had told Laban that they had been commanded of God to obtain the plates (see 1 Ne. 3:12), since Nephi said "he would not hearken unto the commandments of the Lord" (1 Nephi 4:11). This was the second offense. The third offense was when Laban "had taken away our property" (1 Nephi 4:11). Earlier Nephi had recorded "that when Laban saw our property, and that it was exceedingly great, he did lust after it, insomuch that he thrust us out, and sent his servants to slay us, that he might obtain our property" (1 Nephi 3:25).

The three offenses against Nephi fit the law of retaliation that the Lord revealed to Joseph Smith concerning the persecution of the saints in Missouri in 1833:

23 Now, I speak unto you concerning your families—if men will smite you, or your families, once, and ye bear it patiently and revile not against them, neither seek revenge, ye shall be rewarded;

24 But if ye bear it not patiently, it shall be accounted unto you as being meted out as a just measure unto you.

25 And again, if your enemy shall smite you the second time, and you revile not against your enemy, and bear it patiently, your reward shall be an hundredfold.

26 And again, if he shall smite you the third time, and ye bear it patiently, your reward shall be doubled unto you four-fold.

27 And these three testimonies shall stand against your enemy if he repent not, and shall not be blotted out.

28 And now, verily I say unto you, if that enemy shall escape my vengeance, that he be not brought into judgment before me, then ye shall see to it that ye warn him in my name, that he come no more upon you, neither upon your family, even your children's children unto the third and fourth generation.

29 And then, if he shall come upon you or your children, or your children's children unto the third and fourth generation, I have delivered thine enemy into thine hands;

30 And then if thou wilt spare him, thou shalt be rewarded for thy righteousness; and also thy children and thy children's children unto the third and fourth generation.

31 Nevertheless, thine enemy is in thine hands; and if thou rewardest him according to his works thou art justified; if he has sought thy life, and thy life is endangered by him, thine enemy is in thine hands and thou art justified.

*32 Behold, this is the law I gave unto my servant Nephi,
and thy fathers, Joseph, and Jacob, and Isaac, and
Abraham, and all mine ancient prophets and apostles.
(D&C 98:23–32)*

The Lord's reference in modern revelation that he had taught
this law to Nephi seems evident that it was the occasion of Nephi's
being commanded to slay Laban when he was taught this law. The
Lord had delivered Laban into Nephi's hands, and he knew that he
must slay Laban. Although the Doctrine and Covenants revelation
states that the offended person will be rewarded if he spares the
offender's life after the three offenses, the situation with Nephi was
uniquely different. He was commanded to slay Laban so that the
future nation of the Nephites would not perish in unbelief (see 1
Nephi 4:13). This was the will of the Lord, and by following his
will one will exemplify faith unto life and salvation. The Prophet
Joseph taught the same principle in these words:

> God said, "Thou shalt not kill"; at another time
> He said, "Thou shalt utterly destroy." This is the principle
> on which the government of heaven is conducted—by
> revelation adapted to the circumstances in which the
> children of the kingdom are placed. Whatever God
> requires is right, no matter what it is, although we
> may not see the reason thereof till long after the events
> transpire. (*TPJS*, 256)

The people of Ammon, who had been willing to sacrifice
their very lives, knew that it was the Lord's will for them to go and
live among the Nephites. They knew through Ammon's inquiring
of the Lord (see Alma 27:1–14). They exercised faith unto life and
salvation through following the prophet.

The Book of Mormon tells of several individuals who had
salvation assured to them. Just before his death, Lehi told his
sons: "But behold, the Lord hath redeemed my soul from hell; I
have beheld his glory, and I am encircled about eternally in the

arms of his love" (2 Nephi 1:15). In the last chapter written by Nephi, he testified: "I glory in plainness; I glory in truth; I glory in my Jesus, for he hath redeemed my soul from hell" (2 Nephi 33:6). The Lord covenanted with Alma: "Thou art my servant; and I covenant with thee that thou shalt have eternal life" (Mosiah 26:20). Moroni testified that "we shall meet before the judgment-seat of Christ, where all men shall know that my garments are not spotted with your blood. And then shall ye know that I have seen Jesus, and that he hath talked with me face to face, and that he told me in plain humility, even as a man telleth another in mine own language, concerning these things" (Ether 12:38–39). There were undoubtedly many others who attained faith unto life and salvation.

Faith unto life and salvation is to know the course you pursue is the will of the Lord. As Paul taught the Romans, "whatsoever is not of faith is sin" (Rom. 14:23, see vv. 17–23). Those who endure in faith on his name unto the end must attain this principle of faith to be saved in the kingdom of God.

21

JUSTIFICATION THROUGH GRACE

"And we know that justification through the grace of our Lord and Savior Jesus Christ is just and true." (D&C 20:30)

One of the doctrines that is not commonly talked about among Church members is justification; at least it is not talked about in those terms. Perhaps we in the Church should familiarize ourselves with the scriptural meaning of the word, because it is spoken of in all of the four standard works, not just in the Book of Mormon.

What Is Justification?

The most common Book of Mormon synonym for justification is "born again." The Book of Mormon teaches us about rebirth repeatedly. The doctrine of being born again is also referred to in various ways, such as "born of the Spirit," "baptized of the Spirit," and "baptism of fire and the Holy Ghost."

When Nephi, son of Lehi, spoke concerning the doctrine of Christ, he taught: "For the gate by which ye should enter is repentance and baptism by water; and then cometh a remission of your sins by fire and by the Holy Ghost" (2 Nephi 31:17). The baptism of fire is a cleansing power that comes upon a person after baptism. Moroni gives a second witness to Nephi's declaration:

"And after they had been received unto baptism, and were wrought upon and cleansed by the power of the Holy Ghost" (Moro. 6:4). The baptism of fire is further qualified by Mormon: "And the first fruits of repentance is baptism; and baptism cometh by faith unto the fulfilling the commandments; and the fulfilling the commandments bringeth remission of sins" (Moro. 8:25).

From the teachings above, we learn the following about the baptism of fire and the Holy Ghost: (1) it is not the ordinance of baptism itself that brings a remission of sins but the fulfilling of the commandments; (2) because a person is willing to keep the commandments (i.e., is humble), the Father will visit him with fire and the Holy Ghost; and (3) the Holy Ghost acts as a cleansing agent on the body and actually removes the sin. This is the literal remission of one's sins.

Another synonym for "justification" is "redeemed of God." Alma described his rebirth: "I have repented of my sins, and have been redeemed of the Lord; behold I am born of the Spirit" (Mosiah 27:24). Alma said he had repented of his sins; and when true repentance is complete, being born again brings a remission of sins. Enos equated his rebirth with having received a remission of his sins (see Enos 1:2–5). The subjects of King Benjamin received a remission of their sins when the Spirit of the Lord came upon them (see Mosiah 4:2–3).

Those who repent and are baptized of water and of the Spirit, thus receiving a remission of their sins, are in the Savior's words "guiltless before my Father" (3 Nephi 27:16). Nephi spoke of the righteous being justified, "wherefore, the guilty taketh the truth to be hard" (1 Nephi 16:2). Enos knew from his experience that his "guilt was swept away" (Enos 1:6). Thus justification, as taught in the Book of Mormon, is to experience a rebirth that takes away our past sins and leaves us, at that point in our lives, guiltless before God.

Who Must Be Justified?

The Lord said unto Alma, the younger: "Marvel not that all mankind, yea, men and women, all nations, kindreds, tongues and people, must be born again; yea, born of God, changed from their carnal and fallen state, to a state of righteousness, being redeemed of God, becoming his sons and daughters; And thus they become new creatures; and unless they do this, they can in nowise inherit the kingdom of God" (Mosiah 27:25–26). Thus the "born again" experience must come to all people, even those who are born into the Church. Alma, the younger, asked his "brethren of the church, have ye spiritually been born of God?" (Alma 5:14). To these same brethren he testified: "I say unto you the aged, and also the middle aged, and the rising generation; yea, to cry unto them that they must repent and be born again" (Alma 5:49). Since salvation requires this "born again" experience, we must examine more closely what it entails.

How Is One Justified?

Joseph Smith taught that "being born again, comes by the Spirit of God through ordinances" (*TPJS*, 162). The ordinances are baptism by water and the conferral of the gift of the Holy Ghost by the laying on of hands (see 3 Nephi 18:37; Moro. 2:1–2). All the members of The Church of Jesus Christ of Latter-day Saints have the Holy Ghost conferred upon them. However, many may not be using the gift: "A man may receive the Holy Ghost, and it may descend upon him and not tarry with him" (D&C 130:23). President Joseph Fielding Smith made this alarming observation:

> Now I am going to say something that maybe I could not prove, but I believe is true, that we have a great many members of this Church who have never reached a manifestation through the Holy Ghost. Why? Because they have not made their lives conform to the truth. And the Holy Ghost will not dwell in

unclean tabernacles where perhaps the light of Christ remains. But the Holy Ghost will not dwell in unclean tabernacles or disobedient tabernacles. The Holy Ghost will not dwell with that person who is unwilling to obey and keep the commandments of God or who violates those commandments willfully. In such a soul the spirit of the Holy Ghost cannot enter.

That great gift comes to us only through humility and faith and obedience. Therefore, a great many members of the Church do not have the guidance. Then some cunning, crafty individual will come along teaching that which is not true, and without the guidance which is promised to us through our faithfulness, people are unable to discern and are led astray. It depends on our faithfulness and obedience to the commandments of the Lord if we have the teachings, the enlightening instruction, that comes from the Holy Ghost.[68]

As Joseph the Prophet said: "You might as well baptize a bag of sand as a man, if not done in view of the remission of sins and getting of the Holy Ghost. Baptism by water is but half a baptism, and is good for nothing without the other half—that is, the baptism of the Holy Ghost" (*TPJS*, 314). On another occasion he said, "The baptism of water, without the baptism of fire and the Holy Ghost attending it, is of no use; they are necessarily and inseparably connected" (*TPJS*, p. 360).

A Mighty Change of Heart

A person being immersed in the Spirit brings a change of heart, a mighty change of heart. King Benjamin's subjects believed all the words the king had spoken to them: "We know of their surety and truth, because of the Spirit of the Lord Omnipotent,

---

68 Smith, J. F. (1961). *Church News*, November 4, p.14.

which has wrought a mighty change in us, or in our hearts" (Mosiah 5:2). Alma, the younger, described to his sons the great change that he had experienced when an angel of God appeared to him. After his soul was racked with eternal torment for three days because of his past sins and persecution of the Church, he testified:

> *17 And it came to pass that as I was thus racked with torment, while I was harrowed up by the memory of my many sins, behold, I remembered also to have heard my father prophesy unto the people concerning the coming of one Jesus Christ, a Son of God, to atone for the sins of the world.*

> *18 Now, as my mind caught hold upon this thought, I cried within my heart: O Jesus, thou Son of God, have mercy on me, who am in the gall of bitterness, and am encircled about by the everlasting chains of death.*

> *19 And now, behold, when I thought this, I could remember my pains no more; yea, I was harrowed up by the memory of my sins no more.*

> *20 And oh, what joy, and what marvelous light I did behold; yea, my soul was filled with joy as exceeding as was my pain!*

> *21 Yea, I say unto you, my son, that there could be nothing so exquisite and so bitter as were my pains. Yea, and again I say unto you, my son, that on the other hand, there can be nothing so exquisite and sweet as was my joy.* (Alma 36:17–21)

Alma's heart was changed, as his later life illustrates. However, there is a difference in changing your mind, changing your actions, and changing your heart. To change the mind is to change your thinking, and a change of action may even follow; but, that change will only be temporary unless the heart is also changed.

No Disposition to Do Evil but to Do Good

The subjects of King Benjamin proclaimed "that we have no more disposition to do evil, but to do good continually" (Mosiah 5:2). While we are in mortality, we will experience the temptations of the flesh from time to time; but at the time we have the Spirit upon us, we cannot sin and will not sin unless the Spirit leaves us. Some people quote from one of the epistles of John as evidence that the born again person no longer sins; and even if they make mistakes, they are not accountable. However, in his translation of the Bible, Joseph Smith made this clarification: "Whosoever is born of God doth not *commit sin*; for his seed remaineth in him: and he cannot sin, because he is born of God" (JST 1 John 3:9; italics added). This is in contrast with the King James Version: "Whosoever is born of God doth not *continue in* sin; *for the Spirit of God* remaineth in him; and he cannot continue in sin, because he is born of God, having *received that holy spirit of promise*" (1 John 3:9; italics added).

When we follow our natural tendencies in a mortal world, as we all do from time to time, the Spirit withdraws and we may sin. Our challenge is to live that we might have the constant companionship of the Holy Ghost (see D&C 121:46), and then we will not sin because of that Spirit. But even without the Spirit, we have no desire to do evil, but desire to do good. The real evidence of our rebirth comes by our attempts to constantly do good. Alma, the younger, explains to his sons his own desire to always do good, after his being born again: "Yea, and from that time even until now, I have labored without ceasing, that I might bring souls unto repentance; that I might bring them to taste of the exceeding joy of which I did taste; that they might also be born of God, and be filled with the Holy Ghost" (Alma 36:24). While we may have shortcomings and make mistakes, they will be temporary if we have as our major goal an eye single to the glory of God.

Great Views of Things to Come

A third characteristic of a born-again person (as Jesus taught Nicodemus) is that they see the kingdom of God (see John 3:3). Although we may have knowledge of the kingdom, to one degree or another, when the Spirit is manifest we are able to see the kingdom of God functioning upon the earth. As King Benjamin's people said: "And we, ourselves, also, through the infinite goodness of God, and the manifestations of his Spirit, have great views of that which is to come; and were it expedient, we could prophesy of all things" (Mosiah 5:3). As Alma recounted his rebirth experience to his sons, he said: "Yea, methought I saw, even as our father Lehi saw, God sitting upon his throne, surrounded with numberless concourses of angels, in the attitude of singing and praising their God; yea, and my soul did long to be there" (Alma 36:22). Alma probably thought he had seen God because, although he had never seen him before, the vision which he had was so glorious that he assumed it had to be God. The manifestation of the Spirit was so sweet and so exquisite, he knew it must be of God.

Willing to Enter a Covenant

When people have glorious manifestations, they are willing to follow whatever the Lord's will may be for them. They recognize it as a fruit of their faith:

> *4 And it is the faith which we have had on the things which our king has spoken unto us that has brought us to this great knowledge, whereby we do rejoice with such exceedingly great joy.*

> *5 And we are willing to enter into a covenant with our God to do his will, and to be obedient to his commandments in all things that he shall command us, all the remainder of our days, that we may not bring upon ourselves a*

never-ending torment, as has been spoken by the angel,
that we may not drink out of the cup of the wrath of God.
(Mosiah 5:4–5)

To enter into a covenant is first of all to be baptized by water.
The baptism of water is the initial step of being born again.

A Son or Daughter of Christ

An unborn baby lives immersed in a sack of water in its
mother's womb. As a person is immersed in water by the authority
of the priesthood, he or she is symbolically participating in a
newness of life. As Paul taught the Romans:

1 What shall we say then? Shall we continue in sin, that
grace may abound?

2 God forbid. How shall we, that are dead to sin, live any
longer therein?

3 Know ye not, that so many of us as were baptized into
Jesus Christ were baptized into his death?

4 Therefore we are buried with him by baptism into
death: that like as Christ was raised up from the dead
by the glory of the Father, even so we also should walk in
newness of life.

5 For if we have been planted together in the likeness of his
death, we shall be also in the likeness of his resurrection:

6 Knowing this, that our old man is crucified with him,
that the body of sin might be destroyed, that henceforth
we should not serve sin. (Rom. 6:1–6)

As a newborn babe is an individual spirit and body at birth,
so the baptized individual is given the right to become a new
creature by the baptism of the Spirit to follow. If they have entered
into the water:

> *. . . with full purpose of heart, acting no hypocrisy and no deception before God, but with real intent, repenting of [their] sins, witnessing unto the Father that [they] are willing to take upon [them] the name of Christ, by baptism—yea, by following your Lord and your Savior down into the water, according to his word, behold, then shall ye receive the Holy Ghost; yea, then cometh the baptism of fire and of the Holy Ghost. (2 Nephi 31:13)*

This is the second phase of a symbolic rebirth: the spirit entering the body. At birth, after the umbilical cord is cut, a child is dependent upon its own blood instead of its mother's. When a person is born again, he becomes dependent upon the blood of Christ for his eternal life instead of his own blood. He or she is symbolically a son or daughter of Jesus Christ because of the covenant to take his name:

> *7 And now, because of the covenant which ye have made ye shall be called the children of Christ, his sons, and his daughters; for behold, this day he hath spiritually begotten you; for ye say that your hearts are changed through faith on his name; therefore, ye are born of him and have become his sons and his daughters.*
>
> *8 And under this head ye are made free, and there is no other head whereby ye can be made free. There is no other name given whereby salvation cometh; therefore, I would that ye should take upon you the name of Christ, all you that have entered into the covenant with God that ye should be obedient unto the end of your lives. (Mosiah 5:7–8)*

Thus a person is born again, having experienced three phases of birth as patterned after his mortal birth: being immersed in water, being dependent upon the blood of Christ, and having the Spirit of the Holy Ghost within him (compare 1 John 5:4–8). He or she has subscribed to the articles of adoption, as the Prophet Joseph said: "It is one thing to see the kingdom of God, and another thing to enter into it. We must have a change of heart to see the kingdom of God, and subscribe the articles of adoption to enter therein" (*TPJS*, 328).

The second birth comes through the grace of Christ, a gift towards salvation to those who desire to take his name upon them and exercise faith in him (see Enos 1:6–8). They have wrestled with the natural man (see Enos 1:24), have become adopted sons and daughters of Jesus Christ, and will inherit eternal life if they continue faithful (see Ether 3:14).

The Book of Mormon gives several different experiences of people being born again. Some go into more detail than others. There are accounts of Nephi (see 2 Nephi 31); Enos (see Enos 1:1–18); King Benjamin's subjects (see Mosiah 5); Alma (see Mosiah 27:11–31 and Alma 36:5–24); Alma's teachings (see Alma 5); the Lamanite king Lamoni (see Alma 18:40–41; 19:6–13); the Lamanite queen and her servants (see Alma 19:29–34); the Lamanites at the time Nephi and Lehi were cast into prison (see Hel. 5); and others in lesser detail.

None of the accounts are exactly the same, in fact, some are very dissimilar. This seems significant. Just as natural births differ, so do rebirth experiences differ. Some born-again people need and have a greater change of heart, just as some natural births are more strenuous than others. Some who have been born again do not have as great a desire to do good as others, just as one naturally born child is more faithful than another. Another reborn person has greater views of the kingdom than another, just as one naturally born child is endowed with greater intellect than another. One member of the Church is more committed to his baptismal covenant, just as one natural child seems to be naturally more obedient to his parents than another. All born-again people come into the family of Christ, but some are more family-oriented than others, just as are some children in human families. Nevertheless, there are consistent characteristics of the rebirth that all must experience, as we have tried to show above.

Have You Been Born Again?

There are variant views in the Christian world, and in the Church, regarding the meaning of being "born again." Whenever it is discussed, the question often arises, "Have I been born again?" The answer to this question is given in the account of the subjects of King Benjamin crying for the mercy of the Atonement to come upon them:

> 2 And they had viewed themselves in their own carnal state, even less than the dust of the earth. And they all cried aloud with one voice, saying: O have mercy, and apply the atoning blood of Christ that we may receive forgiveness of our sins, and our hearts may be purified; for we believe in Jesus Christ, the Son of God, who created heaven and earth, and all things; who shall come down among the children of men.
>
> 3 And it came to pass that after they had spoken these words the Spirit of the Lord came upon them, and they were filled with joy, having received a remission of their sins, and having peace of conscience, because of the exceeding faith which they had in Jesus Christ who should come, according to the words which King Benjamin had spoken unto them. (Mosiah 4:2–3)

The joy of peace and conscience, however, may also come in varying degrees. Therefore, there is another question that arises: Can a person be born again and not know it? The answer is "yes."

The Savior commanded the Nephites, when he spoke to them after their cities were destroyed, to no more offer blood sacrifices:

> And ye shall offer for a sacrifice unto me a broken heart and a contrite spirit. And whoso cometh unto me with a broken heart and a contrite spirit, him will I baptize

> *with fire and with the Holy Ghost, even as the Lamanites,*
> *because of their faith in me at the time of their conversion,*
> *were baptized with fire and with the Holy Ghost, and*
> *they knew it not. (3 Nephi 9:20)*

Although the Lamanites did not know they had been baptized with fire and the Holy Ghost, did they know that something had happened to them? Again the answer must be "yes." One could not explain the immersion of the Spirit without knowing something had happened to him, although each experience is somewhat different. This is what Jesus was explaining to Nicodemus in Jerusalem. He equated the born-again experience with the wind. Some had experienced stronger winds than others. Only those who had experienced the wind could understand it. But they still did not know why or how it came (see John 3:6–8). The same was true of a rebirth. It was a spiritual experience, and only those who had experienced it would know, but they could not explain the why or how of it. Nonetheless, they knew that something good had happened to them.

Some want to describe being born again as a lifetime experience. This description is not consistent with the scriptures, nor with the parallel to natural birth. Although there is a normal gestation period for a child to come to birth, there is a variation of a few days or weeks. There are also longer periods of labor for a mother, extending from a few minutes to several days. However, it is an experience that has a beginning and an end; it is not a lifetime process.

Repeated Justifications

People born into mortality enter to "prove them herewith, to see if they will do all things whatsoever the Lord their God should command them" (Abr. 3:25). Persons becoming sons or daughters of Christ must also prove that they are fit candidates to enter back into the presence of God. Just as mortals may go astray, so may sons or daughters of Christ. Alma asked the people of Zarahemla: "And now behold, I say unto you, my brethren, if ye have experienced a change of heart, and if ye have felt to sing the song of redeeming love, I would ask, can ye feel so now?" (Alma 5:26). Alma then asked the people several thought-provoking questions that all of us should consider (see Alma 5:27). Our purpose is to define the born-again person, or justification, so we will not pursue these questions here.

There are some who teach that a person needs to be reborn periodically in his lifetime. Again, this is not consistent with the natural birth parallel. Baptism of water and the Holy Ghost is the initial justification. This is a complete immersion of the Spirit. We need other justifications in our life, but there is only one complete immersion required for salvation. People may be justified when they are healed (see James 5:14–15) or receive other blessings of God. The Holy Spirit of Promise (the Holy Ghost's "stamp of approval") must come upon "all covenants, contracts, bonds, obligations, oaths, vows, performances, connections, associations, or expectations" (D&C 132:7).[69] Every experience that the Spirit accompanies gives us a remission of sins and is a justification that comes by the grace of Jesus Christ and his atoning blood.

Nephi taught that the baptism of fire and the Holy Ghost put us on the path to eternal life. He then asked: "And now, my beloved brethren, after ye have gotten into this strait and narrow path, I would ask if all is done? Behold, I say unto you, Nay; for ye have not come thus far save it were by the word of Christ with unshaken faith in him, relying wholly upon the merits of him who is mighty to save" (2 Nephi 31:19). What we do to remain on the path and obtain eternal life is the subject of our next chapter.

Summary

The importance of the gift of the Holy Ghost is best illustrated by some statements of the Prophet Joseph Smith. In seeking redress for the suffering of the Saints in Missouri, the Prophet and Elias

---

69 See Smith, J. F., *Doctrines of Salvation,* 1:55.

Higbee met with President Van Buren in Washington. In a letter to Hyrum Smith and the high council Higbee wrote:

> In our interview with the President, he interrogated us wherein we differed in our religion from the other religions of the day. Brother Joseph said we differed in mode of baptism, and the gift of the Holy Ghost by the laying on of hands. We considered that all other considerations were contained in the gift of the Holy Ghost.[70]

President David O. McKay's words provide a fitting conclusion to this chapter:

> No man can sincerely resolve to apply to his daily life the teachings of Jesus of Nazareth without sensing a change in his own nature. The phrase, "born again," has a deeper significance than many people attach to it. This changed feeling may be indescribable, but it is real. Happy is the person who has truly sensed the uplifting, transforming power that comes from this nearness to the Savior, this kinship to the Living Christ.[71]

---

70 *History of the Church,* 4:42.

71 McKay, D. O. (1962). *Conference Report,* April, p. 7.

22

SANCTIFICATION THROUGH GRACE

*"And we know also, that sanctification through the grace of our Lord
and Savior Jesus Christ is just and true." (D&C 20:31)*

As discussed in the previous chapter, justification is to qualify for a remission of past sins. Sanctification is to arrive at a state or condition to prevent future sin in our lives, even though we live in an environment of sin. To be sanctified is to become pure and holy. Through the grace of Christ those who are sanctified are becoming like God: they "cannot look upon sin with the least degree of allowance" (D&C 1:31).

The Book of Mormon teaches us about two types of sanctification: (1) Sanctification in the flesh; and (2) sanctification in the Spirit. The three Nephites who were blessed to remain upon the earth until the Second Coming had "a change wrought upon them, insomuch that Satan could have no power over them, that he could not tempt them; and they were *sanctified in the flesh*, that they were holy, and that the powers of the earth could not hold them" (3 Nephi 28:39, italics added). However, those who are sanctified in the spirit are still subject to the temptations of the world, because they have not had a change come upon their bodies. The latter is the subject of this chapter.

The Sanctification Process

As discussed above, justification comes through events in our lives: baptism of the Spirit, healings, acts of kindness, fulfillment of assignments, or others. By comparison, sanctification is a lifetime process. The Prophet Joseph Smith apparently described this process in the following statement:

> We consider that God has created man with a mind capable of instruction, and a faculty which may be enlarged in proportion to the heed and diligence given to the light communicated from heaven to the intellect; and that the nearer man approaches perfection, the clearer are his views, and the greater his enjoyments, till he has overcome the evils of his life and lost every desire for sin; and like the ancients, arrives at that point of faith where he is wrapped in the power and glory of his Maker and is caught up to dwell with Him. But we consider that this is a station to which no man ever arrived in a moment: he must have been instructed in the government and laws of that kingdom by proper degrees, until his mind is capable in some measure of comprehending the propriety, justice, equality, and consistency of the same. For further instruction we refer you to Deut. 32, where the Lord says, that Jacob is the lot of His inheritance. He found him in a desert land, and in the waste, howling wilderness; He led him about, He instructed him, He kept him as the apple of his eye, etc.; which will show the force of the last item advanced, that it is necessary for men to receive an understanding concerning the laws of the heavenly kingdom, before they are permitted to enter it: we mean celestial glory. (*TPJS*, 51)

The Book of Mormon teaches three general principles to follow in attaining a sanctified state: receiving the gift of the Holy Ghost, righteous use of the priesthood, and fasting and prayer.

The Gift of the Holy Ghost

When people are baptized, they receive the gift of the Holy Ghost. The recipient is entitled to the constant companionship of this Spirit but must learn to use this precious gift. In defining his gospel to the Nephite disciples, Jesus said:

> 20 Now this is the commandment: Repent, all ye ends of the earth, and come unto me and be baptized in my name, that ye may be sanctified by the reception of the Holy Ghost, that ye may stand spotless before me at the last day.

> 21 Verily, verily, I say unto you, this is my gospel; and ye know the things that ye must do in my church; for the works which ye have seen me do that shall ye also do; for that which ye have seen me do even that shall ye do. (3 Nephi 27:20–21)[72]

The promptings of the Holy Ghost will direct your life if you receive it and give heed. As Nephi, son of Lehi, taught, "if ye will enter in by the way, and receive the Holy Ghost, it will show unto you all things what ye should do" (2 Nephi 32:5).

Nephi also testified that the Holy Ghost will teach them that they must pray and will teach them the things for which they should pray (see 2 Nephi 32:8). When Christ visited this continent, his disciples prayed unceasingly, being filled with desire. The source of this desire was attributed by Christ to the Holy Ghost:

> 17 And it came to pass that when they had all knelt down upon the earth, he commanded his disciples that they should pray . . .

---

72 The New Testament also teaches the process of sanctification by the Holy Ghost (see Romans 15:16; 1 Peter 1:2; 2 Thess. 2:13).

18 Father, I thank thee that thou hast given the Holy Ghost unto these whom I have chosen; and it is because of their belief in me that I have chosen them out of the world.

19 And it came to pass that when Jesus had thus prayed unto the Father, he came unto his disciples, and behold, they did still continue, without ceasing, to pray unto him; and they did not multiply many words, for it was given unto them what they should pray, and they were filled with desire. (3 Nephi 19:17, 20, 24)

This teaching of Christ is consistent with biblical teachings: "Likewise the Spirit also helpeth our infirmities: for we know not what we should pray for as we ought: but the Spirit itself maketh intercession for us with groanings which cannot be uttered" (Romans 8:26; see also Eph. 6:18; Jude 1:20). The Prophet Joseph Smith clarified the wording of the Hebrew passage: "It would be better thus: 'The Spirit maketh intercession for us with *striving* which cannot be *expressed*'" (*TPJS*, 278, italics added).

As we learn to pray through the guidance of the Holy Ghost, we experience a full and satisfying prayerful life. This rewarding experience is a continuing blessing given without cost or obligation and exemplifies the Holy Ghost as a constant gift in our lives (D&C 121:46).

A Revealer of the Mysteries of God

The Holy Ghost will reveal a knowledge of the great blessings of God to those who prove themselves followers of his principles and commandments. These are termed "mysteries," because the world will not receive them.

After hearing the prophecies of his father; Nephi was desirous to know these same things which came by the power of the Holy Ghost:

And it came to pass after I, Nephi, having heard all the words of my father, concerning the things which he saw in a vision, and also the things which he spake by the power of the Holy Ghost, which power he received by faith on the Son of God—and the Son of God was the Messiah who should come—I, Nephi, was desirous also that I might see, and hear, and know of these things, by the power of the Holy Ghost, which is the gift of God unto all those who diligently seek him, as well in times of old as in the time that he should manifest himself unto the children of men. (1 Nephi 10:17)

Nephi desired to have the experiences his father had had, to see (visions), to speak by the power of the Holy Ghost (receive revelation), and to know by the power of the Holy Ghost (a witness or testimony). Not only did Nephi have these experiences (2 Nephi 4:23–25), but he also tells us that everyone has this same opportunity to learn of the mysteries of God through the power of the Holy Ghost: "For he that diligently seeketh shall find; and the mysteries of God shall be unfolded unto them, by the power of the Holy Ghost, as well in these times as in times of old, and as well in times of old as in times to come; wherefore, the course of the Lord is one eternal round" (1 Nephi 10:19).

Lehi received the power of the Holy Ghost through faith on the Son of God (1 Nephi 10:17, quoted above). Many mysteries of God were revealed to Nephi under the direction of the Holy Ghost. Nephi was instructed to reveal some of these mysteries in his writings on the small plates. He was given visions of future events in Jerusalem among the Nephites and the Gentiles in America (see 1 Nephi 11–14). In the last verse preceding Nephi's recording of these visions, he noted: "And the Holy Ghost giveth authority that I should speak these things, and deny them not" (1 Nephi 10:22).

As we accept and understand the mysteries already revealed, we can gain even greater knowledge. The amount of knowledge gained is limited only by our failing to make the necessary effort. Ammon gave this admonition: "Yea, he that repenteth and exerciseth faith, and bringeth forth good works, and prayeth continually without ceasing—unto such it is given to know the mysteries of God; yea, unto such it shall be given to reveal things which never have been revealed" (Alma 26:22). Of course, the revelation must be within the realm of our stewardships.

What a great time-saver and means of personal development the Holy Ghost could be in our lives individually and collectively if we would all pursue knowledge through this source. The Lord was undoubtedly referring to learning through the Holy Ghost when he said to seek knowledge "by study and also by faith" (D&C 88:118; see also Alma 17:2–3). The real challenge to those who have received the gift of the Holy Ghost is to use that gift.

The Priesthood

Priesthood power is another principle for becoming sanctified. Alma spoke of those who were ordained to the holy order of the high priesthood:

10 Now, as I said concerning the holy order, or this high priesthood, there were many who were ordained and became high priests of God; and it was on account of their exceeding faith and repentance, and their righteousness before God, they choosing to repent and work righteousness rather than to perish.

11 Therefore they were called after this holy order, and were sanctified, and their garments were washed white through the blood of the Lamb.

12 Now they, after being sanctified by the Holy Ghost, having their garments made white, being pure and spotless before God, could not look upon sin save it were with abhorrence; and there were many, exceeding great many, who were made pure and entered into the rest of the Lord their God. (Alma 13:10–12)

Because they used the priesthood in righteousness, the Holy Ghost was their companion, sanctifying and renewing their bodies (see D&C 84:33), exemplifying the grace of Jesus Christ coming upon them.

The priesthood is a call to serve the Lord. As Lehi recognized in his son Nephi, it is to become "an instrument in the hands of God" (2 Nephi 1:24). Alma was an instrument in the Lord's hands in bringing many to the truth and organizing them into the Lord's Church. Those given the priesthood "did nourish them with things pertaining to righteousness" (Mosiah 23:10–18). The Lord promised the sons of Mosiah that he would make them an instrument "in my hands unto the salvation of many souls" (Alma 17:11). At the end of their fourteen-year ministry, Ammon boasted in their having "been made instruments in the hands of God to bring about this great work. Behold, thousands of them do rejoice, and have been brought into the fold of God" (Alma 26:3–4). Alma went forth in the holy order by which he was called (Alma 6:8). Later he took his sons, and "they preached the word, and the truth, according to the spirit of prophecy and revelation; and they preached after the holy order of God by which they were called" (Alma 43:2). The only glory that Alma sought was "that perhaps I may be an instrument in the hands of God to bring some soul to repentance; and this is my joy" (Alma 29:9). Thus the righteous use of the priesthood and the companionship of the Holy Ghost directed the sons of Mosiah and Alma and his sons in the sanctification process, "for they were all men of God" (Alma 48:18).

Fasting and Prayer

A third principle of sanctification from the Book of Mormon was given in the days of Helaman, son of Helaman. In a period of pride and persecution of the Church members, the more humble Saints were sanctified:

> Nevertheless they did fast and pray oft, and did wax stronger and stronger in their humility, and firmer and

*firmer in the faith of Christ, unto the filling their souls
with joy and consolation, yea, even to the purifying and
the sanctification of their hearts, which sanctification
cometh because of their yielding their hearts unto God.
(Hel. 3:35)*

An increase of humility and firmness of faith brought the
Spirit. The Spirit purified their hearts, turning them to God and
yielding them to his will. That sanctification is a process is shown
in the wording, "stronger and stronger in their humility, and firmer
and firmer in the faith of Christ." All three of the above scriptures
regarding sanctification refer to this process as being attained over
a long period of time.

The process of sanctification is closely akin to faith unto
salvation, discussed in chapter 20: to know the course you pursue is
the will of the Lord. To wax stronger in humility means to increase
in humility. It is a deeper realization and appreciation for what the
Lord has done for us. To be firmer in the faith means to be more
secure and immovable in our faith. It is to trust fully that he will
show us the course we should pursue. As one yields his heart unto
God, he will know the will of the Lord. The Holy Ghost will direct
him in doing the things the Savior did (see 3 Nephi 27:21 above).
As he further humbles himself, and further experiences the Spirit,
it will further build his testimony and faith in Christ. The joy and
consolation of the Holy Ghost experienced by the Nephites will
also be felt. Through fasting and prayer, the solution to problems
will be revealed, and one can know the will of the Lord. Progress in
the kingdom of God comes through service in the priesthood, and
those who magnify "their calling, are sanctified by the Spirit unto
the renewing of their bodies" (D&C 84:33). Through receiving
the Holy Ghost the knowledge of good and evil will become so
keen, and the spirit so sensitive, that no longer can sin be justified
but will be looked upon with abhorrence (see Alma 13:12 quoted
above). The promise of the Lord will thus be fulfilled:

67 And if your eye be single to my glory, your whole bodies shall be filled with light, and there shall be no darkness in you; and that body which is filled with light comprehendeth all things.

68 Therefore, sanctify yourselves that your minds become single to God, and the days will come that you shall see him; for he will unveil his face unto you, and it shall be in his own time, and in his own way, and according to his own will. (D&C 88:67–68)

Such is the description of the sanctified man.

Sanctification in This Life

Some people rationalize that sanctification is an unrealistic goal and is only taught as an attempt to help people live better lives, not actually to attain that condition. The Book of Mormon describes for us a sanctified man and shows that it was attained among the Nephites.

As Nephi is recording on the small plates, he pauses to write the things of his soul (see 2 Nephi 4:15–35). In doing so, he exemplifies a man who is sensitive to sin and well on his way to sanctification. Too often, the concept of sin brings the external violations to mind at the expense of "weightier matters" of the gospel (compare Matt. 23:23). While breaking the Word of Wisdom or the sabbath, or failing to pay tithing or to attend church, are certainly examples of sin, the sanctified man is sensitive to weightier sins. Note the things that Nephi identifies as iniquities, temptations, and sins:

26 O then, if I have seen so great things, if the Lord in his condescension unto the children of men hath visited men in so much mercy, why should my heart weep and my soul linger in the valley of sorrow, and my flesh waste away, and my strength slacken, because of mine afflictions?

27 And why should I yield to sin, because of my flesh? Yea, why should I give way to temptations, that the evil one have place in my heart to destroy my peace and afflict my soul? Why am I angry because of mine enemy?

28 Awake, my soul! No longer droop in sin. Rejoice, O my heart, and give place no more for the enemy of the soul.

29 Do not anger again because of mine enemies. Do not slacken my strength because of mine afflictions. (2 Nephi 4:26–29)

Nephi's remorse for slackening his strength and being angry with his enemies exemplifies that he is very sensitive to sin. His fervent prayer is that he might shake at the appearance of sin. Nephi pleaded, "O Lord, wilt thou redeem my soul? Wilt thou deliver me out of the hands of mine enemies? Wilt thou make me that I may shake at the appearance of sin?" (2 Nephi 4:31). Sanctification is obtainable in this life and is a realistic goal. The devil would discourage us and have us believe it is an unrealistic goal, thus helping us rationalize in committing sin. The fact that sanctification in this life is a realistic goal is an incentive for living a good life as well as a goal for eternal life.

Sanctification Is Attainable for All

If the devil cannot convince us that sanctification is an unrealistic goal, his next attempt is to have us believe that, if sanctification is possible, it is only so for the prophets, apostles, or other Church leaders. The Book of Mormon proves that idea wrong. In the scripture quoted previously, Alma records that "there were many, exceedingly great many" who had attained sanctification (see Alma 13:12 above). Earlier, Alma had chastised those in the land of Zarahemla who had been born of God and were persecuting those who had become sanctified:

Yea, will ye persist in supposing that ye are better one than another; yea, will ye persist in the persecution of your brethren, who humble themselves and do walk after the holy order of God, wherewith they have been brought into this church, having been sanctified by the Holy Spirit, and they do bring forth works which are meet for repentance. (Alma 5:54)

Those who were being persecuted were brethren of the Church who honored their priesthood and followed the inspiration of the Holy Spirit. "Brethren" is plural and implies there were many who were being persecuted. Sanctification is not limited to an elect few but is possible for all who receive the blessings of the priesthood and the Holy Ghost.

Sanctification by Fulfilling One's Stewardship

Those who so live by the Spirit attain sanctification regardless of what position they hold in the Church or what station in life they hold. As previously cited, "sanctification comes by their yielding their hearts to God" (see Hel. 3:35). When one yields his heart to God and follows the will of the Lord, the Spirit sanctifies him. This is exemplified in the life of the great general, Moroni. Not only was he faithful unto the Lord, but he also endeavored to get his people to do the same: "Now it came to pass that while Amalickiah had thus been obtaining power by fraud and deceit, Moroni, on the other hand, had been preparing the minds of the people to be faithful unto the Lord their God" (Alma 48:7). Moroni was appointed chief captain over all the Nephite armies when he was only twenty-five years of age and was engaged in war and killing for at least fourteen years, possibly more.[73] He sought the guidance

---

73 Alma 43:17 tells of his appointment at age twenty-five but does not say the year that he was appointed. It is assumed that it was in the 18th year of the reign of the judges, the year his appointment is mentioned in the Book of Mormon, but he may have been appointed earlier. He died in the 36th year of

of the Lord continually in his calling and used Christ and the scriptures to inspire his armies and the Nephite people to maintain their lands and freedom (see Alma 43–46). The description of this great individual exemplifies the sanctified man:

> *11 And Moroni was a strong and a mighty man; he was a man of a perfect understanding; yea, a man that did not delight in bloodshed; a man whose soul did joy in the liberty and the freedom of his country, and his brethren from bondage and slavery;*

> *12 Yea, a man whose heart did swell with thanksgiving to his God, for the many privileges and blessings which he bestowed upon his people; a man who did labor exceedingly for the welfare and safety of his people.*

> *13 Yea, and he was a man who was firm in the faith of Christ, and he had sworn with an oath to defend his people, his rights, and his country, and his religion, even to the loss of his blood . . .*

> *16 And also, that God would make it known unto them whither they should go to defend themselves against their enemies, and by so doing, the Lord would deliver them; and this was the faith of Moroni, and his heart did glory in it; not in the shedding of blood but in doing good, in preserving his people, yea, in keeping the commandments of God, yea, and resisting iniquity.*

> *17 Yea, verily, verily, I say unto you, if all men had been, and were, and even would be, like unto Moroni, behold, the very powers of hell would have been shaken forever;*

---

the reign of the judges (Alma 63:3). If he was appointed in the 18th year, he would have been only 43 years old at his death. He yielded up his command three years earlier to spend the rest of his days in peace (Alma 62:43). This statement seems to suggest he was older than 40 and thus was appointed earlier than the 18th year of the judges.

*yea, the devil would never have power over the hearts of
the children of men. (Alma 48:11–13, 16–17)*

"A man of perfect understanding" does not mean that he
knew everything about everything. Such perfection attained by
Moroni can be known only through the Holy Ghost, which is the
source to become sanctified. His perfect understanding was that
he knew the will of the Lord and followed it. General Moroni had
all the characteristics of the people of Helaman described above
(see Hel. 3:35). He not only experienced joy and consolation, as
Helaman's people did, but he also sought that same joy for all the
people of his country. He was strong in his humility, as exemplified
by his heart swelling "in thanksgiving to his God" (v. 12 above).
He was also firm in his faith, willing to enter into an oath to defend
his people in their faith that they would be delivered. He is not the
only one of this time period to reach this blessed state.

As Mormon abridged the record, he compared General
Moroni to other men of God. Their calling happened to be in
missionary service as mentioned above: "Behold, he was a man
like unto Ammon, the son of Mosiah, yea, and even the other
sons of Mosiah, yea, and also Alma and his sons, for they were all
men of God" (Alma 48:18). Thus we see that whosoever will yield
their hearts unto God, as described in Helaman 3:35, in whatever
capacity their lives may lead them, will receive the guidance of
the Spirit and the blessings of the priesthood to bring about their
sanctification. These are the general requirements. More specific
requirements will be discussed in the next chapter.

The importance of our using the gift which we are given is
shown by an account of Brigham Young dreaming of visiting with
Joseph Smith after Joseph had left this mortal life:

Tuesday, 23 [Feb. 1847]—I met with the
brethren of the Twelve in the Historian's office.
Conversation ensued relative to emigration westward.

I related the following dream: While sick and asleep about noonday of the 17th inst., I dreamed that I went to St. Joseph. He looked perfectly natural, sitting with his feet on the lower round of his chair. I took his right hand and kissed him many times, and said to him: "Why is it that we cannot be together as we used to be. You have been from us a long time, and we want your society and I do not like to be separated from you."

Joseph rising from his chair and looking at me with his usual, earnest, expressive and pleasing countenance replied, "It is all right."

I said, "I do not like to be away from you."

Joseph said, "It is all right; we cannot be together yet; we shall be by and by; but you will have to do without me for a while, and then we shall be together again."

I then discovered there was a hand rail between us, Joseph stood by a window and to the southwest of him it was very light. I was in the twilight and to the north of me it was very dark; I said, "Brother Joseph, the brethren you know well, better than I do; you raised them up, and brought the Priesthood to us. The brethren have a great anxiety to understand the law of adoption or sealing principles; and if you have a word of counsel for me I should be glad to receive it."

Joseph stepped toward me, and looking very earnestly, yet pleasantly said, "Tell the people to be humble and faithful, and be sure to keep the spirit of the Lord and it will lead them right. Be careful and not turn away the small still voice; it will teach you what to do and where to go; it will yield the fruits of the kingdom. Tell the brethren to keep their hearts open to conviction, so that when the Holy Ghost comes to them, their hearts will be ready to receive it. They can tell the Spirit of the Lord from all other spirits; it will whisper peace and joy to their souls; it will take malice, hatred, strife and all evil from their hearts; and their whole desire will be to do good, bring forth righteousness and build up the kingdom of God. Tell the brethren if they will follow the spirit of the Lord they will go right. Be sure to tell the people to keep the Spirit of the Lord; and if they will, they will find themselves just as they were organized by our Father in Heaven before they came into the world. Our Father in Heaven organized the human family, but they are all disorganized and in great confusion."

Joseph then showed me the pattern, how they were in the beginning. This I cannot describe, but I saw it, and saw where the Priesthood had been taken from the earth and how it must be joined together, so that there would be a perfect chain from Father Adam to his latest posterity. Joseph again said, "Tell the people to be sure to keep the Spirit of the Lord and follow it, and it will lead them just right."[74]

Through studying the Book of Mormon, we can better assure ourselves of having the Holy Ghost as our companion. It gives us the formula for obtaining the power of the Holy Ghost through the gift we have received and gives many examples of what it will do for us.

Sanctification should be the goal of every member of the Church, because the Lord "dwelleth not in unholy temples, but in the hearts of the righteous doth he dwell; yea, and he has also said that the righteous shall sit down in his kingdom, to go no more out; but their garments should be made white through the blood [grace] of the Lamb" (Alma 34:36).

---

74 Watson, E. J., Ed. *Manuscript History of Brigham Young, 1846–1847,* pp. 528–30.

23

LOVE AND SERVE GOD

Sanctification comes "to all those who love and serve God with all their mights, minds, and strength." (D&C 20:31)

Those who love God with all their might, mind, and strength "are true followers of his Son, Jesus Christ" and will be filled with the love of Christ, which is charity (Moro. 7:47–48). Therefore, to be sanctified is to obtain charity. Although being filled with the love of Christ and being sanctified are synonymous (and an extension of the previous chapter), charity is treated separately because of the extensive teachings on the subject in the Book of Mormon. Moroni concluded the Book of Mormon record with an invitation that confirms what is said above:

> *32 Yea, come unto Christ, and be perfected in him, and deny yourselves of all ungodliness; and if ye shall deny yourselves of all ungodliness, and love God with all your might, mind and strength, then is his grace sufficient for you, that by his grace ye may be perfect in Christ; and if by the grace of God ye are perfect in Christ, ye can in nowise deny the power of God.*
>
> *33 And again, if ye by the grace of God are perfect in Christ, and deny not his power, then are ye sanctified in Christ by the grace of God, through the shedding of the*

*blood of Christ, which is in the covenant of the Father
unto the remission of your sins, that ye become holy,
without spot. (Moro. 10:32–33)*

Thus, Moroni outlines a three-step process by which we can
be sanctified in Christ: (1) deny yourself of all ungodliness; (2)
love God with all your might, mind, and strength; and (3) obtain
perfection in Christ by his grace. Let us consider each of these
separately.

Deny All Ungodliness

The word "ungodliness" is not used in the Book of Mormon
except by Moroni above, but there are many other passages that
identify ungodly actions. In defining charity, Moroni lists several
things that charity is not: it "envieth not, is not puffed up, seeketh
not her own, is not easily provoked, thinketh no evil, and rejoiceth
not in iniquity" (Moro. 7:45). Nephi testified that the Lord had
commanded that all men should have charity and "should not
envy" (2 Nephi 26:30–32). Alma asked the born-again people of
Zarahemla if they were stripped of envy and warned them that, if
not, they were not prepared and would not be found guiltless before
Christ (see Alma 5:29). There are many other general labelings of
envy as a cause of wickedness among the Nephites (see Alma 1:32;
4:9; 16:18; Hel. 13:22; 3 Nephi 21:19; 30:2; Morm. 8:28, 36). In
contrast, the Zion society that followed the ministry of Jesus Christ
among the Nephites was characterized as having "no envyings" (4
Nephi 1:16).

Pride causes people to be puffed up. This was also a repeated
problem among the Nephites. Jacob, brother of Nephi, said the
people of Nephi under the second king "began to search much
gold and silver, and began to be lifted up somewhat in pride"
(Jacob 1:16). There is a relationship between pride and materialism
in the Book of Mormon. In his temple speech that followed, Jacob
said: "And the hand of providence hath smiled upon you most
pleasingly, that you have obtained many riches; and because some

of you have obtained more abundantly than that of your brethren ye are lifted up in the pride of your hearts, and wear stiff necks and high heads because of the costliness of your apparel, and persecute your brethren because ye suppose that ye are better than they (Jacob 2:13; see also Alma 4:6).

Jacob went on to warn his people to "let not this pride of your hearts destroy your souls" (Jacob 2:16). Wicked King Noah's people were characterized as being "lifted up in the pride of their hearts" (Mosiah 11:5, 19). Alma also asked the people of Zarahemla if they were stripped of pride; and if not, they were not prepared to meet God (see Alma 5:28). He went on to equate pride with trampling

> 53 . . . the Holy One under your feet; yea, can ye be puffed up in the pride of your hearts; yea, will ye still persist in the wearing of costly apparel and setting your hearts upon the vain things of the world, upon your riches?
>
> 54 Yea, will ye persist in supposing that ye are better one than another; yea, will ye persist in the persecution of your brethren, who humble themselves and do walk after the holy order of God, wherewith they have been brought into this church, having been sanctified by the Holy Spirit, and they do bring forth works which are meet for repentance. (Alma 5:53–54)

This last verse is repeated from the previous chapter to remind us of the general requirements of sanctification and also to show its contrast, pride. Those "who humble themselves and do walk after the holy order of God" are sanctified by the Holy Spirit. Those who are not stripped of pride "trample the Holy One under [their] feet" (1 Nephi 19:7). There are many other warnings of pride among the Nephites, and there are also many prophecies of pride being prevalent among the Gentiles in the latter days (see 2 Nephi 26:10, 20; 28:12–15). We will not expound on these warnings and prophecies but close the subject with this Doctrine and Covenants admonition: "But beware of pride, lest ye become as the Nephites of old" (38:39).

Charity does not seek her aggrandizement but seeks the welfare of Zion. It has an eye single to the glory of God (see Morm. 8:15). Priestcraft, on the other hand, seeks "not the welfare of Zion" but labors for money (2 Nephi 26:29–31). Priestcraft is counter to priesthood. The wickedness of King Noah is a prime example of priestcraft among the Nephites. Nephite kings held the priesthood and, thus, would be guilty of priestcraft if it were not honored. Noah sought his own desires and built a kingdom of wickedness (see Mosiah 11:1–19; 29:17–18).

To be patient in suffering is to be not easily provoked. The Lord told the sons of Mosiah, as they went on their mission among the Lamanites, to "be patient in long-suffering and afflictions, that ye may show forth good examples" (Alma 17:11). That they followed the Lord's instructions is exemplified by Ammon in the land of Ishmael (see Alma 17:20–25) and by Aaron, Muloki, and Ammah in prison in the land of Middoni (see Alma 20:2, 29). Their patience resulted in the conversion of thousands of Lamanites (see Alma 26:4, 27–31).

Those who are pure in heart think no evil. To avoid evil thoughts, we must keep our mind on the Savior. In the negative context, Alma said: "For how knoweth a man the master whom he has not served, and who is a stranger unto him, and is far from the thoughts and intents of his heart?" (Mosiah 5:13). Alma admonished his son Helaman to "let all thy thoughts be directed unto the Lord" (Alma 37:36). To do so will help us become pure in heart.

Alma advised Shiblon to "bridle all your passions, that ye may be filled with love" (Alma 38:12). "Wickedness never was happiness" (Alma 41:10). The Lamanites at the time of Alma were "delighting in all manner of wickedness and plunder, except it were among their own brethren" (Mosiah 24:7). Wickedness was prevalent among the Nephites, as well. Without enumerating these many occasions, the warning of Alma is appropriate: "All ye that will persist in your wickedness . . . shall be hewn down and cast into the fire except they speedily repent" (Alma 5:56). To deny ungodliness is to deny all forms of wickedness and iniquity. As said by King Benjamin:

> 29 And finally, I cannot tell you all the things whereby ye may commit sin; for there are divers ways and means, even so many that I cannot number them.
>
> 30 But this much I can tell you, that if ye do not watch yourselves, and your thoughts, and your words, and your deeds, and observe the commandments of God, and continue in the faith of what ye have heard concerning the coming of our Lord, even unto the end of your lives, ye must perish. And now, O man, remember, and perish not. (Mosiah 4:29–30)

Love God with All Your Might, Mind, and Strength

Nephi taught that "the Lord God hath given a commandment that all men should have charity, which charity is love. And except they should have charity they were nothing. Wherefore, if they should have charity they would not suffer the laborer in Zion to perish. But the laborer in Zion shall labor for Zion" (2 Nephi 26:30–31). To love God is to labor for him or for the building of Zion.

One of the best-known scriptures in the Book of Mormon is Mosiah 2:17: "When ye are in the service of your fellow beings ye are only in the service of your God." The real value of this scripture is appreciated much more when it is used in the context of King Benjamin's sermon. Although he was their king, he looked upon his stewardship as service to God. He wanted his people not to fear him or think that he was "more than a mortal man":

> But I am like as yourselves, subject to all manner of infirmities in body and mind; yet I have been chosen by this people, and consecrated by my father, and was suffered by the hand of the Lord that I should be a ruler and a

*king over this people; and have been kept and preserved
by his matchless power, to serve you with all the might,
mind and strength which the Lord hath granted unto me.
(Mosiah 2:10–11)*

His desire was to love God by serving the people with all
the might, mind, and strength that the Lord had given him.
He enumerated what he had done and had not done for them
during his service as king. He was not boasting but merely telling
the people of his conscience being clear before God: "for I have
only been in the service of God" (Mosiah 2:16). He then gave his
well-known adage on service quoted above. After this statement,
he urged them to serve one another and to give thanks to their
heavenly king (see Mosiah 2:18–19). After recounting all that the
heavenly King had done for them, King Benjamin said that "if
ye should serve him with all your whole souls yet ye would be
unprofitable servants. And behold, all that he requires of you is to
keep his commandments," for which they were blessed (Mosiah
2:21–22). This pattern of service is one we should emulate.

The teaching of Amulek is another testimony of the
importance of serving God through serving those around you:

*27 Yea, and when you do not cry unto the Lord, let your
hearts be full, drawn out in prayer unto him continually
for your welfare, and also for the welfare of those who are
around you.*

*28 And now behold, my beloved brethren, I say unto you,
do not suppose that this is all; for after ye have done all
these things, if ye turn away the needy, and the naked,
and visit not the sick and afflicted, and impart of your
substance, if ye have, to those who stand in need—I say
unto you, if ye do not any of these things, behold, your
prayer is vain, and availeth you nothing, and ye are as
hypocrites who do deny the faith.*

29 Therefore, if ye do not remember to be charitable, ye are as dross, which the refiners do cast out, (it being of no worth) and is trodden under foot of men. (Alma 34:27–29)

While Amulek's examples of charity appear to be physical, the spiritual dimension of their welfare will follow. As the New Testament apostle James wrote:

15 If a brother or sister be naked, and destitute of daily food,

16 And one of you say unto them, Depart in peace, be ye warmed and filled; notwithstanding ye give them not those things which are needful to the body; what doth it profit? (James 2:15–16)

Having provided for physical needs, the recipient will be more susceptible to the spiritual.

To serve God with our might represents the physical. To serve with our mind represents the mental or intellectual. And to serve with our strength is to use all of the power of our resources to do his will.

Perfection in Christ

Perfection in Christ must come through the grace of God, or as a gift from him. Mormon, speaking to those "of the church, that [were] the peaceable followers of Christ, and that [had] obtained a sufficient hope by which [they could] enter into the rest of the Lord" (Moro. 7:3), urged them:

. . . pray unto the Father with all the energy of heart, that ye may be filled with this love, which he hath bestowed upon all who are true followers of his Son, Jesus Christ; that ye may become the sons of God; that when he shall appear we shall be like him, for we shall see him as he is;

*that we may have this hope; that we may be purified even
as he is pure. Amen. (Moroni 7:48)*

There are several things to learn from Mormon's teaching.
First of all, he was speaking to those who were devout Church
members, who were already committed to Christ. Secondly, his
urging these people to pray shows that they were to ask for his
love, something that comes as a gift or by grace. This gift came
only to those who were true followers of the Son. Those who are
true followers of Christ are "yielding their hearts unto God" and
on the road to sanctification (Hel. 3:35). Wherefore, they are being
sanctified in the Spirit as discussed in chapter 22. Those who are
thus sanctified will be sanctified in the flesh and become like Christ
when he appears. This is also a gift by the grace of God. The apostle
John teaches this same doctrine in the New Testament: "Beloved,
now are we the sons of God, and it doth not yet appear what we
shall be: but we know that, when he shall appear, we shall be like
him; for we shall see him as he is" (1 John 3:2).

There are a few people in the Book of Mormon record, some
of whom were discussed in the previous chapters, that attained
this perfection in Christ. Nephi, son of Lehi, was one of these. He
testified:

> *6 I glory in plainness; I glory in truth; I glory in my Jesus,
> for he hath redeemed my soul from hell.*
>
> *7 I have charity for my people, and great faith in Christ
> that I shall meet many souls spotless at his judgment-seat.*
>
> *8 I have charity for the Jew—I say Jew, because I mean
> them from whence I came.*
>
> *9 I also have charity for the Gentiles. But behold, for none
> of these can I hope except they shall be reconciled unto
> Christ, and enter into the narrow gate, and walk in the
> strait path which leads to life, and continue in the path
> until the end of the day of probation. (2 Nephi 33:6–9)*

He gloried in truth; charity rejoiceth in the truth (see Moro. 7:45). He gloried in Jesus. To confess that Jesus is the Christ by the power of the Holy Ghost requires charity (see Moro. 7:44). He sought not for himself but for his Nephite people, the Jews, and the Gentiles. He was sanctified in the Spirit and had become perfected in Christ, through grace.

Another Book of Mormon character who became perfected in Christ was Moroni, son of Mormon. He spoke to the Lord about charity being exemplified by Jesus "laying down his life for the world" and then prayed further that the Lord "would give unto the Gentiles grace, that they might have charity" (Ether 12:33–36). In response to Moroni's prayer, the Lord said unto him:

If they have not charity it mattereth not unto thee, thou hast been faithful; wherefore, thy garments shall be made clean. And because thou hast seen thy weakness thou shalt be made strong, even unto the sitting down in the place which I have prepared in the mansions of my Father. (Ether 12:37)

Moroni testified further of his having seen Jesus and commended the reader "to seek this Jesus of whom the prophets and apostles have written, that the grace of God the Father, and also the Lord Jesus Christ, and the Holy Ghost, which beareth record of them, may be and abide in you forever. Amen" (Ether 12:41). He later wrote to the posterity of the Lamanites, who were seeking his life, that his writings might be of help to them in obtaining eternal life (Moro. 1:1–4). This is certainly an example of the pure love of Christ. When he closed the Book of Mormon by inviting all to come unto Christ and be perfected in him, he was not asking the reader to do something he had not done. He himself had become perfected in Christ.

Apparently the Jaredite prophet Ether was also perfected in Christ. Although we have only a brief account of his ministry, his closing words, as abridged by Moroni, reflect his having yielded his heart unto God: "Whether the Lord will that I be translated, or that I suffer the will of the Lord in the flesh, it mattereth not, if it so be that I am saved in the kingdom of God. Amen" (Ether 15:34). He was totally dedicated to do the Lord's will.

There were undoubtedly many others among the Nephites who were perfected in Christ, such as Nephi the son of Helaman (see Hel. 10:4–11), and among the Jaredites, such as the brother of Jared (see Ether 3:17–20). The examples cited above are those most completely detailed in the scriptures who show their perfection in Christ. Sanctification or charity is bestowed upon "all those who love and serve God with all their mights, minds, and strength" (D&C 20:31).

24

MAN MAY FALL FROM GRACE

*"But there is a possibility that man may fall from grace
and depart from the living God."*
(D&C 20:32)

The doctrines of justification and sanctification, discussed in the previous chapters, are true because of the grace of Christ (see D&C 20:30–31). To fall from the grace of Christ is to lose the gifts of justification and/or sanctification. Departing from the living God would imply a discontinuance of yielding your heart to him, with the subsequent loss of the Spirit and the power of the priesthood. This chapter will consider the fall from justification, and the fall from sanctification will be considered in chapter 24.

Fall From Justification

In Alma's great discourse to the people of Zarahemla on being born again, he presented several questions as determining factors for whether a person had had this experience. He then posed this question: "And now behold, I say unto you, my brethren, if ye have experienced a change of heart, and if ye have felt to sing the song of redeeming love, I would ask, can ye feel so now?" (Alma 5:26). The question posed above confirms that man may lose his status of justification.

Alma follows with several other questions that were asked as criteria for whether or not their rebirth experience, bringing a remission of sins, had been retained. The basic question was whether they had kept themselves blameless before God since being justified. This query was followed by suggestions of self-examination. Alma asked if they "were called to die at this time," what would be their status before God regarding humility, pride, envy, mockery of fellow Church members, and persecution of the same? Those who would answer negatively to these questions are told by Alma that they are not prepared for the judgment bar, for they will not be found guiltless, and must repent or they cannot be saved (see Alma 5:27–31). Alma's announcement is another way of saying they have fallen from the grace of the doctrine of justification.

Alma's call to repentance of these people who have fallen from grace illustrates the principle that those who have lost their justification can regain it. However, if they do not repent but continue in wickedness, they are worse off than had they not been born again. Mormon's editorial comment, as he abridged the records of the mission of the sons of Mosiah to the Lamanites, is another example of the seriousness of falling from grace: "And thus we can plainly discern that after a people have been once enlightened by the Spirit of God, and have had great knowledge of things pertaining to righteousness, and then have fallen away into sin and transgression, they become more hardened, and thus their state becomes worse than though they had never known these things" (Alma 24:30). The conclusion drawn by Mormon was apparently based on the fact that none of the Amalekites, except one, nor any of the Amulonites, both of whom were apostate Nephites who had merged with the Lamanites, were converted by the Nephite missionaries preaching among the Lamanites (see Alma 23:14). These apostates had fallen from the grace of justification.

There are many ways to lose the grace of justification. King Benjamin warned his people to "beware lest there shall arise contentions among you, and ye list to obey the evil spirit" (Mosiah

2:32). The evil spirit is the father of contention. When Jesus appeared to the Nephites, he cautioned: "He that hath the spirit of contention is not of me, but is of the devil, who is the father of contention, and he stirreth up the hearts of men to contend with anger, one with another. Behold, this is not my doctrine, to stir up the hearts of men with anger, one against another" (3 Nephi 11:29–30). Satan stirs people "up to anger against that which is good" (2 Nephi 28:20). The Book of Mormon "speaketh harshly against sin . . . wherefore, no man will be angry at the words which I [Nephi] have written save he shall be of the spirit of the devil" (2 Nephi 33:5). Through contention and anger we lose the Spirit of the Lord and become subject to the spirit of the devil.

Complacency is another danger of which we must be warned. To not do what we should do constitutes a sin of omission (see James 4:17). This is another tool of Satan identified by Nephi: "And others will he pacify, and lull them away into carnal security, that they will say: All is well in Zion; yea, Zion prospereth, all is well—and thus the devil cheateth their souls, and leadeth them away carefully down to hell" (2 Nephi 28:21). In writing to Pahoran, General Moroni accused him (albeit falsely because of lack of information) of sitting in idleness, and then asked: "Do ye suppose that God will look upon you as guiltless while ye sit still and behold these things?" (Alma 60:23). To not be looked upon as guiltless signifies that we are no longer justified. We must "make use of the means which the Lord has provided for us," as Alma wrote to Pahoran in the same epistle (Alma 60:21). If we don't use these means, the devil will cheat our souls, as Nephi said.

A third way of losing the grace of justification is also instigated by Satan. Still speaking of the devil, Nephi said, "And behold, others he flattereth away, and telleth them there is no hell; and he saith unto them: I am no devil, for there is none— and thus he whispereth in their ears, until he grasps them with his awful chains, from whence there is no deliverance" (2 Nephi 28:22). The prime example in the Book of Mormon of one who was grasped by the awful chains of Satan is Korihor. After he was struck dumb following his encounter with Alma for teaching anti-Christ doctrine, Korihor confessed in writing:

> 52 I know that I am dumb, for I cannot speak; and I know that nothing save it were the power of God could bring this upon me; yea, and I always knew that there was a God.
>
> 53 But behold, the devil hath deceived me; for he appeared unto me in the form of an angel, and said unto me: Go and reclaim this people, for they have all gone astray after an unknown God. And he said unto me: There is no God; yea, and he taught me that which I should say. And I have taught his words; and I taught them because they were pleasing unto the carnal mind; and I taught them, even until I had much success, insomuch that I verily believed that they were true; and for this cause I withstood the truth, even until I have brought this great curse upon me. (Alma 30:52–53)

In spite of enjoying success and having experiences that are pleasing unto our carnal reasoning, we must recognize that it may be Satan who is working upon us.

After King Benjamin instructed his people how to retain a remission of the sins they had just obtained and warned them of many pitfalls, he wisely cautioned:

> 29 And finally, I cannot tell you all the things whereby ye may commit sin; for there are divers ways and means, even so many that I cannot number them.
>
> 30 But this much I can tell you, that if ye do not watch yourselves, and your thoughts, and your words, and your deeds, and observe the commandments of God, and continue in the faith of what ye have heard concerning the coming of our Lord, even unto the end of your lives, ye must perish. And now, O man, remember, and perish not. (Mosiah 4:29–30)

There are many ways to commit sin, but we must always remember another admonition given by Alma, to "humble yourselves before the Lord, and call on his holy name, and watch and pray continually, that ye may not be tempted above that which ye can bear, and thus be lead by the Holy Spirit, becoming humble, meek, submissive, patient, full of love and all long-suffering" (Alma 13:28). Paul taught the same principle (see 1 Cor. 10:13).

More important than why people fall from grace is how we can maintain grace. General Moroni knew "that it was easier to keep the city from falling into the hands of the Lamanites than to retake it from them" (Alma 59:9). The same is true of living the gospel. Prevention is more economical than repentance. The Book of Mormon teaches us how to retain a remission of sins, or our justification.

Retaining Justification

As discussed in chapter 23, to be justified is to receive a remission of one's sins. However, as the Lord revealed to the Prophet Joseph Smith, when a person is forgiven and then returns to his old habits, "the former sins return" (D&C 82:7). Therefore, we must learn the formula to remain guiltless before God.

To those who had just been born again, King Benjamin counseled:

> And again I say unto you as I have said before, that as ye have come to the knowledge of the glory of God, or if ye have known of his goodness and have tasted of his love, and have received a remission of your sins, which causeth such exceedingly great joy in your souls, even so I would that ye should remember, and always retain in remembrance, the greatness of God, and your own nothingness, and his goodness and long-suffering towards you, unworthy creatures, and humble yourselves even in the depths of humility, calling on the name of the Lord daily, and standing steadfastly in the faith of that which

is to come, which was spoken by the mouth of the angel.
(Mosiah 4:11)

Remembering God, calling on his name, being aware of
our own nothingness, and being faithful, as advocated by King
Benjamin, are ways to maintain a relationship between God and
man. We must also maintain a relationship with our fellow men.
King Benjamin also advised his subjects how this was done.

> *And now, for the sake of these things which I have spoken*
> *unto you—that is, for the sake of retaining a remission of*
> *your sins from day to day, that ye may walk guiltless before*
> *God—I would that ye should impart of your substance*
> *to the poor, every man according to that which he hath,*
> *such as feeding the hungry, clothing the naked, visiting*
> *the sick and administering to their relief, both spiritually*
> *and temporally, according to their wants. (Mosiah 4:26)*

King Benjamin's formula for retaining justification could be
summarized as keeping the first two commandments: "Love the
Lord thy God with all thy heart, and with all thy soul, and with all
thy mind"; and "Love thy neighbour as thyself" (Matt. 22:37–39).
If we really love ourselves, we will want to retain a remission of our
sins.

As Alma, son of Alma, went about the Church teaching, he
described those who were retaining a remission of sins:

> *13 Now this [pride] was a great cause for lamentations*
> *among the people, while others were abasing themselves,*
> *succoring those who stood in need of their succor, such*
> *as imparting their substance to the poor and the needy,*
> *feeding the hungry, and suffering all manner of afflictions,*
> *for Christ's sake, who should come according to the spirit*
> *of prophecy;*
>
> *14 Looking forward to that day, thus retaining a*
> *remission of their sins; being filled with great joy because*

of the resurrection of the dead, according to the will and power and deliverance of Jesus Christ from the bands of death. (Alma 4:13–14)

The suffering of afflictions for Christ's sake again suggests a spiritual dimension of the man-to-man relationship. It should be emphasized that there is an obligation to care for spiritual as well as temporal needs.

There is another point in this man-to-man relationship made earlier by the same Alma:

And thus, in their prosperous circumstances, they did not send away any who were naked, or that were hungry, or that were athirst, or that were sick, or that had not been nourished; and they did not set their hearts upon riches; therefore they were liberal to all, both old and young, both bond and free, both male and female, whether out of the church or in the church, having no respect to persons as to those who stood in need. (Alma 1:30)

All people are God's children, and those who have become spiritually adopted sons and daughters of Christ through rebirth (see Mosiah 5:7) should not be respecters of persons. They should respect all, as does God: "black and white, bond and free, male and female; and he remembereth the heathen; and all are alike unto God, both Jew and Gentile" (2 Nephi 26:33).

An example of retaining a remission of sins is again Alma, son of Alma. He later testified to his son Helaman that from the time of his being born again [justified] "even until now, I have labored without ceasing, that I might bring souls unto repentance; that I might bring them to taste of the exceeding joy of which I did taste; that they might also be born of God, and be filled with the Holy Ghost" (Alma 36:24). That his labors were a labor of love for his fellow men is illustrated in his answer to Korihor regarding the charge of usurping authority over the people. Alma testified:

32 Thou knowest that we do not glut ourselves upon the labors of this people; for behold I have labored even from the commencement of the reign of the judges until now, with mine own hands for my support, notwithstanding my many travels round about the land to declare the word of God unto my people.

33 And notwithstanding the many labors which I have performed in the church, I have never received so much as even one senine for my labor; neither has any of my brethren, save it were in the judgment seat; and then we have received only according to law for our time.

34 And now, if we do not receive anything for our labors in the church, what doth it profit us to labor in the church save it were to declare the truth, that we may have rejoicings in the joy of our brethren? (Alma 30:32–34)

King Benjamin is another example that was cited earlier (see Mosiah 2:10–19). There are certainly other examples of justification in the Book of Mormon. "Keeping yourselves blameless before God" (Alma 5:27) is crucial to salvation.

To retain the grace of justification, we must be spiritually alive. We become spiritually alive when we are born again. When we lose the grace of justification, we become spiritually dead. Elder Spencer W. Kimball admonished: "There are many people in this church today who think they live, but they are dead to the spiritual things. And I believe even many who are making pretenses of being active are also spiritually dead."[75] With the help of the Lord and his Spirit, we can remain alive in Christ as his son or daughter.

---

75 Kimball, S. W. (1951). *Conference Report,* April, p. 105.

25

LET THE CHURCH TAKE HEED

"Therefore let the church take heed and pray always, lest they enter

into temptation." (D&C 20:33)

The Book of Mormon speaks in detail of times when the Church collectively went astray. There are also several warnings or descriptions of false churches or apostate factions of the Church. The caution made known by the Book of Mormon addresses the true Church, not the other churches that were in existence or false branches of the true Church. The causes of the Church going astray are given to us as warnings in the Book of Mormon.

Priestcraft

One of the major problems within the church of Christ in the Book of Mormon was priestcraft. Although it was first introduced among the Nephites about 91 B.C. (see Alma 1:12), it is an age-old problem. Priestcraft is Satan's counterfeit of priesthood and, in one form or another, has been practiced since Satan influenced Cain to offer inappropriate sacrifices (see Moses 5:18–21).

While priestcraft has always existed, it is not specifically labeled as such in the Bible. The term may have been deleted when many plain and precious parts were taken away (1 Nephi 13:23–29). However, the Book of Mormon is a great revealer of priestcraft and the evils it engendered in the times of the Nephites. It confirms that priestcraft existed among the Jews and was the cause of the Savior's crucifixion (see 2 Nephi 10:5). It also warns against priestcraft in the latter dispensation (see 3 Nephi 30:2). The Doctrine and Covenants likewise refers to priestcraft as causing error in the last days among the few who do good in his corrupted vineyard (see D&C 33:4).

As the Book of Mormon is studied, priestcrafts should not be confused with the anti-Christs. These two evils are not identical and should be considered separately. The anti-Christs, such as Korihor and Sherem, spoken of in chapter one, openly rebel against Christ, while the user of priestcraft claims a belief in Christ but perverts his teachings. Nephi, in warning against priestcraft in the days when the Book of Mormon would come forth, defined it as follows:

> *He commanded that there shall be no priestcrafts; for, behold, priestcrafts are that men preach and set themselves up for a light unto the world, that they may get gain and praise of the world; but they seek not the welfare of Zion. (2 Nephi 26:29)*

A close analysis of the Book of Mormon definition of priestcraft will show that it parallels yet contradicts the priesthood. Priesthood bearers should set Christ up as the light of the world (see 3 Nephi 18:24), while those guilty of priestcraft set themselves up as a light of the world. They do this, either consciously or inadvertently, by proclaiming that a teaching of the scriptures or of one of God's servants is false and substituting another teaching in its place. Priesthood bearers are to have an eye single to the glory of God (see D&C 27:2; 88:67), while those guilty of priestcraft seek the gain and praise of the world. They do this, again either consciously or inadvertently, by trying to obtain popularity among Church members, by doing things for monetary increase beyond the normal remuneration for their time, or by seeking favorable positions or rewards. The greatest object of the priesthood bearer should be the building up of Zion (see *TPJS*, 160), while those guilty of priestcraft have only selfish desires and little or no concern for the building of Zion. This last parallel is a fairly stern castigation towards Church members, since Zion is not a common goal spoken of in circles outside the Church.

The Book of Mormon describes priestcraft as a major problem during the last one hundred years before the birth of Christ. Priestcraft was first introduced among the Nephites by one Nehor in the land of Zarahemla about 91 B.C. He taught three basic doctrines which clearly illustrate Nephi's definition of priestcraft. Nehor bore down against the Church, teaching that "every priest and teacher ought to become popular; and they ought not to labor with their hands, but that they ought to be supported by the people" (Alma 1:3). This is a good example of "seeking the gain and praise of the world." Nehor also taught "that all mankind should be saved at the last day, and that they need not fear nor tremble, but that they might lift up their heads and rejoice; for the Lord had created all men, and had also redeemed all men; and, in the end, all men should have eternal life" (Alma 1:4). This is contrary to the Book of Mormon and Bible teaching of working out your own salvation (see Alma 34:37; Morm. 9:27; Philip. 2:12). Nehor's bearing down against the Church, and the persecutions against the Church by his followers, are the third example of Nephi's definition: "They seek not the welfare of Zion." These three criteria are a test to determine whether it is priesthood or priestcraft in any age of the world.

The Order of Nehor

Although Nehor suffered an ignominious death for the murder of Gideon and finally acknowledged that his teachings were contrary to the word of God, priestcraft among the Nephites was not abolished (see Alma 1:16). In fact, it became a constant threat until Christ came among them. Nehor's followers become known as members of the "order of Nehor" throughout the rest of the Book of Mormon. A few examples will illustrate its influence.

Amlici was one major Book of Mormon character who was of the order of Nehor. Rising to leadership among Nehor's followers, he sought to destroy the Church of God (see Alma 2:4). Again, this indicates that those who practice priestcraft do not seek the welfare of Zion. Amlici stirred up his people to war against the Nephites and joined also with the Lamanites. He retained the order of Nehor in fighting against the establishment of Zion.

The next stronghold for the order of Nehor was in the land of Ammonihah. The judge responsible for burning the people who believed in the word of God, and also their holy scriptures, was "after the order and faith of Nehor" (Alma 14:8–16). That all the lawyers who opposed Alma and Amulek (see Alma 8–11) were of the order of Nehor is probable but not certain, but their desire was to get gain of the world (see Alma 10:32). The entire population, it seems, had become influenced as they sought to destroy the liberty of the people (see Alma 8:17). The entire populace "did not believe in the repentance of their sins" (Alma 15:15) but believed that all would be saved, a characteristic of Nehor's teaching. When the land of Ammonihah was utterly destroyed, it became known as the "Desolation of Nehors; for they were of the profession of Nehor, who were slain" (Alma 16:11). Their destruction illustrated the eventual outcome of priestcraft in the land.

Again, the destruction of the city of Ammonihah, and those of the order of Nehor, did not end the order in other areas. In the Nephite city of Jerusalem, the apostates known as Amalekites "had built synagogues after the order of the Nehors" (Alma 21:3–4). The Amalekites and Amulonites were always stirring the Lamanites up against the Nephite and Lamanite converts, and no Amalekites or Amulonites were ever among those who were converted, except one (see Alma 23:18; 24:28–29). Their presence was a lasting evil influence among the Nephites and Lamanites.

As previously stated, the Book of Mormon also warns about priestcraft in the latter days. Therefore, the Church must take heed against this pernicious practice. There are many descriptions and warnings of priestcraft that was to be among the Gentiles after the coming forth of the Book of Mormon (see 2 Nephi 26:14). Nephi, quoting Isaiah, defined the learned, to whom the words of the Book of Mormon were to be taken, as guilty of priestcraft, seeking gain and the glory of the world:

> *15 But behold, it shall come to pass that the Lord God shall say unto him to whom he shall deliver the book: Take these words which are not sealed and deliver them to another, that he may show them unto the learned, saying: Read this, I pray thee. And the learned shall say: Bring hither the book, and I will read them.*

> *16 And now, because of the glory of the world and to get gain will they say this, and not for the glory of God. (2 Nephi 27:15–16)*

Martin Harris's account of taking the characters that had been copied from the plates and translated by Joseph Smith to New York verified the fulfillment of Isaiah's prophecy and discloses why Professor Charles Anthon reacted the way he did (see JS–H 1:63–65).

The Savior also recognized the existence of priestcraft in the latter days. He informed the Nephites that one of the reasons that the fulness of the gospel would be taken from the Gentiles would be priestcraft (see 3 Nephi 16:10). The Savior later quoted Micah to the Nephites and prophesied that all priestcrafts, along with other iniquities, "shall be done away" (3 Nephi 21:19).

Through a study of the Book of Mormon, one can see the effects of priestcraft upon a people. One can also see how clearly the Nephites and the Savior, himself, forewarned of this evil practice in the latter days. Let us remember that the best way to combat priestcraft is to honorably magnify the priesthood and follow its righteous leadership. If we will always set up Christ as our light and the light to the world, have an eye single to the glory of God, and labor with love for the establishment of Zion, we will never become victims of the evil practice of priestcraft.

Pride

A second major problem of the Church was pride. Individual pride was previously discussed, but now we will consider its effect upon the Church. After overcoming the problems of Nehor and Amlici, the Church was more fully established and prospered spiritually and temporally (see Alma 4:1–5). However, in the eighth year of the reign of the judges:

> *6 . . . the people of the church began to wax proud, because of their exceeding riches, and their fine silks, and their fine-twined linen, and because of their many flocks and herds, and their gold and their silver, and all manner of precious things, which they had obtained by their industry; and in all these things were they lifted up in the pride of their eyes, for they began to wear costly apparel . . .*
>
> *8 . . . the people of the church began to be lifted up in the pride of their eyes, and to set their hearts upon riches and upon the vain things of the world, that they began to be scornful, one towards another, and they began to persecute those that did not believe according to their own will and pleasure.*
>
> *9 . . . there began to be great contentions among the people of the church; yea, there were envyings, and strife, and malice, and persecutions, and pride, even to exceed the pride of those who did not belong to the church of God.*
>
> *10 . . . and the wickedness of the church was a great stumbling-block to those who did not belong to the church; and thus the church began to fail in its progress. (Alma 4:6, 8–10)*

Note the relationship of pride and riches. The Book of Mormon shows that pride is almost always associated with riches. The effect upon the Church is also almost always internal conflict and an eventual decline. Jacob, brother of Nephi, cited riches as the cause of his people being lifted up in pride in his great temple speech delivered after the death of Nephi:

> *12 And now behold, my brethren, this is the word which I declare unto you, that many of you have begun to search for gold, and for silver, and for all manner of precious ores, in the which this land, which is a land of promise unto you and to your seed, doth abound most plentifully.*

> *13 And the hand of providence hath smiled upon you most pleasingly, that you have obtained many riches; and because some of you have obtained more abundantly than that of your brethren ye are lifted up in the pride of your hearts, and wear stiff necks and high heads because of the costliness of your apparel, and persecute your brethren because ye suppose that ye are better then they. (Jacob 2:12–13)*

Jacob gave the solution to the problem of pride and riches. The solution has the same basic ingredients as our present-day welfare system to help the people help themselves (see Jacob 2:17–19). The people of Jacob apparently did not respond to Jacob's message, and the righteous were led out from among them, as Jacob had prophesied (see Jacob 3:4; Omni 1:12).

Pride came into the Church in the days of Helaman, son of Helaman, with the same effect:

> *33 . . . there was peace also, save it were the pride which began to enter into the church—not into the church of God, but into the hearts of the people who professed to belong to the church of God—*

> *34 And they were lifted up in pride, even to the persecution of many of their brethren. Now this was a great evil, which did cause the more humble part of the people to suffer great persecutions, and to wade through much affliction. (Hel. 3:33–34)*

Although many were strengthened because of their persecutions and afflictions (v. 35), in the following year exceedingly great pride "had gotten into the hearts of the people; and it was because of their exceedingly great riches and their prosperity in the land; and it did grow upon them from day to day" (Hel. 3:36).

Ten years later, the results of the growth of pride and riches in the Church was summarized in these words:

> *11 Now this great loss of the Nephites, and the great slaughter which was among them, would not have happened had it not been for their wickedness and their abomination which was among them; yea, and it was among those also who professed to belong to the church of God.*

> *12 And it was because of the pride of their hearts, because of their exceeding riches, yea, it was because of their oppression to the poor, withholding their food from the hungry, withholding their clothing from the naked, and smiting their humble brethren upon the cheek, making a mock of that which was sacred, denying the spirit of prophecy and of revelation, murdering, plundering, lying, stealing, committing adultery, rising up in great contentions, and deserting away into the land of Nephi, among the Lamanites. (Hel. 4:11–12)*

Again, the Church must take heed of the conditions that result from riches lest they collectively fall from grace.

Not Observe the Commandments

Another example of the Church collectively going astray was the Zoramites, in about 75 B.C. The Zoramites:

> *8 ... were dissenters from the Nephites; therefore, they had had the word of God preached to them.*

9 But they had fallen into great errors, for they would not observe to keep the commandments of God, and his statutes according to the law of Moses.

10 Neither would they observe the performances of the church, to continue in prayer and supplication to God daily, that they might not enter into temptation. (Alma 31:8–10)

They became one-day-only worshipers, adopted a false concept of God, believed in the doctrine of election in the flesh, and used one set prayer for everyone (see Alma 31:12–23). Their hearts were also set upon all manner of fine goods and were lifted up unto great boasting in their hearts (see 31:24–25). The effect upon the Church of not keeping the commandments of God is evident.

Having considered the effects upon the Church of priestcraft, pride, and not keeping the commandments and performances of God, let us consider some ways, as taught in the Book of Mormon, for the Church to take heed.

Pure Testimony

Alma resigned as chief judge to:

. . . go forth among his people, or among the people of Nephi, that he might preach the word of God unto them, to stir them up in remembrance of their duty, and that he might pull down, by the word of God, all the pride and craftiness and all the contentions which were among his people, seeing no way that he might reclaim them save it were in bearing down in pure testimony against them. (Alma 4:19)

When pure testimony is borne, the Spirit will confirm that testimony and enter into the hearts of the people (see 2 Nephi 33:1). President Brigham Young testified:

There is not a man or woman that loves the truth, who has heard the report of the Book of Mormon, but the Spirit of the Almighty has testified to him or her of its truth; neither has any man heard the name of Joseph Smith, but the Spirit has whispered to him— He is a true Prophet. (*Journal of Discourses* 1:93)

Other Solutions

Jacob taught the people: "think of your brethren like unto yourselves" (Jacob 2:17). As brothers and sisters in the gospel, we should have a desire to do what we would want done for ourselves. We should put the golden rule into effect: "Therefore, all things whatsoever ye would that men should do to you, do ye even so to them, for this is the law and the prophets" (3 Nephi 14:12). Jacob said further to "be familiar with all and free with your substance, that they may be rich like unto you" (Jacob 2:17). To become "familiar with all" is a program of church welfare—to analyze the assets and the debits and how to balance them more effectively. In the meantime, we must be "free with [our] substance" and supply the people with their basic needs of food, clothing, and shelter while they are making preparations to become self-sufficient. However, we must prioritize our objectives. Jacob admonished: "But before ye seek for riches, seek ye for the kingdom of God. And after ye have obtained a hope in Christ ye shall obtain riches, if ye seek them; and ye will seek them for the intent to do good—to clothe the naked, and to feed the hungry, and to liberate the captive, and administer relief to the sick and the afflicted" (Jacob 2:18–19).

The obtaining of the kingdom of God must be our top priority. We may obtain riches if we seek them for the right reasons. However, we still must help the needy help themselves. We can find ways for people to obtain employment or opportunities to earn money to buy food and clothing. We can donate to the missionary fund to help people be liberated from spiritual captivity as well as financial captivity. We can generously contribute to the fast offering funds to help the sick and afflicted. If we follow these guidelines, riches will not canker our souls (see D&C 56:16).

Alma later went forth among the Zoramites, preaching the word of God unto them, because "it had had more powerful effect upon the minds of the people than the sword, or anything else" (Alma 31:5). His success was among those who were poor as to the things of the world and therefore humbled (see Alma 32:2–4, 13). Those who were lifted up in pride because of their riches were not receptive of the gospel. As quoted previously, the people of Helaman "did fast and pray oft, and did wax stronger and stronger in their humility, and firmer and firmer in the faith of Christ, unto the filling their souls with joy and consolation, yea, even to the purifying and the sanctification of their hearts, which sanctification cometh because of their yielding their hearts unto God" (Hel. 3:35).

If we will individually live the gospel, the Church will be strong collectively. The Church must "meet together oft, to fast and to pray, and to speak one with another concerning the welfare of their souls" (Moro. 6:5). They must meet oft to partake of the sacrament "in remembrance of the Lord Jesus" (Moro. 6:.6) and be "strict to observe that there shall be no iniquity among them" (Moro. 6:7). As General Moroni stated: "Remember that God has said that the inward vessel shall be cleansed first, and then shall the outer vessel be cleansed also" (Alma 60:23). If the members of the Church will individually retain their justification and sanctification, they will not fall from grace, and the Church will collectively be blessed and prepared for the Second Coming of Christ.

26

THE SANCTIFIED TAKE HEED

"Yea, and even let those who are sanctified take heed also."
(D&C 20:34)

We learn from the Book of Mormon that the sanctified may also fall from grace. The sanctified spoken of are those who are sanctified in the spirit but not yet sanctified in the flesh or the body. They have qualified for entrance into the celestial kingdom, but they are also candidates for becoming sons of perdition if they fall from grace. One does not become a son or daughter of perdition all at once. It is a process, just as becoming sanctified is a process. The Book of Mormon identifies various steps in the process of falling from the grace of sanctification and warns against taking those steps.

Sons of Perdition

The Book of Mormon says little directly about becoming sons of perdition. However, it does warn about Satan and the process that leads to that awful fate. As Mormon abridged the record of Alma he observed: "And thus we see how great the inequality of man is because of sin and transgression, and the power of the devil, which comes by the cunning plans which he hath devised to ensnare the hearts of men" (Alma 28:13). Nephi testified that the words he had written "speaketh harshly against sin, according to the plainness of the truth; wherefore, no man will be angry at the words which I have written save he shall be of the spirit of the devil" (2 Nephi 33:5). The spirit and power of the devil lead us to sin. In his great sermon on the Atonement, Jacob warned of the consequences of following the devil when the day of judgment arrives:

> *45 O, my beloved brethren, turn away from your sins; shake off the chains of him that would bind you fast; come unto that God who is the rock of your salvation.*
>
> *46 Prepare your souls for that glorious day when justice shall be administered unto the righteous, even the day of judgment, that ye may not shrink with awful fear; that ye may not remember your awful guilt in perfectness, and be constrained to exclaim: Holy, holy are thy judgments, O Lord God Almighty—but I know my guilt; I transgressed thy law, and my transgressions are mine; and the devil hath obtained me, that I am a prey to his awful misery.*
>
> *47 But behold, my brethren, is it expedient that I should awake you to an awful reality of these things? Would I harrow up your souls if your minds were pure? Would I be plain unto you according to the plainness of the truth if ye were freed from sin?*
>
> *48 Behold, if ye were holy I would speak unto you of holiness; but as ye are not holy, and ye look upon me as a teacher, it must needs be expedient that I teach you the consequences of sin. (2 Nephi 9:45–48)*

King Benjamin warns against obeying the evil spirit and of the consequences which follow:

> *33 For behold, there is a wo pronounced upon him who listeth to obey that spirit; for if he listeth to obey him, and remaineth and dieth in his sins, the same drinketh*

*damnation to his own soul; for he receiveth for his wages
an everlasting punishment, having transgressed the law of
God contrary to his own knowledge.*

*34 I say unto you, that there are not any among you,
except it be your little children that have not been taught
concerning these things, but what knoweth that ye are
eternally indebted to your heavenly Father, to render to
him all that you have and are; and also have been taught
concerning the records which contain the prophecies which
have been spoken by the holy prophets, even down to the
time our father, Lehi, left Jerusalem. (Mosiah 2:33–34)*

The greater the knowledge, the greater the sin. The Lord has
said, "For of him unto whom much is given much is required;
and he who sins against the greater light shall receive the greater
condemnation" (D&C 82:3; see also Luke 12:48). There are only
two places in the Book of Mormon that seem to describe those who
have sinned to the degree that they have fallen from the grace of
sanctification. The first is King Benjamin's great sermon partially
quoted above, and the second is Mormon's description of the last
generation of the Nephites before their destruction.

King Benjamin reminds his people that they have been
taught:

*35 . . . all that has been spoken by our fathers until now.
And behold, also, they spake that which was commanded
them of the Lord; therefore, they are just and true.*

*36 . . . brethren, that after ye have known and have
been taught all these things, if ye should transgress and
go contrary to that which has been spoken, that ye do
withdraw yourselves from the Spirit of the Lord, that it
may have no place in you to guide you in wisdom's paths
that ye may be blessed, prospered, and preserved—*

> *37 I say unto you, that the man that doeth this, the same cometh out in open rebellion against God; therefore he listeth to obey the evil spirit, and becometh an enemy to all righteousness; therefore, the Lord has no place for him, for he dwelleth not in unholy temples. (Mosiah 2:35–37)*

Therefore, King Benjamin refers to their having been taught justice and truth sufficiently to have become sanctified. His warning of the spirit withdrawing would leave the people in the state that Mormon describes when the Spirit withdrew from the fourth generation of Nephites after the time of Christ.

> *13 But wickedness did prevail upon the face of the whole land, insomuch that the Lord did take away his beloved disciples, and the work of miracles and of healing did cease because of the iniquity of the people.*

> *14 And there were no gifts from the Lord, and the Holy Ghost did not come upon any, because of their wickedness and unbelief. . . .*

> *16 And I did endeavor to preach unto this people, but my mouth was shut, and I was forbidden that I should preach unto them; for behold they had wilfully rebelled against their God; and the beloved disciples were taken away out of the land, because of their iniquity.*

> *17 But I did remain among them, but I was forbidden to preach unto them, because of the hardness of their hearts; and because of the hardness of their hearts the land was cursed for their sake. (Morm. 1:13–14, 16–17)*

Open rebellion against God is incited by Satan. Those who follow him become his sons.

The Lord described the sons of perdition, through Joseph Smith, after Joseph and Sidney Rigdon had seen them in vision: "Thus saith the Lord concerning all those who know my power, and have been made partakers thereof, and suffered themselves through the power of the devil to be overcome, and to deny the truth and defy the power—They are they who are the sons of perdition, of whom I say that it had been better for them never to have been born" (D&C 76:31–32). To know God's power is to have light and knowledge of Him. To have been partakers of God's power is to have had spiritual experiences that made known that light and power. To have suffered [allowed] themselves to be overcome by the power of the devil shows that it was their choice; they did wilfully sin. To deny the truth is to know truth but refuse to acknowledge it. Finally, to defy the power of God is to fight against his work. Their state is worse than before they were born. They had an opportunity to gain salvation by coming to the earth but forfeited that right.

Joseph Smith's description of the sons of perdition confirms the above interpretation of the vision:

> All sins shall be forgiven, except the sin against the Holy Ghost; for Jesus will save all except the sons of perdition. What must a man do to commit the unpardonable sin? He must receive the Holy Ghost, have the heavens opened unto him, and know God, and then sin against Him. After a man has sinned against the Holy Ghost, there is no repentance for him. He has got to say that the sun does not shine while he sees it; he has got to deny Jesus Christ when the heavens have been opened unto him, and to deny the plan of salvation with his eyes open to the truth of it; and from that time he begins to be an enemy. This is the case with many apostates of the Church of Jesus Christ of Latter-day Saints.

> When a man begins to be an enemy to this work, he hunts me, he seeks to kill me, and never ceases to thirst for my blood. He gets the spirit of the devil—the same spirit that they had who crucified the Lord of

Life—the same spirit that sins against the Holy Ghost.
You cannot save such persons; you cannot bring them
to repentance; they make open war, like the devil, and
awful is the consequence. (*TPJS*, 358)

Joseph's description fits those who were sanctified but fell
from grace.

From the following warning, given by King Benjamin, we
gather that repentance is still possible even after open rebellion,
but:

*38 ...if that man repenteth not, and remaineth and
dieth an enemy to God, the demands of divine justice
do awaken his immortal soul to a lively sense of his own
guilt, which doth cause him to shrink from the presence
of the Lord, and doth fill his breast with guilt, and pain,
and anguish, which is like an unquenchable fire, whose
flame ascendeth up forever and ever.*

*39 And now I say unto you, that mercy hath no claim on
that man; therefore his final doom is to endure a never-
ending torment. (Mosiah 2:38–39)*

The unrepentant would become like Mormon's people, of
whom he said: "I saw that the day of grace was passed with them,
both temporally and spiritually; for I saw thousands of them hewn
down in open rebellion against their God" (Morm. 2:15). They
were filled with the fear of death, and yet they were obsessed with
killing by the sword and other weapons of war (Morm. 6:7–15).
The Jaredites came to the same obsession (see Ether 15:19–31).
Spiritually, the Spirit of the Lord was so foreign to them that they
had lost all desire to repent.

The warning of never-ending torment given by King
Benjamin is the eternal condition of sons of perdition. Men
may suffer endless punishment, or eternal punishment, which is
the demands of justice (God's punishment), and still attain an

eternal glory, even the celestial glory. Alma was in an everlasting burning and torment; yet, because of the grace of Christ, his soul was "redeemed from the gall of bitterness and bonds of iniquity" (Mosiah 27:28–29). "Eternal" and "Endless" are God's names, wherefore these punishments are God's punishments (D&C 19:6–12). But there is an end to this torment for those who have paid the demands of justice, themselves. Mercy hath no claim on them, because they knowingly and wilfully sinned (see Heb. 10:26).

Those who suffer never-ending torment are they who deny the Holy Ghost: "For behold, if ye deny the Holy Ghost when it once has had place in you, and ye know that ye deny it, behold, this is a sin which is unpardonable" (Alma 39:6). Jesus sorrowed over "the fourth generation from this generation [Mormon's generation], for they are led away captive by him even as was the son of perdition; for they will sell me for silver and for gold, and for that which moth doth corrupt and which thieves can break through and steal. And in that day will I visit them, even in turning their works upon their own heads" (3 Nephi 27:32; see also 29:7). All of the wicked people of Mormon's day were probably not eternal sons of perdition. Some were undoubtedly victims of their society; but based upon their individual knowledge, they will be judged with a proper balance of justice and mercy. Those who were sanctified but willfully fought against and fell from the Savior's grace were sons of perdition.

The Second Death

Another step in the process of falling from grace is to be carnally minded. Jacob reminded his people that "to be carnally minded is death" (2 Nephi 9:39; see also Rom. 8:6). The death spoken of is spiritual death. Samuel the Lamanite speaks of the Atonement of Christ redeeming all mankind from spiritual death and bringing them back into the presence of the Lord. He then proclaims: "Yea, and it bringeth to pass the condition of repentance, that whosoever repenteth the same is not hewn down and cast into the fire; but whosoever repenteth not is hewn down and cast into the fire; and there cometh upon them again a spiritual death, yea, a second death, for they are cut off again as to things pertaining to righteousness" (Hel. 14:18). Being cut off from things pertaining to righteousness describes being out of the presence of the Lord, or the celestial kingdom. They would thus still be candidates for terrestrial or telestial glory. Alma speaks of the time when we appear before the judgment bar of God and will "acknowledge to our everlasting shame that all his judgments are just" (Alma 12:15). Following our judgment, Alma says, "then cometh a death, even a second death, which is a spiritual death; then is a time that whosoever dieth in his sins, as to a temporal death, shall also die a spiritual death; yea, he shall die as to things pertaining unto righteousness" (Alma 12:16).

Dying "as to things pertaining unto righteousness" is not necessarily a complete second death. People may be cut off from the principles pertaining to the celestial kingdom but may still receive the testimony of Jesus and be good, honorable terrestial beings (see D&C 76:74–79). They have rejected the plan of redemption, "the penalty thereof being a second death, which was an everlasting death as to things pertaining unto righteousness; for on such the plan of redemption could have no power, for the works of justice could not be destroyed, according to the supreme goodness of God" (Alma 12:32).

Those who receive "not the gospel of Christ, neither the testimony of Jesus . . . who deny not the Holy Spirit, . . . who are thrust down to hell [to suffer for their sins during the Millennium] . . . who shall not be redeemed from the devil until the last resurrection" (D&C 76:82–85) are telestial beings and have been cut off from additional "things pertaining to righteousness." Their glory will still "surpass all understanding" (D&C 76:114) according to our earthly comprehension; nevertheless, they have suffered a second death and are assigned to a telestial glory. But those who suffer a complete second death are sons of perdition and are cast into outer darkness where there is no glory (see Alma 40:13).

Alma testified that "according to justice, the plan of redemption could not be brought about, only on conditions of repentance" (Alma 42:13). Mercy will pay the demands of justice on condition of repentance, but "otherwise justice claimeth the creature and executeth the law, and the law inflicteth the punishment; if not so, the works of justice would be destroyed, and God would cease to be God" (Alma 42:22).

Those people who refuse the principles of repentance, according to Jacob, are devoid of the Atonement:

> *16 . . . and they who are filthy shall be filthy still; wherefore, they who are filthy are the devil and his angels; and they shall go away into everlasting fire, prepared for them; and their torment is as a lake of fire and brimstone, whose flame ascendeth up forever and ever and has no end.*

> *17 O the greatness and the justice of our God! For he executeth all his words, and they have gone forth out of his mouth, and his law must be fulfilled. (2 Nephi 9:16–17)*

The mental anguish of the filthy is symbolically like burning in a fire of brimstone, a high-temperature flame. The soul [spirit] can never die (see Alma 42:9); however, it can fail to qualify to remain eternally in the presence of God. Being cut off from the presence of the Lord may be partial or full. When fully cut off, a person suffers a complete spiritual death and becomes a son or daughter of perdition. The souls of God are precious, and those sent "out of this world into an eternal world, unprepared to meet their God" (Alma 48:23), bring sorrow to God and the righteous who realize the value of a soul. May even the sanctified take heed.

27

WE KNOW THESE THINGS ARE TRUE

"And we know that these things are true." (D&C 20:35)

Moroni promised the readers of the Book of Mormon: "when ye shall receive these things [the Book of Mormon]," you should ask God if they "are not true"; and "he will manifest the truth of it unto you, by the power of the Holy Ghost. And by the power of the Holy Ghost ye may know the truth of all things" (Moro. 10:4–5). In the April 6th revelation, the Lord confirms that "by *these things* we know" the truth of the many individual doctrines taught in the Book of Mormon (see D&C 20:17–34, italics added. Note that "these things" refers to the Book of Mormon in both scriptures. The subject of D&C 20:5–16 is the coming forth of the Book of Mormon, its content, and its purposes. These facts support the conclusion that "these things" refer to the Book of Mormon). The promise of Moroni was conditional, and the same conditions apply to the various doctrines taught in the Book of Mormon. Sometimes these conditions are not realized by the reader, and thus they do not qualify for the fulfillment of the promise.

Read the Book

The first condition for knowing the Book of Mormon (or the doctrines in the Book of Mormon) to be true is to "read these things," (Moro. 10:3). Depending upon other conditions, this knowledge may come from the reading of one verse or from a thorough study of the book. There is, however, an unusual clause attached to the condition of reading, "if it be wisdom in God that ye shall read them" (Moro. 10:3). Under what circumstances may it not be within God's wisdom for a person to read the Book of Mormon? It would seem that the intent of the reader is the answer to this question. If a person reads with the purpose of disproving or finding fault with the book or the doctrine, or if one's heart is not right, the Holy Ghost will not bear witness. The conditions that follow the first condition bear this out.

Earlier, as Moroni was finishing his father's record, and not knowing he would have time and plates to write more, he spoke to those who were not receptive to the revelations of God: "And again I speak unto you who deny the revelations of God, and say that they are done away, that there are no revelations, nor prophecies, nor gifts, nor healing, nor speaking with tongues, and the interpretation of tongues; Behold I say unto you, he that denieth these things knoweth not the gospel of Christ; yea, he has not read the scriptures; if so, he does not understand them" (Morm. 9:7–8). Those who read for understanding will come to know by the power of the Holy Ghost that the Book of Mormon is true.

Remember the Lord's Mercy

The second condition given by Moroni for knowing the truth of the Book of Mormon was to "remember how merciful the Lord hath been unto the children of men, from the creation of Adam even down until the time that ye shall receive these things" (Moro. 10:3). The only way to remember how merciful the Lord has been unto the children of men from Adam to the present time is to study the Bible and note the principles and doctrines through which God deals with men. Having studied the Bible in such a manner, a person who studies the Book of Mormon will recognize that God deals with people in the Book of Mormon world in the same manner as he did in the biblical world and thus see that he is the same God yesterday, today, and forever (see D&C 20:12; Heb. 13:8). An analysis of the Book of Mormon writings will show that God did deal with both the biblical and the Book of Mormon people by the same governing principles and doctrines. The incidents may not always be exact parallels (which, of course, should not be expected), but both records contain similar teachings, principles, doctrines, or historical proceedings. As Mormon said: "if ye believe [the Bible] you will believe [the Book of Mormon] also" (Morm. 7:9).

Ponder in Your Heart

After reading and comparing the Book of Mormon with the biblical record, Moroni instructs us to "ponder it in your hearts" (Moro. 10:3). To ponder is to weigh or consider alternatives. The heart represents the spirit, or the internal feelings of man. However, the pondering must involve the mind as well as the feelings. To consider only in the mind is just an intellectual weighing. To consider only the feelings may be just an emotional experience. The Lord described revelation to Oliver Cowdery: "I will tell you in your *mind* and in your *heart*, by the Holy Ghost, which shall come upon you and which shall dwell in your heart" (D&C 8:2; italics added). To ponder in your heart is, therefore, to carefully think through the possibilities with a desire to feel which of the alternatives are true. Therefore, Moroni's third condition is a brief restatement of the experiment upon the word doctrine, as outlined by Alma to the humbled Zoramites (see Alma 32:27–43).

Ask God in the Name of Christ

The fourth condition given by Moroni is the one that is almost always cited: "And when ye shall receive these things, I would exhort you that ye would ask God, the Eternal Father, in the name of Christ, if these things are not true" (Moro. 10:4). The law of Christ teaches us: "Ask, and it shall be given unto you"

(3 Nephi 14:7). However, the law implies that if you do not ask, you will not receive. The implication is confirmed in the Book of Mormon. Nephi's question to Laman and Lemuel when they could not understand their father's teachings was: "Have ye inquired of the Lord? And they said unto me: We have not; for the Lord maketh no such thing known unto us" (1 Nephi 15:8–9). Later, he closed his record by speaking concerning the doctrine of Christ (see 2 Nephi 31:2) and, in that final admonition, said that if we did not understand the words of Christ, "it will be because ye ask not, neither do ye knock" (2 Nephi 32:4).

Moroni also outlines the proper approach: to "ask God, the Eternal Father, in the name of Christ" (Moro. 10:4). While any sincere request will be honored by our Father in Heaven, Moroni took this opportunity to reinforce the teaching of the Book of Mormon concerning to whom and how to pray (discussed in chapter ten).

Sincere Heart and Real Intent

Moroni further qualifies how we should pray: "And if ye shall ask with a sincere heart, with real intent, having faith in Christ, he will manifest the truth of it unto you, by the power of the Holy Ghost" (Moro. 10:4). We must honestly and conscientiously seek to know and act upon our belief. As King Benjamin said about the beliefs of his people, "and now, if you believe all these things see that ye do them" (Mosiah 4:10).

When someone reads the Book of Mormon and claims to have prayed about its truthfulness without a positive answer, a common response from members (who do believe in the book) is to say that the person was not sincere. This response is not appropriate even if it is true; but more importantly, it may not be a valid evaluation of why the Holy Ghost did not bear record. The reason for not receiving a positive response may have been any one of the previous four conditions or any of the yet-to-be-discussed conditions not having been met. Rather than giving this inappropriate response, we should help the reader to analyze why he or she has not had a witness of truth and encourage him or her to seek again.

All That Is Good Acknowledges Christ

The sixth qualifier listed by Moroni is a statement more than a condition: "And whatsoever thing is good is just and true; wherefore, nothing that is good denieth the Christ, but acknowledgeth that he is" (Moro. 10:5–6). If we revise the statement into a condition, we ask the following questions: Is what you read in the Book of Mormon good? Does it acknowledge Christ? Does following the book's teachings or avoiding its warnings make you a better person? Nephi put it this way:

> 4 The words which I have written in weakness will be made strong unto them; for it persuadeth them to do good; it maketh known unto them of their fathers; and it speaketh of Jesus, and persuadeth them to believe in him, and to endure to the end, which is life eternal.
>
> 5 And it speaketh harshly against sin, according to the plainness of the truth; wherefore, no man will be angry at the words which I have written save he shall be of the spirit of the devil. (2 Nephi 33:4–5)

For over thirty years, the writer has challenged his students to show him anything in the Book of Mormon, in its context, that would not make them better people by applying it to their lives or by heeding its warnings. The majority of the students have recognized the futility of the exercise, but there has never been anyone able to fulfill the challenge. Nephi gave a similar challenge: "And now, my beloved brethren, and also Jew, and all ye ends of the earth, hearken unto these words and believe in Christ; and if ye believe not in these words believe in Christ. And if ye shall believe in Christ ye will believe in these words, for they are the words of

Christ, and he hath given them unto me; and they teach all men that they should do good" (2 Nephi 33:10).

Once more, the reader of the Book of Mormon, who recognizes its spiritual value, will know of its truth.

Deny Not the Power of God

The next two conditions given by Moroni are warnings not to deny (1) the power of God and (2) the gifts of God. Both of the denials are associated with the power of the Holy Ghost and the knowledge of Jesus Christ. The first one reads: "And ye may know that he is, by the power of the Holy Ghost; wherefore I would exhort you that ye deny not the power of God; for he worketh by power, according to the faith of the children of men, the same today and tomorrow, and forever" (Moro. 10:7). The power of God may suggest sensational experiences but, because of the warning not to deny it, seems otherwise. We are reminded of Elijah's experiences in Horeb, the mount of God. The word of the Lord said:

> *11 Go forth, and stand upon the mount before the Lord. And, behold, the Lord passed by, and a great and strong wind rent the mountains, and brake in pieces the rocks before the Lord; but the Lord was not in the wind: and after the wind an earthquake; but the Lord was not in the earthquake:*
>
> *12 And after the earthquake a fire; but the Lord was not in the fire: and after the fire a still small voice. (1 Kings 19:11–12)*

Those who may be expecting something sensational may not recognize the still small voice of the Spirit. Therefore, Moroni warns us to deny not the power of God.

Deny Not the Gifts of God

It may seem strange that Moroni launches into a rather lengthy expose on the gifts of the Spirit in the middle of his final chapter. However, when the chapter is analyzed, it fits very well into Moroni's overall scheme. The operation of the gifts of the Spirit should be understood in the context of knowing if the Book of Mormon is true. Moroni warns:

> *And again, I exhort you, my brethren, that ye deny not the gifts of God, for they are many; and they come from the same God. And there are different ways that these gifts are administered; but it is the same God who worketh all in all; and they are given by the manifestations of the Spirit of God unto men, to profit them. (Moro. 10:8)*

Moroni then enumerates some of the many gifts of the Spirit. The various gifts were analyzed in chapter sixteen. Our purpose here is not to analyze the gifts again but to see how they relate to knowing the Book of Mormon is true. The Prophet Joseph Smith gave three great treatises on the gifts of the Spirit.[76] To understand how the gifts relate to knowing the Book of Mormon is true, it is important to know a few things that were said by the Prophet. First of all, Joseph Smith cautioned:

> Some people have been in the habit of calling every supernatural manifestation the effects of the Spirit of God, whilst there are others that think there is no manifestation connected with it at all; and that it is nothing but a mere impulse of the mind, or an inward feeling, impression, or secret testimony or evidence, which men possess, and that there is no such a thing as an outward manifestation. (*TPJS*, 242)

Joseph went on to say that "there are only two gifts that could be made visible—the gift of tongues and the gift of prophecy," and then declared, "The greatest, the best, and the most useful gifts would be known nothing about by an observer" (*TPJS*, 246).

From these observations made by the Prophet, we gain insight into why Moroni spent some time describing the gifts.

---

76 See *TPJS*, pp. 202–215, 223–229, 242–248.

There are many ways that the Spirit may manifest the truth to an individual. Mortal man is prone to advertise the spectacular; so, when an observable gift is given to a person to let him or her know of the truth of the Book of Mormon, others want and expect to have the same experience. When the Lord chooses to manifest the truth to them through another gift, they may not recognize it; therefore, Moroni warns the reader not to deny the gifts of God. The gift is given to profit not only the receiver but others, and only the Lord knows which is the best gift for the person at that time. Moroni's exhortation is important: "remember that every good gift cometh of Christ" (Moro. 10:18). The challenge is to recognize the gift that is manifest.

Faith, Hope, Charity

Tied closely with the gifts of God are the principles of faith, hope, and charity. Moroni makes two important declarations about these three principles before he ties them back to the power of God. The first declaration is that there must be (involved in our lives) all three principles: faith, hope, and charity. Then he states that no one can be saved in the kingdom of God without these principles (Moro. 10:20–21). Moroni next speaks of the despair that comes when there is no hope, which despair comes because of iniquity, and quotes Christ that through faith "ye can do all things which are expedient unto me" (Moro. 10:22–23). He then makes a connection to the knowledge of the truth of the Book of Mormon. Speaking "unto all the ends of the earth," he declares that if the power of God (condition number seven) and the gifts of God (condition number eight) "shall be done away among you, it shall be because of unbelief" (Moro. 10:24). Moroni then refers back to condition number six: if the gifts and power of God are gone, there shall be no one doing good, and none shall be saved in the kingdom of God (Moro. 10:25–26). Without faith, hope, and charity, the knowledge of the truth of the Book of Mormon will not be made known, and salvation will not be attained. One follows the other; the Book of Mormon brings salvation.

Bible Prophecies

The tenth and last condition for knowing the Book of Mormon is true, as outlined by Moroni, is the fulfilling of the Bible prophecies. When people realize that the Bible foretells of the coming forth of the Book of Mormon, they will be more receptive to the Spirit because of their willingness to read the Book of Mormon for the right reason, to ponder it in their hearts, and to pray with a sincere heart and real intent. While the Spirit may bear witness without the realization of Bible prophecies, a lack of knowledge of Bible prophecies may be a factor in preventing the Spirit to bear witness.

There are many biblical prophecies concerning the Book of Mormon. Some of the better known ones are Genesis 49:22–26 (branches of Joseph's seed running over the wall of the ocean to the Americas); Isaiah 29 (a people being destroyed, but speaking out of the ground through their records); Ezekiel 37:15–20 (two sticks, the record of Judah and the record of Joseph coming together in the last days); Psalms 85:11 (truth [the Book of Mormon] coming out of the earth and righteousness [angels restoring authority] coming down from heaven); John 10:14–16 (the Lord's sheep hearing the voice of the Good Shepherd); and Revelation 14:6–7 (another angel having the everlasting gospel go to every nation, kindred, tongue, and people). These prophecies, read with an open heart and mind, will help bring people to a knowledge of the truth of the Book of Mormon.

Summary

Moroni gave ten conditional factors that may influence one's knowing of the truthfulness of the Book of Mormon. It is not necessary for all of these conditions to be met by every reader. Any one of them may be sufficient to bring the Spirit to testify, or the neglect of any one of them may be the reason that the Spirit doesn't come. If readers do not come to know that the book is true, we should help them understand which factors given by Moroni have not been met: "I, the Lord, am bound when ye do what I say; but when ye do not what I say, ye have no promise" (D&C 82:10).

There are thousands, even millions, of people who have come to know that the Book of Mormon is true. We can learn from their testimonies, but we must obtain our own. As we are prepared, the Lord will have his Spirit bear witness.

After we know the Book of Mormon is true, we must continue to study it that we may know of the truth of the principles and doctrines that it teaches. The truth will be revealed "line upon line, precept upon precept, here a little and there a little" (2 Nephi 28:30; Isaiah 28:13).

Moroni's Ten Conditions to Know the Book of Mormon Is True

1. Read the book, if it is wisdom in God (Moroni 10:3; Mormon 9:7–8).

2. Remember the mercy of God from Adam to the present (Moroni 10:3; Mormon 7:8–9).

3. Ponder in your hearts (Moroni 10:3; D&C 8:2) and experiment upon the word (Alma 32:27–43).

4. Pray. Ask God in the name of Christ (Moroni 10:4; 1 Nephi 15:1–11; 2 Nephi 32:4).

5. Ask with a sincere heart, with real intent, and with faith in Christ (Moroni 10:4; Mosiah 4:10).

6. Know it is good if it acknowledges Christ (Moroni 10:5–6; 2 Nephi 33:4–5, 10).

7. Deny not the power of God (Moroni 10:7; 1 Kings 19:11–12).

8. Deny not the gifts of God (Moroni 10:8–19; *TPJS,* pp. 242, 246).

9. Deny not faith, hope, or charity (Moroni 10:20–23; 2 Nephi 33:7–11).

10. Recognize the Bible prophecies (Moroni 10:27–31; Genesis 49:22–26; Isaiah 29; Psalms 85:10–11; Ezekiel 37:15–20; John 10:14–16; Rev. 14:6–7).

Again, it is not necessary for all of these conditions to be met by every reader; any one of them may be sufficient to bring the Spirit to testify, or the neglect of any one of them may be the reason that the Spirit doesn't come.

28

NEITHER ADDING TO NOR DIMINISHING FROM

"And we know these things are true and according to the revelations of John, neither adding to, nor diminishing from the prophecy of his book, the holy scriptures, or the revelations of God which shall come hereafter by the gift and power of the Holy Ghost, the voice of God, or the ministering of angels." (D&C 20:35)

A very common response when the Book of Mormon is presented or spoken of is the quoting of the last chapter of the last book in the Bible, as it is presently compiled:

8 For I testify unto every man that heareth the words of the prophecy of this book, If any man shall add unto these things, God shall add unto him the plagues that are written in this book:

19 And if any man shall take away from the words of the book of this prophecy, God shall take away his part out of the book of life, and out of the holy city, and from the things which are written in this book. (Revelation 22:18–19)

Jesus Christ, knowing that this objection would be given, refuted the argument in the April 6th revelation introducing this chapter. Other evidence supports what the Lord stated above. The book of Revelation was not the last one written. John's epistles, which are believed to have been written later than his Revelation, would thus add to his own work. The Book of 2 Peter is thought by many to have been written much later than the other books.[77]

A careful analysis of the verses from the book of Revelation quoted above shows that they refer only to the book of Revelation and not to the whole Bible. Both of the above verses are singular, in reference to the book of Revelation itself and the prophecy within the book. The book of Revelation is introduced with a similar singular reference: "Blessed is he that readeth, and they that hear the words of this prophecy, and keep those things which are written therein: for the time is at hand" (Revelation 1:3). As Moroni abridged the records of the Jaredites, the Lord told him that the revelations written by John would be understood when the sealed portion of the Book of Mormon plates come forth (Ether 4:16). The foretelling of the coming forth of that record shows that the Lord intended to give more revelation than that given to John. The historical setting of the compilation of the Bible further substantiates this position. A similar statement by Moses would suggest that nothing should have been written after his words: "Ye shall not add unto the word which I command you, neither shall ye diminish ought from it, that ye may keep the commandments of the Lord your God which I command you" (Deut. 4:2; see also 29:20). Most Bible scholars would certainly agree with the interpretation of the verses from the end of the book of Revelation as applying only to the book, itself. Only the layperson is misled to believe in the broader application.

The Book of Mormon does not add to what God has revealed in the Holy Scriptures, the Bible. However, it does clarify and expound the biblical teachings. In the words of Elder Harold

---

77 Cadbury, Henry J. (1951). The New Testament and Early Christian Literature. *The Interpreter's Bible,* ed. G. A. Buttrich. 7:7. Although the author of this work on the Book of Mormon does not agree with the conclusions of the article cited here, it represents the thinking of many biblical scholars regarding the dating of these books.

B. Lee: "There is nothing better that we can do to prepare ourselves spiritually than to read the Book of Mormon. Many doctrines of the Bible that are only partially covered there are beautifully explained in the Book of Mormon, the Doctrine and Covenants and the Pearl of Great Price."[78]

Elder Lee's statement is confirmed in the April 6 revelation outlining the doctrines taught in the Book of Mormon (D&C 20:17–34) and discussed in the previous chapters of this work. The Book of Mormon verifies and clarifies the biblical doctrines, but it does not add to the book of prophecy and revelation written by John.

Failure to gather all of the original teachings of the Bible upon any one subject will probably lead to a misunderstanding or misinterpretation of that subject. On the other hand, a comprehension of all of the biblical teachings will bring one to an acceptance of the teachings of the Book of Mormon on any given subject.

The Book of Mormon does not diminish from the Holy Scriptures, either. Both have the same vital messages. The Old Testament is basically an account of the descendants of Abraham who made a covenant to be the Lord's servants in bringing the opportunity of eternal life to the rest of the world. This covenant was passed on through Isaac and Jacob, whose name was changed to Israel. This has become known as the covenant made with the house of Israel. The Book of Mormon is written as another witness of this covenant and its fulfillment in these latter days. During the Savior's visit to the Nephites, he taught that when the words of Isaiah "shall be fulfilled then is the fulfilling of the covenant which the Father hath made unto his people, O house of Israel." He further taught that the remnants of Israel which were scattered abroad upon the face of the earth would be gathered and "be brought to the knowledge of the Lord their God, who hath redeemed them" (3

---

78 Lee, Harold B. (1969). *Improvement Era, 72* (1), pp. 13–14.

Nephi 20:12–14, see also 3 Nephi 21:1–7). Mormon also testified to the remnant of his people who had been spared that God would give unto them Mormon's words, "that they may know of the things of their fathers"; know that they were of the house of Israel; and know that they "must come unto repentance, or [they could] not be saved" (Morm. 7:1–3).

The New Testament is a witness that Jesus is the Christ, the Son of God, and the source for the obtaining of eternal life. The Book of Mormon bears the same witness. This is best exemplified by comparing the purpose of the Gospel of John, the same author as the book of Revelation, with the purpose of the writers of the Book of Mormon. John declared that he had not written all the signs or miracles that Jesus had done before his disciples, "But [the ones he had written] are written, that ye might believe that Jesus is the Christ, the Son of God; and that believing ye might have life through his name" (John 20:31). Mormon's concluding words to his people were that they must come to the knowledge of their fathers; repent of all their sins and iniquities; and believe that Jesus Christ is the Son of God, believe that he was slain by the Jews, and believe that by the power of the Father he had brought to pass "the resurrection of the dead, whereby man must be raised to stand before his judgment-seat." Those who are found guiltless may dwell in the presence of God in his kingdom (Morm. 7:4–7). Mormon continues:

> 8 Therefore repent, and be baptized in the name of Jesus, and lay hold upon the gospel of Christ, which shall be set before you, not only in this record but also in the record which shall come unto the Gentiles from the Jews, which record shall come from the Gentiles unto you.

> 9 For behold, this is written for the intent that ye may believe that; and if ye believe that ye will believe this also; and if ye believe this ye will know concerning your fathers,

and also the marvelous works which were wrought by the power of God among them. (Mormon 7:8–9)

The title page of the Book of Mormon also identifies this same purpose: "And also to the convincing of the Jew and Gentile that JESUS is the CHRIST, the ETERNAL GOD, manifesting himself unto all nations."

Practically every page of the Book of Mormon in some way bears testimony of the divinity of Jesus Christ and his gospel. Nephi testified of this as he concluded the small plates:

And now, my beloved brethren, and also Jew, and all ye ends of the earth, hearken unto these words and believe in Christ; and if ye believe not in these words believe in Christ. And if ye shall believe in Christ ye will believe in these words, for they are the words of Christ, and he hath given them unto me; and they teach all men that they should do good. (2 Nephi 33:10)

The Book of Mormon is truly "Another Testament of Jesus Christ" (The Book of Mormon subtitle). It stands as a second witness to the sacred record of the Bible. The Book of Mormon has the same objective as the Old Testament: to bring the reader to know of the fulfillment of the covenant made with Abraham. It has the same objective as the New Testament: to believe in and accept Jesus as the Christ and to obtain eternal life through these means.

The entire twenty-ninth chapter of 2 Nephi would be a fitting summary, but two verses will suffice:

8 Wherefore murmur ye, because that ye shall receive more of my word? Know ye not that the testimony of two nations is a witness unto you that I am God, that I remember one nation like unto another? Wherefore, I speak the same words unto one nation like unto another. And when the two nations shall run together the testimony of the two nations shall run together also.

*9 And I do this that I may prove unto many that I am
the same yesterday, today, and forever; and that I speak
forth my words according to mine own pleasure. And
because that I have spoken one word ye need not suppose
that I cannot speak another; for my work is not yet
finished; neither shall it be until the end of man, neither
from that time henceforth and forever. (2 Nephi 29:8–9)*

Other Records Promised

According to the Book of Mormon, other records were destined to come forth, and the Book of Mormon would not add to nor diminish from revelation from other divine sources. The above announcement is apparently a similar declaration as the ninth Article of Faith of The Church of Jesus Christ of Latter-day Saints: "We believe all that God has revealed, all that He does now reveal, and we believe that He will yet reveal many great and important things pertaining to the Kingdom of God." The Lord's "work is not yet finished; neither shall it be until the end of man, neither from that time henceforth and forever" (2 Nephi 29:9). There are at least six different groups of records mentioned in the Book of Mormon that should be anticipated to come forth. A seventh group is mentioned, but nothing is said about their destiny. We will mention each briefly.

The Plates of Nephi

As Mormon abridged the record that we now have, he said that he did not write even a hundredth part of the teachings of Jesus (see 3 Nephi 26:6). He further said that the (large) plates of Nephi contained the more part of what Jesus had taught, but what he had written would come to his people (the people known to us as the Lamanites) from the Gentiles (see 3 Nephi 26:7–8). The record of Nephi abridged by Mormon was to try the faith of Mormon's people in the latter days: "and if it shall so be that they shall believe these things [that Mormon abridged] then shall the greater things be made manifest unto them" (3 Nephi 26:9).

The Sealed Portion

The sealed portion of the plates that was delivered to Joseph Smith but not translated (2 Nephi 27:6–10) was commented on by both Nephi and Moroni. Nephi, quoting from the original Isaiah text, said it contained "a revelation from God, from the beginning of the world to the ending thereof" (2 Nephi 27:7; see also v. 10). Moroni described it more specifically, saying it contained the vision shown unto the brother of Jared of "all the inhabitants of the earth which had been, and also all that would be . . . unto the ends of the earth." The Lord commanded the brother of Jared to write the things he had seen and to seal them up until the Lord's own time, "until after that he should be lifted up upon the cross; . . . that they should not come unto the world until after Christ should show himself unto his people" (Ether 3:25–27; 4:1). After the Lord's people had all dwindled in unbelief and there were none but Lamanites who had rejected the gospel, Moroni was to seal them up again (see Ether 4:3–5).

Nephi, quoting from the same Isaiah text, said, "Touch not the things which are sealed, for I (the Lord) will bring them forth in mine own due time" (2 Nephi 27:21). Moroni told us that they should not go forth unto the Gentiles until they had repented "of their iniquity, and become clean before the Lord." Moroni said further that "they shall exercise faith in [the Lord] . . . even as the brother of Jared did, that they may become sanctified in me, then will I manifest unto them the things which the brother of Jared saw, even to the unfolding unto them all my revelations, saith Jesus Christ, the Son of God, the Father of the heavens and of the earth, and all things that in them are" (Ether 4:6–7).

The sealed portion will establish once and for all that God (Jesus Christ) did know all things from the beginning and has told them periodically to his prophets so that they would not give credit unto idols or men for the accomplishments and happenings of the earth (see Isaiah 48:3–7; 1 Nephi 20:3–7).

Twenty-Four Gold Plates

The record of the Jaredites was abridged by Moroni from twenty-four plates found by the people of Limhi (Ether 1:2; Mosiah 8:8–9). There are thirty generations of the Jaredites (see Ether 1:6–32) abridged into just thirty-one pages in our present book of Ether in the Book of Mormon. The full account of these twenty-four plates will be available when they are found, "and whoso findeth them . . . will have power that he may get the full account" (Ether 1:4).

The Jaredites left the eastern continent when the Lord scattered the people upon all the face of the earth at the time of the building of the great tower—the Tower of Babel (Ether 1:3; Genesis 11:1–9). The first ten chapters of Genesis, up to the time of the Tower of Babel, cover nearly two thousand years in about sixteen pages. Certainly there is much more to be revealed concerning the dealings of Christ with the people who lived during those two thousand years. To have "power that he may get the full account" suggests that there is more information contained therein than was in the Jewish record, and that he will "have power" from the Lord or the plates will come forth under the Lord's direction.

The Plates of Brass

After Lehi's sons brought him the plates which they had returned to Jerusalem to obtain (see 1 Nephi 3:2–4; 4:38), he studied their content (see 1 Nephi 5:10–16); then, being moved upon by the Spirit, he "began to prophesy concerning his seed":

> 18 *That these plates of brass should go forth unto all nations, kindreds, tongues, and people who were of his seed.*
>
> 19 *Wherefore, he said that these plates of brass should never perish; neither should they be dimmed any more by*

time. And he prophesied many things concerning his seed.
(1 Nephi 5:18–19; see also Alma 37:1–19)

Their great worth to future generations may be in a different perspective than they were unto the Nephites, but they will certainly have their great worth. While the Book of Mormon has served as a second witness to the truth of the holy scriptures (see D&C 20:11), the plates of brass will serve as a third witness to the Bible, the second witness being the 24 gold plates, and also a witness that the Book of Mormon is a witness to the Bible. They shall also make known many of the plain and precious parts that have been lost from the Bible up to the time of Jeremiah (see 1 Nephi 13:26–29; 39–40). The writings of such prophets as Zenos, Zenoch, and Neum will be restored (see 1 Nephi 19:10; Alma 33:3–16; Helaman 8:19–20; 3 Nephi 10:16).

Lamanite Records

In commenting upon his recording only a hundredth part of what he had available to him, Mormon records that "there are many books and many records of every kind, and they have been kept chiefly by the Nephites" (Hel. 3:13–15). This quotation shows that the Lamanites also kept some records and implies that they were in Mormon's possession at the time of his abridgment. There is no promise of these records coming forth; but if Mormon had them, they probably will. The future possession of these records and their translation will give us another view of the history of these people (see Alma 9:16–17). When we have these records and others, the controversial geographical and archaeological problems of the Book of Mormon lands will also receive additional clarification.

Record of the Ten Tribes

Nephi, son of Lehi, quotes the Lord in commanding all men to keep a record as a testimony for the time when the nations come together (see 2 Nephi 29:1–11). He refers to the Jews, the Nephites, and other tribes of the house of Israel which were led away:

> *12 For behold, I shall speak unto the Jews and they shall write it; and I shall speak unto the Nephites and they shall write it; and I shall also speak unto the other tribes of the house of Israel, which I have led away, and they shall write it; and I shall also speak unto all nations of the earth and they shall write it.*

> *13 And it shall come to pass that the Jews shall have the words of the Nephites, and the Nephites shall have the words of the Jews; and the Nephites and the Jews shall have the words of the lost tribes of Israel; and the lost tribes of Israel shall have the words of the Nephites and the Jews. (2 Nephi 29:12–13)*

The Savior told the Nephites that he was going to visit these lost tribes; and when their records come forth, we will have a third witness to the divinity and ministry of Christ after his resurrection (see 3 Nephi 16:1–3). A further purpose of the record of the lost tribes was given by the Savior to show "unto them that fight against my word and against my people, who are of the house of Israel, that I am God, and that I covenanted with Abraham that I would remember his seed forever" (2 Nephi 29:14). Of further importance to those tribes, themselves, will be the rich treasures they will bring to Ephraim, through which they will receive crowns of glory (see D&C 133:30–32).

Other Jaredite Records

The daughter of Jared, a female character of the book of Ether, queried about "the record which our fathers brought across the great deep? Behold, is there not an account concerning them of old, that they by their secret plans did obtain kingdoms and great glory?" (Ether 8:9). This record does not seem to be the same as the twenty-four plates of gold translated into what Moroni called the book of Ether (see Ether 1:2), although the first part of Ether does speak of the creation and the time of Adam to the great tower (see v. 3). There is no mention of it being preserved for the last days, but it was durable enough to be available in the fifth generation of the Jaredites. Since the Jaredites kept records on metal plates, it is possible that the record referred to by the daughter of Jared is still in existence and will come forth and be translated in some future day. If the record is brought forth, there would be much information given on the conditions of the world and the workings of God among the people prior to the time of the Jaredites.

Faith Must Be Tried

All of these six or seven additional records, and possibly many others, are held in store for the Lord's people. When will they come forth? Mormon said that he wrote a lesser part of the things which Jesus taught the people for "the intent that they may be brought again unto this people, from the Gentiles." He said further that it was expedient that they should have the lesser part first to try their faith, and if they would "believe these things then shall the greater things be made manifest unto them." To those who did not believe, "shall the greater things be withheld from them, unto their condemnation" (3 Nephi 26:9–10). When we make full use of the records that we now have, the Lord has promised us many more records, which will greatly benefit us individually and collectively. These records will be consistent with the Book of Mormon in not adding to nor diminishing from the doctrine and messages of the revelations of John or of other scriptures.

EPILOGUE

"And the Lord God has spoken it; and honor, power and glory
be rendered to his holy name, both now and ever. Amen."
(D&C 20:36)

The revelations given on or around 6 April 1830 tell us much about the importance of the Book of Mormon to the Church. This work has emphasized the major doctrines which the book teaches. The revelations given to the elders of the Church conclude with a tribute of worship to the Lord. In addition to the praising of his holy name, the tribute acknowledges the source of the doctrine taught in the Book of Mormon: "The Lord God has spoken it" by revelation.

While there are many in the world today who "draw near unto [Christ] with their mouth, and with their lips do honor [him], but have removed their hearts far from [him], and their fear towards [him] is taught by the precepts of man" (2 Nephi 27:25; see also Isaiah 29:13; JS–H 1:19), those who come to understand and appreciate the Book of Mormon and the doctrines it teaches will also shout praises to his holy name. Evidence for this concept is shown by the praises of those prophets in the Book of Mormon who knew and understood him.

After Lehi was shown the vision of Jerusalem and had read a book given him by Christ (see Nephi 1:11–13), Nephi records:

14 When my father had read and seen many great and marvelous things, he did exclaim many things unto the Lord, such as: Great and marvelous are thy works, O Lord God Almighty! Thy throne is high in the heavens, and thy power, and goodness, and mercy are over all the inhabitants of the earth; and, because thou art merciful, thou wilt not suffer those who come unto thee that they shall perish!

15 And after this manner was the language of my father in the praising of his God; for his soul did rejoice, and his whole heart was filled, because of the things which he had seen, yea, which the Lord had shown unto him. (1 Nephi 1:14–15)

Years later Nephi was bound by his brothers when at sea; and following his being loosed because of the great and terrible tempest that the brothers recognized to be the judgments of God, he also acknowledged the power of God with these words: "Nevertheless, I did look unto my God, and I did praise him all the day long; and I did not murmur against the Lord because of mine afflictions" (1 Nephi 18:16). Still later, Nephi paused in his recording of the Nephite events to "write the things of [his] soul" and said: "Behold, my soul delighteth in the things of the Lord; and my heart pondereth continually upon the things which I have seen and heard" (2 Nephi 4:15–16). Nephi concluded the soliloquy begun with the words above by praising God: "I will lift up my voice unto thee; yea, I will cry unto thee, my God, the rock of my righteousness. Behold, my voice shall forever ascend up unto thee, my rock and mine everlasting God. Amen" (2 Nephi 4:35).

Jacob, the brother of Nephi, told his brethren that "my heart delighteth in righteousness; and I will praise the holy name of my God" (2 Nephi 9:49). He then quoted Isaiah 55:1–2, inviting them to come unto Christ. He later proclaimed:

8 Behold, great and marvelous are the works of the Lord. How unsearchable are the depths of the mysteries of him; and it is impossible that man should find out all his ways. And no man knoweth of his ways save it be revealed unto him; wherefore, brethren, despise not the revelations of God.

9 For behold, by the power of his word man came upon the face of the earth, which earth was created by the power of his word. Wherefore, if God being able to speak and the world was, and to speak and man was created, O then, why not able to command the earth, or the workmanship of his hands upon the face of it, according to his will and pleasure? (Jacob 4:8–9)

Concerning those who had just been baptized and had come to the knowledge of their Redeemer, Alma said: "And how blessed are they, for they shall sing to his praise forever" (Mosiah 18:30).

Ammon rejoiced over what the Lord had done for the Lamanites during the fourteen-year mission of the sons of Mosiah. He blessed the name of God, proposed they sing to his name, and gave thanks to his holy name:

10 . . . His brother Aaron rebuked him, saying: Ammon, I fear that thy joy doth carry thee away unto boasting.

11 But Ammon said unto him: I do not boast in my own strength, nor in my own wisdom; but behold, my joy is full, yea, my heart is brim with joy, and I will rejoice in my God.

12 Yea, I know that I am nothing; as to my strength I am weak; therefore I will not boast of myself, but I will boast of my God, for in his strength I can do all things; yea, behold, many mighty miracles we have wrought in this land, for which we will praise his name forever.

13 Behold, how many thousands of our brethren has he loosed from the pains of hell; and they are brought to sing redeeming love, and this because of the power of his word which is in us, therefore have we not great reason to rejoice?

14 Yea, we have reason to praise him forever, for he is the Most High God, and has loosed our brethren from the chains of hell.

15 Yea, they were encircled about with everlasting darkness and destruction; but behold, he has brought them into his everlasting light, yea, into everlasting salvation; and they are encircled about with the matchless bounty of his love; yea, and we have been instruments in his hands of doing this great and marvelous work.

16 Therefore, let us glory, yea, we will glory in the Lord; yea, we will rejoice, for our joy is full; yea, we will praise our God forever. Behold, who can glory too much in the Lord? Yea, who can say too much of his great power, and of his mercy, and of his long-suffering towards the children of men? Behold, I say unto you, I cannot say the smallest part which I feel. (Alma 26:10–16)

The response by Ammon probably shows us as well as any why we should praise the name of Christ "now and ever" (D&C 20:36). However, the Book of Mormon adds a few more statements that should be considered.

Nephi, son of Lehi, wrote: "But the Lord knoweth all things from the beginning; wherefore, he prepareth a way to accomplish all his works among the children of men; for behold, he hath all power unto the fulfilling of all his words. And thus it is. Amen" (1 Nephi 9:6). He later explained that God "will preserve the righteous by his power, even if it so be that the fulness of his wrath must come, and the righteous be preserved, even unto the destruction of their enemies by fire" (1 Nephi 22:17).

King Benjamin told his subjects that if he merited any thanks from them, "O how you ought to thank your heavenly king" (Mosiah 2:19). He then added this humbling thought:

20 If you should render all the thanks and praise which your whole soul has power to possess, to that God who has created you, and has kept and preserved you, and has caused that ye should rejoice, and has granted that ye should live in peace one with another—

21 I say unto you that if ye should serve him who has created you from the beginning, and is preserving you from day to day, by lending you breath, that ye may live and move and do according to your own will, and even supporting you from one moment to another—I say, if ye should serve him with all your whole souls yet ye would be unprofitable servants. (Mosiah 2:20–21)

The king went on to explain that all God requires of us is to keep his commandments, "for which if ye do, he doth immediately bless you; and therefore he hath paid you. And ye are still indebted unto him, and are, and will be, forever and ever; therefore, of what have ye to boast?" (Mosiah 2:22–24). King Benjamin calls this being eternally indebted to your heavenly father (Mosiah 2:34).

Perhaps a comment should be made about being immediately blessed. The Prophet Joseph remarked:

The inhabitants of this continent anciently were so constituted, and were so determined and persevering, either in righteousness or wickedness, that God visited them immediately either with great judgments or blessings. But the present generation, if they were going to battle, if they got any assistance from God, they would have to obtain it by faith. (*TPJS*, 299)

The generation spoken of above is the dispensation of the fulness of the times that extends into the millennial reign (Ephesians 1:10). Therefore, it is through faith that we today obtain blessings.

May we exercise the faith to have experiences through the Lord Jesus Christ and the Holy Spirit that we may shout praises to their names and to our Heavenly Father. May the chapters of this book help us more fully appreciate the members of the Godhead and the Book of Mormon and bring us to a deeper understanding and appreciation of the doctrine taught in that marvelous work.

INDEX

A

R

PRAISE FOR 28 TRUTHS

I cannot think of anyone more qualified to prepare a commentary on the Book of Mormon than Dr. Monte S. Nyman. Through many years of association I have been impressed with Brother Nyman's thorough understanding of the nature and spirit of the Book of Mormon and of all the holy scriptures. One of his greatest gifts is the ability to see relationships and meanings of one passage of scripture to another, and it shows in his teachings and his writings. He is a true believer and expert teacher.

—The Late Robert J. Matthews
Former Dean of Religious Education, BYU

Dr. Monte S. Nyman's knowledge of the Book of Mormon and Church doctrine is astounding. As a student at BYU Jerusalem, my fellow classmates and I would take turns reading from *Teachings of the Prophet Joseph Smith,* asking Dr. Nyman from which page we were reading. We could never stump him—he had the book memorized! Dr. Nyman is the consummate Latter-day Saint scholar: an expert in ancient scripture and a faithful disciple of Jesus Christ.

—Amy Osmond Cook
Faculty Associate, Arizona State University
Publisher, Sourced Media Books